Milton's Prude

Words and Signs in His Poetry and Prose

Martin Kuester

University Press of America,® Inc.
Lanham · Boulder · New York · Toronto · Plymouth, UK

Copyright © 2009 by
University Press of America,® Inc.
4501 Forbes Boulevard
Suite 200
Lanham, Maryland 20706
UPA Acquisitions Department (301) 459-3366

Estover Road
Plymouth PL6 7PY
United Kingdom

Library of Congress Control Number: 2008942693
ISBN-13: 978-0-7618-4527-0 (clothbound : alk. paper)
ISBN-13: 978-0-7618-4528-7 (paperback : alk. paper)
eISBN-13: 978-0-7618-4529-4

Contents

Preface

  This book is my translation and revision of an earlier version I wrote in German, *"Prudent Ambiguities": Zur Problematik von Sprache und Bedeutung im Werk John Miltons* (Trier: Wissenschaftlicher Verlag Trier, 1999). I would like to thank Erwin Otto of Wissenschaftlicher Verlag Trier for publishing the earlier work and for encouraging me to prepare an English-language version. Further thanks are due to Stephan Kohl, University of Würzburg, who kindly agreed to include the original book in his series "Literatur—Imagination—Realität." For permission to reprint earlier versions of smaller sections of this volume, I would like to thank the editors of *English Studies in Canada*, where my first ideas about the archangel Raphael's role appeared as "The End of Monolithic Language: Raphael's Sematology in *Paradise Lost*," *ESC* XV.3 (1989): 263-276; the editors of *Anglia*, where earlier ideas regarding *Paradise Lost* as a godgame appeared as "Godgames in Paradise: Educational Strategies in Milton and Fowles," *Anglia* 115.1 (1997): 29-43; and the editors of *Zeitschrift für Anglistik und Amerikanistik*, who kindly published "*Comus*—An Educational Godgame," *ZAA* 51.3 (2003): 287-295.

  Audiences at places as far apart as St. Catharines (Ontario), Edinburgh, Beaufort (South Carolina), San Francisco and Budapest have listened to some of the ideas presented here and encouraged me to continue my readings and rereadings of Milton's works. Many students in various classes at the universities of Augsburg and Marburg, my student and research assistants over the years, among them first of all Wolfram R. Keller and Marco Ulm, and especially our departmental librarian, Madeleine Kinsella, have shared and supported my interest in Milton's works.

  My work on Milton started out, somewhat ironically, at the University of Manitoba in Canada, where I had gone to write a dissertation on Canadian literature. I did write this dissertation and have been studying and teaching Canadian literature ever since, but one of my Canadian literature professors in Winnipeg is also an inspiring Miltonist, and the impulses given in David Williams's class have developed not only into a sincere friendship but also into a lasting interest in Milton, which led me to focus on the latter in my work towards a postdoctoral degree back in Germany. Thanks are here also due to my former teacher and *Habilitation* supervisor at the University of Augsburg, the late Walter Pache, and to one of my fellow graduate students at the University of Manitoba, Ted Dyck, who is not only a good friend and colleague but also an expert editor. Stylistic felicities in this book are his responsibility, Germanic barbarisms are mine. As far as editing goes, I would also like to thank Samantha Kirk and Alison Syring of the University Press of America, for expert advice and for promptly answering many questions.

Thanks are also due to Dennis Cooley, another good friend from the University of Manitoba, for granting me permission to include an excerpt from his poem "the II-C of her heart (for Smaro)" from his volume *Dedications* at the beginning of my introductory chapter.

Grateful acknowledgment is also made to the Estate of the late John Fowles for permission to quote from *The Aristos* and *The Magus*, copyright © by J.R. Fowles Ltd.

I would like to finish by thanking my wife, Hildegard, for having suffered and supported my interest in Anglophone literatures and things Miltonic for many years.

Martin Kuester
Marburg, Germany
October 2008

1 Introduction

> if in talking
> sweetly you fall
> on the slippery slope
> between Sig
> Nified & Sig Nifier
>
> the apple may be pretty
> appealing under such appalling
> circumstances chances
> are it is the name of the game
>
> for in his name he called him (A
> dam madam) forth and the whole earth
> was of one language and
> of one speech they were able to find
> they were like one man
> & woman & all things were
> mag nified dei fied de fined
>
> Dennis Cooley[1]

For more than three hundred years, John Milton has been one of the small number of poets dominating the literary tradition of most—if not all—anglophone countries. Hardly any writer in the English language—or any literary scholar for that matter—has been able to escape his influence. In Harold Bloom's terminology, Milton has been one of those "strong poets" serving as vantage points and models to be imitated or rejected all over the English-speaking world. Milton has been emulated, rewritten, parodied and disputed. Not only has his epic *Paradise Lost* caused severe cases of a Bloomian *anxiety of influence*[2] among his followers, but he has even become one of the preferred targets of feminist literary critics focusing on his alleged misogyny found, for example, in his attitude towards his daughters, in Adam's behaviour towards Eve, or in his depiction of Dalila.[3]

For writers representing postcolonial literatures in English, Milton has become an icon of British culture and civilization. For example, David Dabydeen has castigated Milton and his ornate style as examples of an imperial and colonial attitude condemning "the barbaric, broken utterance of black people,"[4] although a seventeenth-century author can hardly be held responsible for nineteenth- or twentieth-century imperialist misreadings of his work.

For more than three hundred years, Milton's ideas and concepts have been the focus of scholarly discussion; his texts have been interpreted, translated and integrated into new contexts. Not least, the critical discussion of his work has developed into a world-wide industry ranging from symposia to book and journal publications and internet discussion lists.

In spite—or perhaps rather because—of this development, a literary scholar such as John P. Rumrich claims that there is an imbalance in contemporary Milton criticism: the John Milton of secondary literature is an "invented Milton" imagined by traditional Miltonists, "a rhetorical artifact or paradigm foundational to contemporary Milton scholarship."[5] Such a traditionalist position feeds the negative attitude towards innovative critical approaches: for example, a psychoanalytical interpretation of *Paradise Lost* does not fit into the traditional Miltonists' concept of "their" John Milton. Still, this traditional image was itself only invented to make Milton fit the requirements of a rather conservative and self-perpetuating form of academic literary criticism. From such a majority position, psychoanalytic critics of Milton are heretics trying to revive the spirit of those who were ostracized long ago for reading Milton against the grain. These heretical critics seemed to have disappeared after the "great controversy"[6] in the 1930s during which T.S. Eliot had condemned Milton and turned him into a *persona non grata*.

One of the unpopular critics offering "heretical" interpretations of Milton's works at the beginning of the twentieth century was the Frenchman Denis Saurat, who claimed to have detected traces of Jewish mysticism in *Paradise Lost* and who also saw God as withdrawing himself from the world he had created.[7] A similar idea was later developed by William Empson in his controversial volume *Milton's God*, where he depicted this God as an unattractive character whose only redeeming grace was his abdication.[8] Among the latest, highly suggestive readings in this vein are David Norbrook's *Writing the English Republic* and Michael Bryson's *The Tyranny of Heaven*, which sees the discussion leading to the Father's abdication as the result of the Son's challenging his ways.[9]

While traditional Miltonists have time and again tried to characterize Milton as a basically conservative and orthodox Christian, some contemporary critics and historians—among them Christopher Hill—have been drawing our attention to aspects that would characterize him as a revolutionary not only in his political function during the Puritan Interregnum but also as a revolutionary Christian who had much in common with Ranters, Quakers, and other radical sects of the seventeenth century. From the point of view of conservative traditionalists, these unloved "heretical" critics intend "to recapture Milton for the Saurats and Hills and . . . the Waldocks and Empsons of this world."[10]

As will be obvious, I have not always been able to resist the temptation of complementing a basically linguistic approach—which in itself is no longer that unusual in Milton studies—with some ideas adopted from Saurat, Hill, and Empson, such as the concept of *retraction*. My interpretation of *Paradise Lost*, which is at the centre of this study, thus concentrates not only on the analysis of linguistic concepts underlying Milton's epic but also—based on these linguistic concepts—on a new reading of *Paradise Lost* and on the role that the archangel Raphael plays in it. Relying on a narrative model which was already well-known in the seventeenth century and was baptized *godgame* by the twentieth-century British novelist John Fowles, I reinterpret the role of the archangel (based, to a certain extent, on that of his predecessor, the Attendant Spirit in *Comus*) as that of a tool in the great plan of Milton's Father's "ironic" teaching. My interpretation shares some, but by far not all, features with Victoria Silver's recent sophisticated analysis of Milton's irony and with Michael Bryson's reading of the epic. I would go along with Silver in seeing irony as "comprehensive" and "assumption-altering," but while she sees irony as a means "to invite and to constrain the reader from Satan's sort of analogy"[11] between creator and creature, heaven and earth, mimesis and allegory, I see irony more in the sense of a Socratic teaching strategy. Thus I arrive at views that structurally resemble Saurat's ideas—at least as far as they concern God's retraction from his governing position in the universe. Mostly focusing on the role and meaning of language in Milton's work, this study thus can be seen as one of those "heretical" readings that may be subsumed under John Rumrich's title: "Uninventing Milton."[12]

Cedric Brown mentions in his recent biography that "the meanings of Milton's texts were constantly reformed by readers of later centuries."[13] Even structuralist, poststructuralist, and deconstructionist theories have been applied to his texts, often resulting in interpretations which conservative critics might claim that Milton does not "deserve," as they were invented in ideological contexts he would hardly have recognized as relevant and/or useful. But it is an accepted practice in contemporary literary studies to apply contemporary theory and theories even to works belonging to the traditional literary canon. For example, psychoanalytical approaches to Milton's works or Stanley Fish's reader-response approach have by now been accepted as classical readings of Milton's texts.

For this reason, I feel justified in analyzing Milton's works with regard to their underlying concept of language and to study Milton's own statements in his prose and poetry with respect to the question of how concepts and words arise and how they can then be transferred or translated from one context (whether it be heavenly, earthly, cultural, geographic, or historic) to another one. Such an approach touches on questions of semiotics, translation theory, and intertextuality. While my interpretation naturally focuses on the relevant theories developed in Milton's times first of all, it does not refrain from more recent insights about the function of language that are founded, for example, on Saussurean structuralism. Therefore, parallels and structural similarities between seventeenth-century philosophy of language and twentieth-century linguistic concepts come to the surface.

Confronted with a theme such as "Milton and language," readers will first of all think of the poet's style rather than of his ideas regarding the creation and function of language, of words and signs. Even some his contemporaries were not certain whether his style qualified as idiomatic English at all. All the prejudices which exist nowadays were presumably already present in Philip Neve's statement of 1789 that, to an unskilled reader, "the sense and spirit of *Milton*'s phrase must be often unattainable."[14]

Literary critics such as Stanley Fish have shown, however, that Milton was aware of the semiotic and philosophical theories of language current in his own time, and twentieth-century linguistic bibliographies even quote *Paradise Lost* as an example of seventeenth-century theories on the origin of language. The most famous example of Milton's interest in semiotic questions may well be his optimistic statement, in the early pamphlet *Of Education*, that it is the aim of education to repair the ruins of our fathers. In this process, language plays an important role, although it is "but the instrument conveying to us things useful to be known" (*CP* II: 369).

As far as the above-mentioned destruction of an original and ideal world is concerned, many critics assume that parallel to Adam and Eve's Fall in paradise—or, according to another theory, somewhat later, at Babel—there occurred a "linguistic Fall." Its result is that we can differentiate between pre-lapsarian and post-lapsarian language. In Milton's version of biblical history, the "linguistic Fall" represents not only a catastrophe in the life of Adam and Eve but also an important station in the history of mankind. From the point of view of semiotics, regarding the role of language as a means of communication, the "linguistic Fall" represents the first step away from a quasi-mathematical, universal language in which there exists a one-to-one relationship between words and things (or rather, between words and their meanings). If all human beings spoke such a universal language, no communication problems would ever be possible. What we have in *Paradise Lost* is, as I intend to show, a development away from a "natural" and stable connection between word and thing (or meaning) towards a looser coordination of the entities that Saint Augustine would have called *verbum* and *res* and which modern semioticians call sign and referent.[15] One of the consequences of this development is that words which would originally have referred to only one element and situation in paradise, in which their meaning (reference) had been clear and defined by their context, would later be applicable to a whole class of similar objects with the same linguistic meaning (denotation).

In this study I will scan the complete works of John Milton for statements regarding underlying theories of semiotics, translation and communication theory. Whereas Milton's prose, written in the context of day-to-day politics of Civil War and Puritan Interregnum, can probably lay no claim whatsoever to be more than a collection of pragmatically oriented political statements, his lyrical and epic works—especially *Paradise Lost* and *Paradise Regained*—deserve a more detailed reading.

Milton's theories will first be interpreted in the seventeenth-century context of "sematology," i.e., of discussions involving seventeenth-century philosophers of language, theologians, and scientists. As indicated above, I will however also refer to modern linguistic theories such as Ferdinand de Saussure's structuralism or John Lyons's lexical semantics in so far as they throw new light on the questions addressed in Milton's works.

Structuralist and poststructuralist theories of literature—even deconstructionist approaches based on Derridean theories—have been applied to Milton's works, but they have rarely been greeted with enthusiasm. Annabel Patterson summarizes their limited success in the following way:

> Although a case could very well be made that Adam's conversations with Raphael in *Paradise Lost* are themselves debates about representation and problems of signification, most of the followers of Jacques Derrida have had difficulty in demonstrating the presence of metaphysical or epistemological aporias in a writer so confident that Truth, though fumbled together on earth, has divine guarantees elsewhere.[16]

I would agree with Patterson that the discussion between Adam and Raphael in *Paradise Lost* is a contribution to the theory of the origin of language, a contribution which is of course accommodated to the horizon and the abilities of Milton's seventeenth-century readers. But I will also claim, and here I am supported by Peter C. Herman's recent book, *Destabilizing Milton*, and his chapter on "Milton and Aporia,"[17] that Milton's treatment of the question of language and the semiotic theories of representation and signification underlying his work give rise to the very aporias that Patterson rejects. One may then wonder whether in Milton's cosmology the "divine guarantees" mentioned by Patterson refer merely to the truth conveyed or also to the language in which this truth is told.

My primary aim in this study is not, however, to uncover aporias and "the Fall into differance"[18] in Milton's text. I will rather start by interpreting his writings with regard to their underlying concept of language. This concept will then be compared with other linguistic theories brought forth by his (and our) contemporaries.

At the beginning of this study, in Chapter 2, I present some of the most important theories of language to which Milton and his contemporaries would probably have referred. Towards the end of this chapter, there will a brief—and at first sight completely anachronistic—digression on semiotic theories of the twentieth century, which nevertheless have important features in common with seventeenth-century concepts. Among these features are the binary character of the linguistic sign, the limitation of these approaches (at least at the beginning) to single words rather than complete sentences, and intertextual references (positive in the seventeenth century, negative in the twentieth) to the biblical creation story.

Chapter 3 analyzes Milton's prose, in which he shows a great sensitivity to questions of language at quite an early age. What also becomes obvious at a very early stage is Milton's almost prophetic attitude towards his mother tongue and the great linguistic optimism he seems to share (at least for a time) with his contemporaries with regard to the ability of restoring an almost paradisal state on earth through mere linguistic reform. In Milton's later works—such as the *Doctrina Christiana* (if it was indeed written by Milton)—and especially when he is looking for a biblical justification of divorce, this optimism tends to give way (at least momentarily) to a position in which he no longer seems to believe in the survival of an ideal language with its clear one-to-one relationship between words and things. Further insights into Milton's attitude towards linguistic and rhetorical figures can be found in his commentary and translation of Ramus's *Logic*, in which he addresses the role of figurative language and the status of divine speech.

Chapter 4 focuses on Milton's statements on language in his poetic, epic and dramatic works. As the poetic texts tend to be relatively brief, linguistic aspects are often dealt with in a more superficial fashion, but they are nevertheless present. The chapter centres of course on *Paradise Lost* as Milton's most important work. His depiction of the creation and role of language in the epic is analyzed in detail, and I will point to significant parallels between Milton's version, Saussurean semiotics, and modern lexical semantics. Finally, the "linguistic" insights gained so far will be applied to *Paradise Regained* and thus be brought to a conclusion which is very positive from a religious point of view but which also gives rise to scepticism from a linguistic perspective. The chapter concludes with an analysis of the archangel Raphael's teaching as part of the Miltonic paradigm of the *godgame* (foreshadowed by the Attendant Spirit's pedagogical strategies in *Comus*).

In *Paradise Lost* criticism, the above-mentioned distinction between prelapsarian and postlapsarian language—i.e., the question as to whether the Fall has any repercussions on the state of human language—has been at the centre of interest for quite some time. For example, Robert Entzminger states in the introduction to his study *Divine Word*: "When Adam falls in *Paradise Lost*, so does his language."[19] And in *Naming in Paradise*, John Leonard comments on "Milton's use of prelapsarian and postlapsarian names and the various ways in which distinctions between them infiltrate *Paradise Lost*, both on a local scale and in larger narrative episodes."[20]

In his dialogue with Adam in *Paradise Lost*, the archangel Raphael depicts the prehistory and motivation of the creation of the world, of human beings and of their language. Adam, who is here addressed by Raphael, has not yet undergone the Fall and all the consequences it has for his life, philosophy and imagination, but the archangel already feels the need to adapt his report to what he thinks is his pupil's limited horizon. Without being aware of it—but still, as I claim, following God's plans—the archangel here encourages attentive readers to question the necessity of his establishing and maintaining a distinction between the languages of heaven and earth. And if, one may ask heretically, even postlapsarian readers do not see the necessity of this distinction, does prelapsarian Adam really need the strategies of accommodation that Raphael employs in his narrative of heavenly events?

Through his strategy of accommodation—his simplifying adaptation of heavenly truths to Adam's earthly capacities—Raphael destroys Adam and Eve's trust in the existence of a "monolithic" language that can mirror God's world as it is. And he does this even before the Fall. Even before Adam and Eve succumb to Satan's temptation, there is a certain loss of "the extraliterary properties that God's 'word' was presumed to have in Milton's religious tradition."[21] *Logos*, God's 'word,' is nothing more than just *a* word.

I would claim, however, that this "prelapsarian" fall of language is not necessarily the catastrophe that it has been claimed to be, as it is only through this Fall that we who live in postlapsarian times are enabled to depict the prelapsarian world. A "linguistic Fall," if it ever took place, would thus be a lucky event, perhaps even an expression of the *felix culpa*, which—according to some critics—underlies *Paradise Lost*.

Another way of relativizing the importance of the linguistic Fall is to interpret it as nothing but the natural consequence of a quality that was already present in the language of Milton's paradise right from the beginning. I am referring here to the arbitrary coordination of sign and referent, although of course the arbitrariness on which it relies is an arbitrariness based on and supported by God's will. The only "glue" that makes this coordination reliable in Milton's paradise is the same one that exists for Milton and his contemporaries: their faith in the divine authority backing up this one-to-one coordination.

Although the language used by Milton is also a religious language, I wonder if it has to be a kind of performative *God-talk* with a "special logical status," if, in other words, it really has to be "a language whose logical conduct is uniquely different from that of so-called ordinary language even down to its very grammar."[22] Admittedly, the type of "regenerative language" that Northrop Frye calls *kerygmatic* plays an important role for Milton in the end, as "myths become, as purely literary myths cannot, myths to live by."[23] But even if Milton did not see the necessity of a Frygian *double vision* in paradise, I intend to show in this study that the situation in which the need for a "regenerative language" might arise was present in Milton's paradise right from the start. The possibility of a split between *res* and *verbum* even in paradise—a view that shatters the traditional concept of paradisal existence— seems to *always already* have been a possibility. Even though Annabel Patterson claims that Milton trusts in the inherent truth of his writing, I would claim that it is most of all faith that sustains his semiotic system that would otherwise be threatened by arbitrariness.

Even though I have used the word *faith*, I would like to insist that this study is first and foremost a critical study of a work of literature, in which the Father, the Son, Satan, and the archangels are primarily all seen as literary characters. Although it touches on the (lost) unity of the linguistic sign as a *word with power* in the context of a religious speech act, and on what Victoria Silver calls the (non-existent) "cognation of logical and theological expressions,"[24] this work is in no way meant to be a theological treatise. As Michael Bryson puts it, "the Son and the Father are *poetic characters, works of fiction, constructions of a writer's imagination.*"[25]

Notes

1. Dennis Cooley, "the II-C of her heart (*for Smaro*)," *Dedications* (Saskatoon: Thistledown, 1988) 45.

2. See Harold Bloom, *The Anxiety of Influence: A Theory of Poetry* (New York: OUP, 1973).

3. See Sandra M. Gilbert and Susan Gubar, "Milton's Bogey: Patriarchal Poetry and Women Readers," *The Madwoman in the Attic: The Woman Writer and the Nineteenth-Century Imagination* (New Haven: Yale UP, 1979) 187-212.

4. David Dabydeen, "On Not Being Milton: Nigger Talk in England Today," *Proceedings of the XIIth Congress of the International Comparative Literature Association / Actes du XIIIe congrès de l'Association internationale de littérature comparée: München 1988 Munich*, ed. Roger Bauer and Douwe Fokkema (Munich: Iudicium, 1990) I: 84. As for Milton's role in the politics of British imperialism from the eighteenth century to the present, see Anne-Julia Zwierlein, *Majestick Milton: British Imperial Expansion and Transformations of Paradise Lost, 1667-1837* (Münster: Lit Verlag, 2001).

5. John Rumrich, *Milton Unbound: Controversy and Reinterpretation* (Cambridge: CUP, 1996) 2.

6. Frank Kermode, Introduction, *The Living Milton: Essays by Various Hands*, ed. Frank Kermode (London: Routledge, 1960) ix. See also T.S. Eliot, *Milton: Two Studies* (London: Faber, 1968).

7. Denis Saurat, *Milton: Man and Thinker* (1925; New York: AMS Press, 1975).

8. William Empson, *Milton's God* (1961; Cambridge: CUP, 1981).

9. See David Norbrook, *Writing the English Republic: Poetry, Rhetoric and Politics, 1627-1660* (Cambridge: CUP, 1999) and Michael Bryson, *The Tyranny of Heaven: Milton's Rejection of God as King* (Newark: U of Delaware P; London: Associated UPs, 2004). For a more balanced view of Milton's theological heresies and the concept of an angry and possibly hateful God than Bryson's, see Michael Lieb's excellent and even more recent *Theologi-*

cal Milton: Deity, Discourse and Heresy in the Miltonic Canon (Pittsburgh: Duquesne UP, 2006).

10. Rumrich, *Milton Unbound* 3. A.J.A. Waldock wrote in Paradise Lost *and Its Critics* (1947; Cambridge: CUP, 1966): "the epic that is *Paradise Lost* stands or falls, as every work of literature ultimately must, by the sense it makes. I do not think that we do it a service, at this time of day, by attempting to inject sense into those parts of it that do not make sense, by attempting to tighten what no ingenuity can ever now make thoroughly firm" (143).

11. Victoria Silver, *Imperfect Sense: The Predicament of Milton's Irony* (Princeton: Princeton UP, 2001) 192, 54.

12. John Rumrich, "Uninventing Milton," *Modern Philology* 87 (1990): 249-265.

13. Cedric C. Brown, *John Milton: A Literary Life* (New York: St. Martin's Press, 1995) ix.

14. Philip Neve, "Milton (1789)," *Milton 1732-1801: The Critical Heritage*, ed. John T. Shawcross (London: Routledge, 1972) 353.

15. The only remaining truly stable relationship between word and thing would thus be the incarnate word, God himself, or a coordination of sign and referent based on the Christian faith.

16. Annabel Patterson, Introduction, *John Milton*, ed. A. Patterson (London: Longman, 1993) 2.

17. Peter C. Herman, *Destabilizing Milton:* Paradise Lost *and the Poetics of Incertitude* (New York: Palgrave Macmillan, 2005) 49-51.

18. Catherine Belsey, *John Milton: Language, Gender, Power* (Oxford: Blackwell, 1988) 25.

19. Robert Entzminger, *Divine Word: Milton and the Redemption of Language* (Pittsburgh: Duquesne UP, 1985) 1.

20. John Leonard, *Naming in Paradise: Milton and the Language of Adam and Eve* (Oxford: Clarendon, 1990) vii.

21. Georgia B. Christopher, *Milton and the Science of the Saints* (Princeton: Princeton UP, 1982) 21.

22. Thomas F. Merrill, *Epic God-Talk:* Paradise Lost *and the Grammar of Religious Language* (Jefferson, NC: McFarland and Company, 1986) 1.

23. Northrop Frye, *The Double Vision: Language and Meaning in Religion* (Toronto: UTP, 1991) 17-18.

24. Silver, *Imperfect Sense* 45.

25. Bryson, *The Tyranny of Heaven* 26 (italics in original).

2 Theories of Language in the Seventeenth Century: From Essentialism to Nominalism, from the Bible to the Royal Society (and Beyond)

> Literature is an art of words, and the student of it may be interested primarily either in the art or in the words. If his interest is in the words, drawing him in the direction of linguistics and semiotics, the ordinary boundary terms that we commonly use within verbal structures begin to dissolve. We find it increasingly difficult to separate, by definition, literature from criticism, criticism from philosophy or history, or philosophy and history from any other type of verbal communication. All we have are the shifting relations of signifiers to signifieds.
>
> Northrop Frye[1]

> . . . throughout the seventeenth century, literary men as never before came to suspect the usefulness of images for depicting the true nature of the material world.
>
> Patrick Grant[2]

Milton's works were published is an age of revolutions, at, in Stevie Davies's words, "a time of maximum instability and stress, not only in the political world but in the fields of scientific, theological and linguistic change."[3] In the realms of politics and science, fundamental changes turned the traditional world upside down.[4] But, as hinted above, seventeenth-century revolutions went even further, and an "educational revolution" also affected institutions such as schools, academies, and universities. This educational revolution began between 1560 and 1640 and led to a degree of academic education that was unequalled in England until the twentieth century.[5] Important changes and developments also took place in the sciences. As Charles Webster shows in his study of seventeenth-century science, Puritanism must not be reduced to a mere fundamentalist fixation upon the Bible, as many prejudiced views would have it.[6] Some representatives of the Puritan Revolution even went so far as to see the sciences as a means and chance to create a new paradise on earth through "an imminent intellectual restoration."[7] After the Restoration, the groups of progressive scientists that had already existed during the Puritan Interregnum became part of the Royal Society, which also was to play an important role in the development of seventeenth-century concepts of language.

Francis Bacon (1561-1626) is of course the best-known and most important one among the philosophers standing behind this development in the field of the sciences, and the newly founded Royal Society "adopted" him as the father of the natural sciences in Britain.[8] One should, however, not make the mistake of interpreting this seventeenth-century scientific revolution as an abrupt passage from a medieval, superstitious, and teleologically oriented world to a modern, enlightened, and empirically oriented one, for the great revolutionaries also tended to hold scientific and religious beliefs that would hardly be reconcilable with a modern view of the world.[9]

The above-mentioned revolutions in the fields of politics, religion, sciences, and education also left their traces in the seventeenth-century concept of language, as there was a growing mistrust of all "artificial realities" such as language and society.[10] But England was by far not the only country in which doubts about the exactness and possibilities of everyday language arose: early modern Europe as a whole felt a certain uneasiness towards language, a feeling that language had become vague and was no longer grounded in real life. A telling example is Francis Bacon's mistrust of linguistic phenomena, when, in the *Novum Organum*, he refers to names and terms as untrustworthy "idols of the marketplace."

This feeling of discontent may also be seen as the outcome of a paradigm change in the course of the seventeenth century from a primarily essentialist to a predominantly nominalist concept of language. While the essentialists had insisted on—to put it in shorthand—a solid inherent relationship between things and the words that stood for them, this relationship became completely arbitrary for the nominalists. Thus Murray Cohen distinguishes between two schools of language philosophy in the seventeenth century: the essentialist (or naturalist) "seekers after Adamic naming" and the nominalist "empiricists":

> Some linguists in the seventeenth century tend to see the goal of their language work as the recovery, in the shapes and sounds of linguistic elements, of the essences of things in nature; others tend to define their work as reproducing, through mostly arbitrary symbols, the composition and coherence of things in nature.[11]

Normally one would subsume the biblical theories of the creation of language under the naturalist model, together with the position held by Plato's Cratylus. The naturalist-essentialist concept of language seems to be the older one, but in the seventeenth century the theories of naturalism and nominalism coexisted, as the concept of language as an arbitrary system in which the coordination of words and things is not motivated had of course been in existence for a long time.[12] Even for Hermogenes in Plato's *Cratylus*, language is "distinctly ambiguous."[13]

Historians of language do not agree on the exact point in time when the seventeenth-century paradigm change occurred. While some deem the "shift from essentialist to nominal epistemologies" to have occurred suddenly as a kind of Foucauldian epistemic break during the Restoration, others prefer to see it as a period of slow change corresponding to the length of the Puritan Interregnum.[14] Others criticize such attempts at teleologically interpreting linguistic development as "the persistence of a narrative model of 'revolutionary' progress that is imposed on the fragmentary and often conflicting evidence about language use..."[15] Most scholars agree, however, on seeing the second (i.e., nominalist) model, which corresponds to the "sceptical-empirical strain of English thought from the mid-17th century on,"[16] as the model underlying and determining the style of neoclassicism.

Milton's *Paradise Lost* is of course one of the chief literary works to have been published in this era of neoclassicism, even though most critics would prefer not to see it in this connection. If one takes the fact into account that even during the Restoration, Milton was apparently in contact with members of the Royal Society,[17] it makes sense to read and interpret Milton's later works not only with regard to his Puritan and revolutionary attitude but also in the historical context in which they were written and published. So *Paradise Lost* can and should be analyzed as "a precedent for neoclassical aesthetics."[18]

In the following pages, I will present some of the most important theories and concepts of language that were developed and/or discussed in the seventeenth century and thus form the background of Milton's works. As can be expected, I will start with the biblical model of the creation of language and with Augustinian semiotics. Then I will refer to ideas developed by Petrus Ramus in the sixteenth century, before I comment on the epistemological changes in the seventeenth century and the philosophy of language of Bacon, Hobbes and Locke as well as on the more pragmatic approach of the Royal Society.

2.1 The Biblical Model

Many authors have described Renaissance theories of the creation of language in more or less detail.[19] Even though the age of Milton is often seen as part of classically oriented Renaissance (or even neoclassicism, see above), the biblical narrative still played an important role in the seventeenth century. Theories concerning language were thus almost always based on the biblical account of the creation of Adam and Eve. In this context, it is Adam who gives their names to all the animals:

> And out of the ground the Lord God formed every beast of the field, and every fowl of the air; and brought them unto Adam to see what he would call them: and whatsoever Adam called every living creature, that was the name thereof.

And Adam gave names to all cattle, and to the fowl of the air, and to every beast of the field. (Gen. 2.19-20, King James Bible)

Even in the seventeenth century, this account could be interpreted in a number of ways so that biblical commentators wondered whether the names that Adam gave to the animals corresponded to the characters (*essences*) of the animals or whether they were bestowed upon them in an arbitrary and conventional way.[20] In a similar way, philosophers such as Bacon, Hobbes and Locke would, while still referring to the biblical creation account, also question the essential coordination of names and things in Adam's actions.

In the seventeenth century, it was generally assumed that the language spoken in paradise was Hebrew.[21] As for Milton, he does not state his opinion in detail, at least not in his prose works. In *Paradise Lost*, he also does not identify pre- or post-lapsarian language with any national or regional tongues, so that we may assume that he would have shared the general opinion of his time.

Margreta de Grazia describes a seventeenth-century "secularization of language" which had the effect of undermining the formerly assumed relationship between human and divine language so that "human words ceased to be related both in kind and quality to the divine Word."[22] This negation of the comparability of divine and human language implies the "Fall" of language from a quasi-prelapsarian state, in which human beings could communicate with God, to a postlapsarian state in which this kind of communication is possible only under certain circumstances.

This interruption of "unproblematic" communication between human beings and God seemed remediable to many philosophers of language in the seventeenth century. Such a positive view of the matter also appears in the young Milton's optimistic promise in *Of Education* that it would be the function of education "to repair the ruins of our first parents by regaining to know God aright" (*CP* II: 366-367).

As for Milton's later attitude, he indicates in the "Pinnacle Scene" of *Paradise Regained*—and not only there—that he has shifted from a reliance on education and science to that on the power of religious faith.

Eden or Babel

In most seventeenth-century theories of language origin that are based on the Bible, the linguistic "Fall" was identified with the episode of the Tower of Babel which resulted in a multitude of languages. This event of course takes place long after Adam and Eve had been expelled from Paradise so that, according to these theories, the Fall in the Garden of Eden did not have any direct linguistic consequences.[23] On the other hand, there was already a multitude of languages in the Bible before the construction of the Tower of Babel, and according to some interpretations, the "Babylonian" events did not affect all of the tribes descended from Noah's sons.[24]

There were, however, also seventeenth-century theories that considered it possible that the Fall had direct linguistic consequences even in Paradise. As Robert Entzminger claims, "many commentators trace the fall of language back to Eden."[25] Obviously, in the seventeenth century, the question of the Fall—and thus also the question of the Fall of language, of the difference between prelapsarian and postlapsarian language—is not only and not foremost a linguistic question but rather a theological and scientific one, as there are still high hopes of remedying the negative consequences of the Fall, whether it be through faith or through any form of scientific endeavour or the "study of second causes."[26] This faith in the possibility of repairing the consequences of the Fall brought together parts of society that otherwise did not have much to do with each other. It was shared by an incredible alliance, "by alchemists, by Paracelsans, by Bacon, by Hakewill, and by George Wither as well as by Familists, Winstanley and Fox."[27] Some radical religious groups, which critics such as Christopher Hill have even linked to Milton, went so far as to deny that the Fall had taken place at all.[28]

"Words with Power": Augustinian Semiotics

In his work, Milton relies on "a theory of language which allowed truth to be produced through an activity in language,"[29] i.e., he relies on words with which one can—to quote John L. Austin's famous title—*do things*. Colin MacCabe summarizes the semiotic basis of Milton's concept of language as "an epistemology in which truth can actually reside in the processes of language and not simply in an external world which language is called to represent."[30] I intend to show that such a position that relies on an essentialist concept granting quite an important role and function to language can only be attributed to the young and optimistic Milton. The older poet—and more experienced politician—would no longer be willing to grant the authority to restore the "unfallen" status of linguistic representation to mere linguistic and etymological arguments (rather than faith).

According to MacCabe, there were two epistemologies on the basis of which the young Milton might have conceived the idea of linguistic activity as a means of changing political reality: on the one hand, a hermetic philosophy seeing language as a system of correspondences between words and things, and, on the other, Augustinian semiotics. Although some critics have in fact established certain connections between Milton and hermeticists such as Robert Fludd (1574-1637), the second alternative seems to be more promising, all the more so since Augustinian semiotics also offers the faithful possibilities of achieving "glimpses of divine truth"[31] through certain uses of language.

Both these attempts to attribute language an active and creative role in the world were strongly criticized in the seventeenth century by the Royal Society and its predecessors. The members of the Royal Society, following mottoes such as *Nul-*

lius in verba, saw it as one of their foremost tasks to rely as little as possible on un-reliable words (*verba*) and to favour instead reliance on scientifically proven facts (*res*) in order "to promulgate a theory of language which destroyed the possibility of truth residing in language except in so far as language functioned as representa-tion."[32]

In the seventeenth century, Augustinian semiotics still had a strong influence on exegesis, preaching, and rhetoric, especially so on the Puritans who had emigrated to North America.[33] Augustine, relying on Greek philosophy and Roman rhetoric,[34] develops his semiotics in *De Doctrina Christiana* as well as in *De Magistro* and in his *Confessiones*. Even as a child, he realizes that language is based on conventions. In his *Confessions*, he describes the process of language acquisition which accord-ing to him relies not so much on his parents pointing at objects and thus establishing a connection between name and thing but rather on the observing child's ability of memory and abstraction.[35]

In his semiotic model developed in *De Doctrina Christiana*, Augustine estab-lishes a binary system which distinguishes between things (*res*) and signs (*signa*). *Res* are those things referring to nothing else but themselves, "things such as logs, stones, sheep, and so on, which are not employed to signify something."[36] A *signum* is

> a thing which of itself makes some other thing come to mind, besides the impression that it presents to the senses. So when we see a footprint we think that the animal whose footprint it is has passed by; when we see smoke we realize that there is fire beneath it; when we hear the voice of an animate being we note its feeling; and when the trumpet sounds soldiers know they must advance or retreat or do whatever else the state of the battle demands.[37]

As far as the *signa* are concerned, Augustine seems to foreshadow the seven-teenth-century schools of essentialism and nominalism as he distinguishes between natural and given signs: "Natural signs are those which without a wish or any urge to signify cause something else besides themselves to be known from them, like smoke, which signifies fire,"[38] and given signs "are those which living things give to each other, in order to show, to the best of their ability, the emotions of their minds, or anything that they have felt or learnt."[39] In contemporary terminology, those signs are conventional, as they receive their meaning only through a general and mutual agreement of language users.[40]

For Augustine there is, however, another possibility of creating signs that are not conventional, a possibility that is reserved for God alone. Thus Augustine com-plements the definition of things quoted above ("things . . . which are not employed to signify something") by adding that

I do not include the log which we read that Moses threw into the bitter waters to make them lose their bitter taste, or the stone which Jacob placed under his head, or the sheep which Abraham sacrificed in place of his son.[41]

Mazzeo speaks about "God's unique power to confer on realities their significance as signs. A stone is a sign only if Jacob sleeps on it in the particular circumstances in which God made him sleep on it in order to make the event a sign." He concludes from this that for Augustine it is only God who can create non-conventional "signs": "Only the Divinity can use things as signs in an intrinsic and natural, and not conventional meaning."[42]

However, when these signs are adopted for the use of human beings—such as in the context of this study—they regain their conventional status, for after their creation by God they become signs like all the others so that it finally becomes impossible to tell whether they are of divine or human origin. Critics thus often run into difficulties when they try to distinguish between the human use of divine signs and the forbidden urge (or ability) of human beings to create these signs for themselves. Difficulties thus arise in trying

to distinguish between man's allusions and references to the divine allegory of realities as signs, and man's power to create such signs. The latter, in strict theology, is impossible. They can only be discovered, in Scripture or in life, and they can be used, but they cannot be invented.[43]

According to Augustine, human beings can either use (*uti*) or enjoy (*frui*) things: "To enjoy something is to hold fast to it in love for its own sake. To use something is to apply whatever it may be to the purpose of obtaining what you love—if indeed it is something that ought to be loved."[44] In the act of communication, *res* are "used" in order to signify something; they become signs that carry messages. But according to Augustine there are also things which have no referential function pointing beyond themselves, which thus cannot be "used" but only "enjoyed." For Augustine, the highest thing to be enjoyed is of course God himself,[45] "the only thing which is absolutely not a sign (because it is the object to be enjoyed par excellence)."[46]

Among the signs that express transcendental truths through earthly things, there are the sacraments. Although the sacraments rely on convention in the sense that they have been given their significance by God, Augustine does not see them as conventional as they cannot be given their meaning by human beings themselves. Men are able to understand signs of this type, but they cannot create them. In addition, sacraments as they are defined by Augustine are adapted to human capacities: "While knowledge of temporal things and of the various branches of knowledge is useful in Scriptural exegesis, we must not forget that the Sacraments are signs only in so far as they are an adaptation to human sensibility of eternal truths."[47]

The signs mentioned so far in the description of Augustinian semiotics are not only and not necessarily linguistic signs, but the principle of *signum* is easily transferable to words or names. Even though for Augustine all words used by human beings are *signa*—for nobody uses words except in order to signify something—every *signum* still also remains a *res*, "since what is not a thing does not exist."[48] For Stanley Fish, this kind of argumentation is "a tour de force of distinctions that are finally without a difference": "Not only are these things signs of other signs which are also signs, but the chain of *sign*ifying all points in the same direction."[49]

All these endeavours of formalizing the act of signification cannot prevent certain difficulties of understanding between human beings. Augustine traces them back to the human pride symbolized by the Tower of Babel, "when wicked men justly received incompatible languages to match their incompatible minds."[50]

As a result of the "Babylonian" linguistic confusion, even God's message in its accommodated form is no longer immediately accessible. In cases of human non- or miscomprehension of the divine message which had been intuitively understood by Adam and Eve, Augustine suggests a pragmatic solution which Stanley Fish called "at once dazzlingly simple and, from the point of view of our normal assumptions about the world and our perceptions of it, wholly subversive":[51] "Anything in the divine discourse that cannot be related either to good morals or to the true faith should be taken as figurative."[52]

For Augustine, it does not seem to be a problem to replace one word by another, as long as one realizes that in the "movement from words to silence, from signs to realities," the "silent voice of God's creation" always has priority over any human voices.[53]

2.2 Seventeenth-Century Models

Ramus

A rival approach to Augustinian and biblical semiotics in seventeenth-century Britain was the logic of the Frenchman Pierre de la Ramée or Petrus Ramus (1515-72), the most influential logician of the sixteenth century.[54] Ramist dialectics with its hierarchical structure of *method* became an important influence on the seventeenth-century system of education, even though it was later seen as a logical failure and "fruitless schematism."[55] Although Ramus saw logic as an *ars bene disserendi*, he clearly distinguished its realm (i.e., *ratio*) from that of rhetoric (*oratio*).[56] For Ramus, rhetoric as such is thus clearly cut off from the realm of logic.

Ramist logic also played an important role for Milton's attitude towards language. First of all, Milton prepared a Latin version of Ramus's *Logic* which I will analyze in more detail in my chapter on Milton's prose work. It was possibly written as part of his educational work with his private students and published towards the end of his life. Milton's original interest in Ramist logic may well derive from the philosophical leanings of his *alma mater*, for there is a whole genealogy of Ramists at Christ's College in Cambridge which was to culminate in Milton.[57]

In the seventeenth century, logic was imagined to share certain religious and numinous characteristics with the original language of Paradise, and these characteristics gave rise to the hope for a reconstruction of an ideal unfallen state of the world. Perry Miller shows in his seminal work on Puritanism that, according to seventeenth-century opinion, logic, even used by pagans, carries with it "a portion of heavenly wisdom, a replica, however faint, of the divine intelligence" and that "By logic '(in some sort) is healed the wound we received in our reason by *Adams* fall.'"[58]

The logic of Petrus Ramus, at least in the way it is described and summarized by anglophone scholars such as Perry Miller and Walter J. Ong, thus obviously shared certain central aspects with Milton's ideas of a prelapsarian language. In this language, as it exists before the linguistic "Fall," communication is still prelapsarian, axiomatical and intuitive, not postlapsarian and syllogistic as it is today. Furthermore, Ramist logic did not always give preference to syllogistic reasoning over axiomatical judgment relying on human or divine testimony:

> Before Adam lost the image of God, Ramus said, almost all of his judgments had been simply axiomatical; in his integrity he had been able to see and to pronounce sentence immediately, as when he named the animals; he had uttered what was true and perceived what was false, and had discoursed by infallible progression from one proposition to its inevitable successor. Ideally all good judgments—sermons, reflections, poems—ought to be such a series of self-evident axioms, arranged in artistic sequence. But fallen man generally comes to conclusions through love, hate, envy, or cupidity rather than through perception. Therefore today men must use the syllogism in order by its constancy to animate their judgments, "otherwise all our assertions will be levity, error, temerity, not judgment."[59]

In addition, the Ramist way of displaying the binary structure of arguments in charts invites comparison with the way in which modern structuralism makes use of binaries, for example in the tree diagrams used in structuralist linguistics. This parallelism illustrates Walter Ong's statement that in the seventeenth century the concept of language—partly under the influence of Ramism—was no longer so much influenced by an aural-oral situation of communication as by written language.[60]

Bacon

In several of his works, Francis Bacon (1561-1626) deals with question of communication. In *The Advancement of Learning* (1605), the philosopher and politician describes the *tradition* or *delivery* of learning: "For the organ of tradition, it is either Speech or Writing: for Aristotle saith well, *Words are the images of cogitations, and letters are the images of words.*"[61] For Bacon, words do not directly refer to things but rather to notions. The coordination of words (Bacon also calls them *notes of Cogitations*) and notions functions in one of two ways: "the one when the note hath some similitude or congruity with the notion; the other *ad placitum*, having force only by contract or acceptation."[62]

As for Bacon's attitude towards the seventeenth-century concepts of language described so far, different tendencies seem to arise from different works. As Alvin Snider puts it, "conventionalist theories of language achieve a kind of equilibrium, or at least an uneasy coexistence, with the mythology of a divine origin." Snider continues claiming that

> Despite repeated allusions to the language of Adam, Bacon insisted on the conventional nature of language and remained sceptical about the value of Platonic (or 'Cratylic') etymologizing. The inquiry into linguistic origins was founded on the assumption that words 'were not arbitrarily fixed at first, but derived and deduced by reason and according to significance.'[63]

Most seventeenth-century philosophers of language and semioticians seem to have been influenced by both the above-mentioned concepts (which G.A. Padley refers to as Sensualism and Rationalism). The issue of an arbitrary and conventionalist coordination of signified and signifier thus seems to have become "a commonplace of late-seventeenth-century speculation." Padley furthermore states that the seventeenth century "espouses however the nominalist variant of that philosophy, which was sceptical of any necessary connection between name and thing, and it is this very scepticism that lies at the root of modern science."[64] This scepticism will also be at the core of my interpretation of Milton's description of the creation of language in *Paradise Lost.*

From a modern point of view, the seventeenth-century concept of language as a convention is generally linked to the name of John Locke and his theory of language as being "arbitrary, voluntary and individual,"[65] but the following excerpt from Bacon's 59th aphorism shows that conventionalist theories existed—at least *in nuce*—well before the end of the seventeenth century. For example, Lia Formigari identifies a full-fledged "theory of the conventionality of signs" in Bacon's contrasting of human and Adamic language.

In the 59th aphorism in *Novum Organum* (1620), Bacon shows that words are nothing but "idols of the marketplace" (*idola fori*), i.e., unnatural and arbitrarily formed "prime misleaders"[66]: They "are the most troublesome of all: idols which have crept into the understanding through the alliances of words and names. For men believe that their reason governs words, but it is also true that words react on the understanding; and this it is that has rendered philosophy and the sciences sophistical and inactive." The negative power of words even goes so far that they often stand in the way of rational change.[67] Bacon here falls back on an earlier argument that he had voiced in *The Advancement of Learning*, when he mentioned "the false appearances that are imposed upon us by words" and praised the wisdom of mathematicians in their way of coordinating signifieds and signifiers:

> . . . so as it is almost necessary in all controversies and disputations to imitate the wisdom of the Mathematicians, in setting down in the very beginning the definitions of our words and terms, that others may know how we accept and understand them, and whether they concur with us or no.[68]

Still, as mentioned above, Bacon's pronouncements on language are also sometimes contradictory, so that he has been cited not only as "an exponent of an outmoded analogical world-view" but also as "a prophet of nominalistic desacralization,"[69] the second view being prevalent today and contributing to his reputation as a prophet of the natural sciences and the father of the Royal Society, which was to be founded after the Restoration.

Many scholars stress the ambivalence of Bacon's attitude, as it does not become completely clear in his discussion of the relationship between thinking and speaking whether words refer to the things themselves or to ideas of these things,[70] whether we are dealing with a "nominalistically scientific" or a "transcendentally hermeneutic notion of language."[71] Jürgen Kamm concludes, however, that Bacon's characteristic preference of sensual perception reverses the traditional approach of mediaeval scholasticism, as one now no longer attaches imprecise notions to phenomena but rather relies on the phenomena themselves to bring forth precise notions in the act of inductive reasoning. Bacon thus justifies his demands for a new scientific language "in which there is a one-to-one relationship between word and thing, between signifier and referent."[72]

Of course, the idea that phenomena are to bring forth their notion by themselves in an act of inductive reasoning almost sounds like the traditional naturalist position and seems to once again question the conventionalist interpretation of the relationship between signified and referent. In spite of his scepticism towards linguistic reform, Bacon still seems to hope for the restoration of a paradisal state of language. This at least may shine through his remark, in *Valerius Terminus of the Interpretation of Nature*, that "the true ends of knowledge" include "a restitution and reinvesting (in great part) of man to the sovereignty and power (for whensoever he shall be able to call the creatures by their true names he shall again command them) which he had in his first state of creation."[73]

Modern Bacon scholars seem to prefer the view, however, that although his interest in a rational or philosophical language shares some "Adamic" or mystical features, Bacon has given up his search for the lost original language. Babel represents for him "the moment of disjuncture that irrevocably split mind and world into the duality of subject and object" and leads to his "anxious concern over the rift between sign and referent" that foreshadows modern semantic theories.[74]

Despite the high regard in which the seventeenth century holds Bacon, some modern scholars also argue against exaggerating his importance and deny the linguistic relevance of his ideas and his true interest in scientific progress, as, "apart from a generic emphasis on experimentation, Bacon provided no adequate methodological tool or model for the practice of Restoration natural philosophy."[75]

Critics are equally split on the question of Bacon's influence on Milton: many see a Baconian influence on Milton's early writing such as the *Prolusions* and on his pamphlet *Of Education*. As I am going to show in my chapter on Milton's prose, critics have become more and more sceptical about the possibility of a larger influence of Bacon on Milton. For example, Don M. Wolfe argues in his introduction to volume IV.1 of the Yale edition that Milton relied in his writings on moral, religious, aesthetic and political values rather than on the natural sciences. There is no proof, for example, that Milton ever read Bacon's *Novum Organum*. On the contrary: "Had he absorbed even the aphorisms of Part II, his capacious mind could not have remained unaware of the explosive power loosed into the world by Bacon's scientific creed."[76]

Hobbes

In questions of language, the other British philosopher of central importance in the mid-seventeenth century, Thomas Hobbes (1588-1679), was about as sceptical as Bacon. Hobbes's ideas about language appear in several works such as *Elements of Law Natural and Politic* (1640), *Leviathan* (1651), *De Corpore* (1655) and *De Homine* (1658) and have recently been discussed by Michael Isermann. As far as the conventionalist and arbitrary coordination of words and things is concerned, researchers seem to agree that Hobbes favoured the idea "of the arbitrariness of the coordination of signified and signifier."[77] While earlier critics had highlighted Hobbes's nominalism, "his belief that when we speak of universals we are speaking only of names rather than of real things,"[78] Jürgen Kamm emphasizes his reliance on speech acts rather than on single words as a revolutionary development in the seventeenth century.[79]

Other scholars point to the fact that, in contrast to the Bible, Hobbes no longer sees any connection between pre- and post-"Babylonian" languages,[80] but on the other hand, for him the coordination of signified and signifier had been conventionalist and arbitrary even in prelapsarian language. While he identifies in *Leviathan*

(1651) four "abuses of language"—"self-deceiving linguistic ambiguity; metaphorical use of words to deceive others; lying; use of language to grieve others"[81]—he also formulates an ideal state of language and of the coordination of names and things in the famous fourth chapter, "Of Speech":

> Seeing then that truth consisteth in the right ordering of names in our affirmations, a man that seeketh precise truth had need to remember what every name he uses stands for, and to place it accordingly, or else he will find himself entangled in words, as a bird in lime twigs, the more he struggles the more belimed. And therefore in geometry, which is the only science that it hath pleased God hitherto to bestow on mankind, men begin at settling the significations of their words; which settling of significations they call *definitions*, and place them in the beginning of their reckoning.[82]

Such an ideal state of a logical one-to-one correspondence between names and things is of course only possible in logical or mathematical formulae and not in a language that has developed and grown historically.

The Royal Society

The scientific revolution of the seventeenth century can best be summarized by the title of Bacon's planned but unfinished overview of the natural sciences, *The Great Instauration*, which was also the title Charles Webster chose for his important work on this topic. Webster's description of the scientific revolution of the seventeenth century was preceded by several decades in the works of Richard Foster Jones.[83] In his studies, Jones also comments on the role of language in this revolutionary process, and he integrates the linguistic development into a teleological process during which "an earlier, ancient, and nonscientific mentality gave way before the advances of a new, modern, and utilitarian conception of the world and of language."[84]

As far as the seventeenth-century attitude towards language is concerned, even in England the influence of the Czech reformer Johann Amos Comenius and of his theories should not be neglected. His ideas of language-teaching, developed in the context of his all-embracing concept of *Pansophia,* had an international reputation and also spread to Great Britain: at the invitation of his "apostle"[85] in Britain, the German Samuel Hartlib, Comenius spent some months in England. He left some traces in an England torn by the Puritan Revolution but did not have the success he had hoped for. Still, Jackson Cope and Harold Whitmore Jones see the "Universal College" projected in Comenius's *Via Lucis* as the model of the British Royal Society.[86]

Among the promoters of scientific progress during the Puritan Interregnum, the above-mentioned Samuel Hartlib plays an important role. He was "the middleman of reform in the English Revolution"[87] and the leading theoretician of education among the 'Comenian group' in England. Hartlib, who had come as a student to Cambridge in 1625,[88] made a name for himself as a mediator between English scientists and philosophers and their continental counterparts such as Comenius, Mersenne, and Descartes, and it was to him, after all, that Milton's *Of Education* was dedicated.

Although the Royal Society did not count linguistic topics among its central interests, it was also somewhat concerned with questions of language and style, as witnessed by some well-known—albeit marginal[89]—excerpts from Thomas Sprat's *History of the Royal Society*. The ideal language looked for by English philosophers of language—among them such leading members of the Royal Society as Bishop John Wilkins, a member of its "committee for improving the English language"[90]— was "a language free of redundancy or ambiguity, i.e., a word-thing language,"[91] in which there existed a one-to-one correspondence between signified and signifier. Those who fought for such a language would, in Sprat's words,

> take the whole Mass of our Language into their hands, as they find it, and would set a mark on the ill Words; correct those, which are to be retain'd; admit, and establish the good; and make some emendations in the Accent, and Grammar.[92]

One may interpret these remarks as a "proposal for an English academy" modelled upon French and Italian institutions such as the Académie Française or the Accademia della Crusca, but linguistic reform was certainly not the foremost objective of the Society.[93] What it aimed at in connection with language was to get rid of a style of impressive but nevertheless empty eloquence and to reestablish a clearer relationship between words and things, *res* and *verba*.[94] Such an interest in language reform was motivated by

> a constant Resolution, to reject all the amplifications, digressions, and swellings of style: to return back to the primitive purity, and shortness, when men deliver'd so many *things*, almost in an equal number of *words*. They have exacted from all their members, a close, naked, natural way of speaking; positive expressions; clear senses; a native easiness: bringing all things as near the Mathematical plainness, as they can: and preferring the language of Artizans, Countrymen, and Merchants, before that, of Wits, or Scholars.[95]

While Sprat took the purpose of the foreign academies upon which the Royal Society was modelled to be, above all, the "smoothing of their Style, and the Language of their Country," he defined the tasks and goals of the British counterpart as "not the Artifice of Words, but a bare knowledge of things," and—referring to "[t]heir *manner of Discourse*"—he condemned "the luxury and redundance of *speech*."[96]

Although the Royal Society was founded only after the Restoration, it had—as mentioned above—predecessors in the Commonwealth, for example the "Invisible

College," of which Comenius and Hartlib are supposed to have been members.[97] There also seem to have been contacts between the Royal Society and Milton himself. Some members of the Society even appear to have been interested in winning him over to become if not *poet laureate*, then at least a contributor to a new "scientific poetry" following to the concepts of the Royal Society.[98]

The *Plain Style* Discussion

In *Self-Consuming Artifacts*, Stanley Fish uses the phrase "Plain Style Question" for discussions of seventeenth-century language attitudes that reach back to the 1920s and 30s and involve scholars such as Morris W. Croll and Richard F. Jones.[99] According to Croll, one can distinguish in seventeenth-century literature between an early and classically symmetrical Ciceronian style "in the service of prevailing orthodoxies" and a later, progressive and asymmetrical Attic style. The latter, modelled upon the Roman writer Seneca and foreshadowed by the language of Bacon,[100] is evident in the plain style of the Puritans. Jones claimed that the Royal Society's "linguistic platform" influenced its members not only in their scientific works but also "in writings other than scientific."[101] More recent critics such as Arakelian and Vickers think, however, that Jones and Croll made a mistake in seeing the influence of Bacon's, Glanvill's and Sprat's demands for a *plain style* as extending beyond the originally intended scientific context and affecting even the realm of *belles lettres*.[102]

Stanley Fish draws the lines between the seventeenth-century linguistic factions in a different way than Jones, who had constructed a radical opposition between the style of the new science (represented by the Royal Society) and "the style of everyone else, that is of everyone whose writings display the rhetorical ornament, convoluted syntax, and interlarding of Greek and Latin quotations that were to be banished in favor of the ideal of so many words to so many things."[103] "The style of everyone else" of course brings together texts and authors that would otherwise be completely incompatible. Thus one might even classify Milton's own prose as classically Ciceronian, which would establish a certain contrast with his political convictions. Fish shows that all the dichotomies that have been used in order to explain seventeenth-century philosophy of language—"Ciceronian-Attic, Scientific-Rhetorical, Puritan-Anglican, Commonwealth-Restoration"—are not really useful. He even wonders whether the plain style itself is nothing but a phantom, and "that the so-called 'rhetorical' preacher was a phantom opponent who could be invoked by anyone who found it convenient to do so, but who could not himself be found."[104] The search for the phantom of plain style even led to the paradoxical situation that the Puritans and nonconformists who had fought for a plain style at the beginning of the seventeenth century were themselves accused of linguistic excesses by conformist Anglicans after 1660:

This conviction that they were on the side of common sense, clarity and good taste enabled conformists to characterize (and stigmatize) nonconformists as literary and linguistic, as well as religious, dissenters, distinguishable by an abuse of language which was an affront to all who valued plain, rational and civil discourse.[105]

After having thus deconstructed existing dichotomies regarding seventeenth-century language, Stanley Fish himself suggests a new dichotomy typically characterized by his interest in the reception of literary texts: *self-satisfying* vs. *self-consuming*. This new epistemological distinction is founded on two different views of the human spirit and its capacities: on the one hand, on an affirmative position insisting on the human spirit's ability to understand and shape the world; on the other, on a negative position relying on "the assumption that the mind is a prisoner of its inherent limitations, and that the apprehension, in rational or discursive terms, of ultimate truth, is beyond it."[106] While the first, affirmative view requires a language that reconfirms human beings in their view of themselves by addressing them in a fashion that they can understand, the other requires a language that challenges and questions itself and the readers' intellectual abilities. Such a kind of "self-consuming artifact" is of course an ideal object of a Fishian phenomenological interpretation.[107]

One may well wonder if the *plain style* can in any way be relevant for the discussion for such a complex style as Milton's, but it is interesting and useful to observe the range and radicalness of positions existing at the time of the publication of *Paradise Lost*, which after all was published in the same year as Sprat's *History of the Royal Society*.

Theories of Language Among Milton's Contemporaries

Partly even before the Royal Society was founded and partly in the context of this society, some of Milton's contemporaries invented a number of purely denotative *word-thing languages* relying on a one-to-one correspondence between words and things. Among the best-known examples are those languages devised by George Dalgarno and John Wilkins. An analogous language is probably also seen to be used in the Adamic act of naming in Book VIII of *Paradise Lost*. For Jun Harada, such a prelapsarian language mirrors "the monolithic honest quality of Edenic language."[108] But as I will argue in my analysis of *Paradise Lost*, Milton seems to have had great reservations about such a "monolithic" language which supposedly existed in the mythical garden of Eden and which the scientists and philosophers of his time were striving to recreate. According to Stanley Fish, "By using language to point up the distortion that results whenever fallen man attempts to make sense of the world around him, Milton passes judgment on the scientific and linguistic optimism of his own century."[109]

As pointed out in the preceding chapter, some of the philosophers of language in Milton's times really seem to have believed that the recreation or reinvention of a universal language that would be "structurally isomorphic to the order of things" would lead to the reinstitution of a paradisal state on Earth.[110] According to Robert Markley—commenting on Robert Boyle's *Considerations Touching the Style of the Holy Scriptures*, "the most penetrating contemporary view of the issues that figure in late 17th-century debates about the nature and function of language"[111]—the Bible served as a "transhistorical model of moral and stylistic authority" stabilizing Restoration society as well as transcending "the fallen, dialogical languages of a postlapsarian world."[112]

Although they were aware of the fact that the Bible hardly qualified as a fundamental work of semiotics any more, optimists still believed in the usefulness and possibility of the political and theological utopia of, as Markley puts it, "a semiotic encoding of the order of the material and political worlds, an ideal of noise-free communication that, in theory, would transcend political and theological controversy."[113] The most impressive example of such an optimism is—besides the work of the Scotsman George Dalgarno—John Wilkins's *An Essay Towards a Real Character, And a Philosophical Language*, which was published at about the same time as Milton's *Paradise Lost*, in 1668. In this volume, which has been called "the most thorough linguistic work of the century,"[114] Wilkins—bishop, Cromwell's brother-in-law, and important member of the Royal Society—claims that

> 'tis evident enough that the first Language was *con-created* with our first Parents, they immediately understanding the voice of God speaking to them in the Garden. And how Languages came to be *multiplyed*, is likewise manifested in the story of the *Confusion of Babel*.[115]

In this work, which later on was "generally admired as a failure,"[116] Wilkins thus shares the view held in Genesis that the Fall of language took place in connection with the events of the Tower of Babel. Nevertheless, Robert Entzminger claims—and I am going to follow him in this argument—that there are good reasons to disagree with this view, at least as far as Milton's *Paradise Lost* is concerned: Here, I would argue, it is Adam and Eve who are responsible for the linguistic "Fall," if one thinks that such a Fall is really required on the level of language.

According to Entzminger, the complete recreation of biblical prelapsarian language, which even Wilkins does not aim at any more, is impossible because "Milton's Adam forfeits at the Fall the insight into things that their Edenic names express, and thus his postlapsarian speech bears at most an external resemblance to the purity and clarity of innocent words."[117] This interpretation is backed up by Kroll's view of the concepts of language held by British neoclassicists when he questions Richard Foster Jones's "thesis that the scientific world view produced an ideology that treated language as transparent or referential—as an instrument, that is, to an unmediated cognitive and experimental grasp of objects in the world."[118]

Locke

The most important philosopher of language in late seventeenth-century England is undoubtedly John Locke (1632-1704), whom Roy Harris calls the "epistemologist to the founders of the Royal Society."[119] Even if he had such a position, it would certainly be wrong to turn Locke into the follower of a simplistic and all too optimistic tendency of language reform. For example, he has the following to say about language reform in *An Essay Concerning Human Understanding*:

> I am not so vain to think, that any one can pretend to attempt the perfect *Reforming* the *Languages* of the world, no not so much as that of his own Country, without rendring himself ridiculous. To require that Men should use their words constantly in the same sense, and for none but determined and uniform *Ideas*, would be to think, that all Men should have the same Notions, and should talk of nothing but what they have clear and distinct *Ideas* of. Which is not to be expected by any one, who hath not vanity enough to imagine he can prevail with Men, to be very knowing, or very silent. And he must be very little skill'd in the world, who thinks that a voluble Tongue, shall accompany only a good Understanding; or that Men's talking much or little, shall hold proportion only to their Knowledge.[120]

As Hans Aarsleff indicates, Locke's argument opposes the most widespread concept of language, "a doctrine that can best be called by the umbrella term the Adamic language." This theory of Adamic language presupposes that contemporary post-Babylonian languages still bear traces of the original perfect language of Paradise. Therefore, the coordination of signs and referents here is not yet arbitrary, or if is arbitrary, then it relies on divine—and not only human—arbitrariness: "the linguistic sign is not double but unitary."[121] From a nominalist point of view, Locke criticizes "the cheat of words" on which such a theory relies. He takes the coordination of words and things to be arbitrary, as otherwise communication would soon become impossible because of the sheer number of words:

> §1. GOD having designed Man for a sociable Creature, made him not only with an inclination, and under a necessity to have fellowship with those of his own kind; but furnished him also with Language, which was to be the great Instrument, and common Tye of Society. *Man* therefore had by Nature his Organs so fashioned, as to be *fit to frame articulate Sounds*, which we call Words. . . .
> §2. Besides articulate Sounds therefore, it was farther necessary, that he should be *able to use these Sounds, as Signs of internal Conceptions*; and to make them stand as marks for the *Ideas* within his own Mind, whereby they might be made known to others, and the Thoughts of Men's Minds be conveyed from one to another.
> §3. But neither was this sufficient to make Words so useful as they ought to be. It is not enough for the perfection of Language, that Sounds can be made signs of *Ideas*, unless those *signs* can be so made use of, as *to comprehend several*

particular Things: For the multiplication of Words would have perplexed their Use, had every particular thing need of a distinct name to be signified by.[122]

Jürgen Kamm thus states in his study of Restoration discourse that for Locke there is "no natural connection" between a word and the object referred to so that a word never refers to the object itself but rather to the idea the speaker holds about this object. For this reason words always only refer to "nominal essences" and never to "real essences."[123]

In his chapter "Of the Signification of Words," Locke himself points out the arbitrariness of the coordination of word and concept:

> The Comfort, and Advantage of Society, not being to be had without Communication of Thoughts, it was necessary, that Man should find out some external sensible Signs, whereby those invisible *Ideas*, which his thoughts are made up of, might be made known to others. For this purpose, nothing was so fit, either for Plenty or Quickness, as those articulate Sounds, which with so much Ease and Variety, he found himself able to make. Thus we may conceive how *Words*, which were by Nature so well adapted to that purpose, come to be made use of by Men, as *the Signs of* their *Ideas*; not by any natural connexion, that there is between particular articulate Sounds and certain *Ideas*, for then there would be but one Language amongst all Men; but by a voluntary Imposition, whereby such a Word is made arbitrarily the Mark of such an *Idea*. The use then of Words, is to be sensible Marks of *Ideas*; and the *Ideas* they stand for, are their proper and immediate Signification.[124]

As I have hinted several times already and will show once again in my interpretation of *Paradise Lost*, the seeming opposition between theories of the creation of language relying on a "Lockean doctrine of linguistic conventionalism"[125] and the mythology of the divine origin of language, which critics such as Snider point out so often, is not necessarily an opposition. Both can, as I intend to show, very well coexist in the cosmos of a work such as *Paradise Lost* without giving rise to any contradiction.

As far as the ideas of the divine origin of language and of a monologic and monolithic Adamic language are concerned, Kamm makes an interesting point concerning Locke's views of paradisal language. He stresses that for Locke an individual's thoughts are free so that he or she also can freely choose the words he or she uses as well as their meaning. As this liberty also existed for Adam, Kamm insists, the position of seventeenth-century Adamic philosophy of language is rendered questionable "through the inversion of its premises"[126]: As Locke puts it, "The same Liberty also, that *Adam* had of affixing any new name to any *Idea*; the same has any one still."[127] This applies as long as one does not take into account the special authority God had bestowed upon Adam.

Kamm sees Locke's theory of Adamic language as an interesting re-interpretation of the biblical account, and this interpretation seems to have been shared by at least some of his contemporaries in their reading of *Paradise Lost*. This reinterpretation affects above all the role played by Adam, who is seen as a free individual able to decide for himself, using his power of reason in order to find his way in the prelapsarian world, but who otherwise is not that different from postlapsarian men.[128] Such an interpretation cannot, however, in the end rely on the role played by language, for Kamm correctly points out that Locke (and, I would claim, Milton, too) negates "the hope for religious deliverance through the purity of paradisal language, for only the ability to use language is God's gift, whereas the use of language is man's responsibility."[129]

2.3 Digression: Looking Ahead to the Twentieth Century

The distinction that philosophers such as Locke make between words and concepts, signs and ideas can on the one hand be traced back to traditional and even classical patterns of thinking, but on the other hand it also points ahead to the distinction made by linguists and semioticians of the twentieth century between sign and referent (or, simplifying the argument a little, between signifier and signified). In the following pages, the name of Ferdinand de Saussure will metonymically stand for these developments in twentieth-century structuralist and poststructuralist linguistics, even though Saussure's own work cannot always be held responsible for all the ideas and theories developed here.[130]

Ferdinand de Saussure's ideas on language in his seminal *Cours de linguistique générale* are based on several central dichotomies, some of which have become generally accepted as fundamental givens of modern linguistics. Among them are the distinction between *langue*—i.e., language as a system of rules and possibilities at the disposal of all speakers—and *parole*—the actual speech acts produced by the speakers using these rules and possibilities.

Saussure's semiotics or theory of signs deals with similar topics as did some of the "sematologies"[131] written by seventeenth-century philosophers of language. Furthermore, the Swiss linguist counts seventeenth-century grammarians such as the authors of the French grammar of Port Royal among his predecessors.[132] Angela Esterhammer even draws parallels between the creation *ex Deo* in *Paradise Lost* and Saussurean linguistics: "The actions performed by the Son as Word dividing chaos and ordering it into a structure of significantly differentiated units resembles Saussure's account of the operation of the linguistic system on sound and thought."[133]

Saussure also questions some of the same attitudes towards language that Milton problematizes in *Paradise Lost*, and he even refers to the same biblical account of Adam naming the animals as Milton, even though he criticizes it. In a similar way as the seventeenth-century philosophers of language, Saussure—on whose *Cours* not only modern structural linguistics but also much contemporary literary theory is based—sees language as a system of signs. But while John Wilkins and many of his contemporaries saw human language as a God-given and originally unambiguous system and thought that it would be possible to recreate—at least in their artificial languages—the one-to-one correspondence between words and things, the modern linguist denies that there is such a possibility of recreating a perfect language. When he introduces his concept of the linguistic sign, Saussure's interpretation differs from that of the Bible and from that given in the process of naming in *Paradise Lost* in that he does not see language as *nomenclature*, not as a list of terms corresponding to an equally long list of things:

> Cette conception est critiquable à bien des égards. Elle suppose des idées toutes faites préexistant aux mots (. . .); elle ne nous dit pas si le nom est de nature vocale ou psychique (. . .); enfin elle laisse supposer que le lien qui unit un nom à une chose est une opération tout simple, ce qui est bien loin d'être vrai.[134]

For Saussure, the Adamic one-to-one correspondence is thus not at all typical of linguistic signs in general, but it is rather a rare exception. Still, there is a certain ray of hope for those who want to apply Saussurean semiotics to language in Paradise, for he remarks that, according to an admittedly somewhat simplistic model, languages are "bi-planar" and the linguistic sign is "bi—partite"[135]: "Cependant cette vue simpliste peut nous rapprocher de la vérité, en nous montrant que l'unité linguistique est une chose double, faite du rapprochement de deux termes."[136]

As the *Cours* in its final, printed version was not written by Saussure himself but rather composed by his former students from their and his own notes, Saussure's sceptical view of biblical semiotics (and thus of the semiotics of *Paradise Lost*) did not make it into the normally quoted final version. His reference to the Bible can be found in the critical edition of the *Cours* edited by Rudolf Engler: "<La plupart des conceptions que se font, ou du moins qu'offrent les> philosophes du langage font songer à <notre premier père> Adam appelant près de lui les <divers> animaux et leur donnant à chacun leur nom."[137]

A connection between seventeenth- and twentieth-century theories of language thus obviously lies in the fact that they both refer back to the biblical account of the creation of language, but one has to keep in mind, of course, that Saussure rejects the biblical version's concept of language as a *nomenclature*. Seventeenth-century authors, on the other hand, among them John Milton, seem to have accepted the biblical version, although one may wonder, how long this could have remained true in the age of the Royal Society. Esterhammer even goes a step further—perhaps a step too far—in her reliance on the Saussurean model, when she writes that Saussure "co-opts the central images of the Garden of Eden myth, once the main evidence for a motivated language, to illustrate the arbitrariness of linguistic relations."[138]

Saussure's rejection of the biblical account of the creation of language and of the concept of language as a nomenclature is a direct consequence of his theory of the dual character of the linguistic sign. For Saussure, the linguistic sign consists of two elements, the signified (or *concept*) on the level of meaning and the signifier (or *sound pattern*) on the level of expression or form. The signified here is a purely imaginary concept and should not be mistaken for the real-world referent which it represents within the sign. As Robert Scholes reminds us, "Saussure, as amplified by Roland Barthes and others, has taught us to recognize an unbridgeable gap between words and things, signs and referents."[139]

An important concept in Saussurean linguistics is that of arbitrariness. Within the context of the original Saussurean model of the linguistic sign, arbitrariness exists not so much in the relationship between the sign and the real-world referent as it does within the linguistic sign, that is, in the arbitrary correspondence between signified and signifier, between the levels of meaning and form: "Le lien unissant le signifiant au signifié est arbitraire, ou encore, puisque nous entendons par signe le total résultant de l'association d'un signifiant à un signifié, nous pouvons dire plus simplement: *le signe linguistique est arbitraire.*"[140]

A question not answered by the Saussurean model of the linguistic sign is, however, how the single words or signs are to be combined to form sentences first and then complete texts. God's message and even Adam's communication soon go beyond the first act of "simple nomination,"[141] and present a complex discourse rather than a list of mere linguistic signs. For this reason, the necessity arises to complement the traditional concept of a word-oriented structuralist semiotics. Otherwise this model would not be able to cover the field of the communicative use of language or, for that matter, the rhetorical strategy of accommodation which will become especially important in the context of *Paradise Lost.*[142]

In his critical commentary on Saussure's *Cours*, Roy Harris interprets Saussurean semiotics as being embedded in a system of communication that resembles Locke's concept displayed in *An Essay on Human Understanding.* Harris describes it as a "translation theory" in which "understanding requires a double process of 'translation': a speaker's thoughts are first translated into sounds, and then the sounds uttered are translated back into thoughts by the hearer."[143] But this system does not deal with the pragmatic context in which linguistic signs are used. The speech act theorist Teun van Dijk, however, points to a solution that leads Saussurean linguistics beyond its being limited to mere words and sentences. He moves towards the field of text linguistics when he claims that "the classical Saussurean tradition of structural linguistics was carried over also to the systematic analysis of discourse, narrative, myth, film or advertising."[144] Even if they themselves do not apply their findings to a purely linguistic analysis of communication and rather analyze the realms of myths and rhetoric, French structuralists such as Roland Barthes and Gérard Genette have created models that are both based on Saussure's model of the sign and able to take into account structures larger and more complex than mere linguistic signs. Barthes, for example, developed his model of myth as a "sign" operating not only on the level of Saussure's *langue* but also on the higher level of metalanguage.[145] Genette uses a model of the same structure, but he sees rhetoric—rather than myth—as the meta-level, and he shows how linguistic signs acquire rhetorical connotations that go beyond their original denotative context.[146] Barthes and Genette have thus developed theories by means of which they can pass from a Saussurean system of *langue* to the discourse and rhetoric of applied language, i.e., Saussurean *parole*.

As far as the distinction between word-oriented and text-oriented linguistics is concerned, it is also interesting to note that the original restriction of Saussure's approach to the realm of signs corresponds to an important feature of many seventeenth-century theories of language. For example, Murray Cohen states in his seminal work on language philosophy of this era that "the basic unit of speech . . . is the word."[147] According to Cohen, it is only in the eighteenth century that linguistic theories start to embed the analysis of single words in the context of a more comprehensive discourse analysis: "linguistic significance depended on the system of language as it operates in human discourse."[148]

In this chapter, I have displayed some of the most important linguistic concepts and models that were developed or current in the seventeenth century and thus form the linguistic background of Milton's work. The first models discussed are, as was to be expected, the biblical story of the creation of language and Augustinian semiotics. The next model discussed is that of Ramist philosophy, which dates back to the sixteenth century but continued to be influential in Milton's own century (and of course in his own work). In the context of a discussion of epistemological changes in the seventeenth century, ideas developed by the philosophers Francis Bacon, Thomas Hobbes and John Locke are discussed as well as the Royal Society's policies as far as language is concerned.

Even though Milton is often seen as a representative of the classically oriented era of the Renaissance, biblical accounts and ideas based on medieval interpretations of the Bible still play a certain role in his times. For this reason, the biblical account of Adam giving their names to the animals still remained the starting point of linguistic discussions. Nevertheless, even seventeenth-century philosophers wondered whether the divine process of naming corresponded to the essences of the objects named or whether it was rather an arbitrary and conventionalist act. Still, the interruption of unproblematic communication between God and mankind that was due to the linguistic equivalent of the Fall seemed to be remediable to many in the seventeenth century.

Concerning the question as to when exactly the linguistic Fall took place in the biblical story—whether it coincided with the Fall in the Garden of Eden or whether it took place later, during the confusion accompanying the construction of the Tower of Babel—the seventeenth century did not have a clear answer. However, the interpretation that the "linguistic Fall" took place in Paradise already (if it ever took place) would have been supported by many of Milton's contemporaries.

The question of the relationship between names and things is of course a problem that philosophers have discussed for several millennia (see, for example, Plato's *Cratylus*). In the seventeenth century, the writings of Saint Augustine were still seen to be among the most important basic texts, all the more since—in opposition to the nominalist approach of the Royal Society—Augustine claimed that at least some signs received their meaning through divine authority and not only through a conventionalist and arbitrary act of coordination. Furthermore, the seventeenth century could still rely on Ramist logic in its distinction between intuitively prelapsarian and syllogistically postlapsarian language.

The dichotomy of these intuitively prelapsarian and syllogistically postlapsarian concepts of language also corresponds to the change from an essentialist to a nominalist concept of language. In the writing of Francis Bacon at the beginning of the century, both concepts are still competing with each other, while for Thomas Hobbes and the Royal Society nominalism has gained the upper hand.

Independently of the question as to whether they were essentialist or nominalist in their orientation, seventeenth-century theories of language in their majority still believed in a *word-thing language*, a type of ideal language about which John Milton, for one, seems to have had his severe doubts. In opposition to some of his contemporaries, he does not seem to have believed that it would in principle be possible to reintroduce paradisal circumstances through mere linguistic reform. In this respect, he can be seen as a precursor of Locke's scepticism regarding language.

There are surprising parallels between seventeenth-century concepts of language and modern linguistic theories such as those developed by the father of structuralist linguistics, the Swiss scholar Ferdinand de Saussure. Saussure and many of the seventeenth-century philosophers of language share a belief in the linguistic sign as a binary entity, even though the dichotomies *word/thing* and *signifiant/signifié* do not exactly correspond to each other as far as the level of abstraction is concerned. In addition, both Saussure's model of the linguistic sign and the concepts of his seventeenth-century predecessors restricted themselves to the level of words and did not really take that of sentences into account. Nevertheless, contemporary structuralists such as Roland Barthes and Gérard Genette have shown that the integration of the model of the Saussurean sign into a more comprehensive model of communication is possible.

Notes

1. Northrop Frye, *Words With Power: Being a Second Study of "The Bible and Literature"* (1990; Harmondsworth: Penguin, 1992) 63.

2. Patrick Grant, *Images and Ideas in Literature of the English Renaissance* (London: Macmillan, 1979) xi.

3. Stevie Davies, *Milton* (New York: Harvester Wheatsheaf, 1991) 19. See also Elizabeth Sauer, *Barbarous Dissonance and Images of Voice in Milton's Epics* (Montreal: McGill-Queen's UP, 1996).

4. See Christopher Hill, *The World Turned Upside Down: Radical Ideas During the English Revolution* (London: Temple Smith, 1972).

5. See Charles Webster, *The Great Instauration: Science, Medicine and Reform 1626-1660* (London: Duckworth, 1975) 102.

6. Webster, *The Great Instauration* xiii. See also Christopher Hill, *A Nation of Change and Novelty: Radical Politics, Religion and Literature in Seventeenth-Century England* (London: Routledge, 1990) 17.

7. Webster, *The Great Instauration* 12.

8. Alvin Snider, *Origin and Authority in Seventeenth-Century England: Bacon, Milton, Butler* (Toronto: UTP, 1994) 70.

9. See Harinder Singh Marjara, *Contemplation of Created Things: Science in Paradise Lost* (Toronto: UTP, 1992) 4.

10. Entzminger, *Divine Word* 6.

11. Murray Cohen, *Sensible Words: Linguistic Practice in England, 1640-1785* (Baltimore: Johns Hopkins UP, 1977) 21. This distinction mirrors that between natural and conventional signs undertaken by Augustine, amongst others, and may be loosely rendered by the dichotomous terms *naturalism* and *nominalism*.

12. See Snider, *Origin and Authority* 250.

13. Marcia L. Colish, *The Mirror of Language: A Study in the Medieval Theory of Knowledge*, rev. ed. (Lincoln: U of Nebraska P, 1983) 8.

14. See Richard W.F. Kroll, *The Material Word: Literate Culture in the Restoration and Early Eighteenth Century* (Baltimore: Johns Hopkins UP, 1991) xix.

15. Robert Markley, *Fallen Languages: Crises of Representation in Newtonian England, 1660-1740* (Ithaca: Cornell UP, 1993) 21.

16. Kroll, *The Material Word* xv.

17. See Nicholas von Maltzahn, "Laureate, Republican, Calvinist: An Early Response to Milton and *Paradise Lost* (1667)," *Milton Studies* 29 (1992): 181-98.

18. Kroll, *The Material Word* 325.

19. See, for example, Arno Borst, *Der Turmbau zu Babel: Geschichte der Meinungen über Ursprung und Vielfalt der Sprachen und Völker*, 4 vols. (Stuttgart: Hiersemann, 1957-

63) 1312-34; Cohen, *Sensible Words*; Lia Formigari, *Language and Experience in 17th-Century British Philosophy* (Amsterdam: Benjamins, 1988).

20. See James Knowlson, *Universal Language Schemes in England and France, 1600-1800* (Toronto: UTP, 1975) 12.

21. See Don Cameron Allen, "Some Theories of the Growth and Origin of Language in Milton's Age," *Philological Quarterly* 28.1 (1949): 5-16. See also Beverley Sherry, "Speech in *Paradise Lost*," *Milton Studies* 8 (1975): 247-66, and David S. Katz, "The Language of Adam in Seventeenth-Century England," *History and Imagination: Essays in Honor of H.R. Trevor-Roper*, eds. Hugh Lloyd-Jones, Valerie Pearl and Blair Worden (1981; New York: Holmes and Meier, 1982) 132-45. Milton's own version of the creation of language in *Paradise Lost* is listed as a variant of the Genesis-tradition in Gordon Winant Hewes, *Language Origins: A Bibliography*, 2nd ed. (The Hague: Mouton, 1975) 2: 503.

22. Margreta de Grazia, "The Secularization of Language in the Seventeenth Century," *Journal of the History of Ideas* 41.2 (1980): 319.

23. See Werner Hüllen, *"Their Manner of Discourse": Nachdenken über Sprache im Umkreis der Royal Society* (Tübingen: Narr, 1989) 151.

24. See Borst, *Der Turmbau zu Babel* 1331 and Katz, "The Language of Adam in Seventeenth-Century England" 137-38.

25. Entzminger, *Divine Word* 69. See also Sherry, "Speech in *Paradise Lost*" 251; and Heinrich Geissler, *Comenius und die Sprache* (Heidelberg: Quelle und Meyer, 1959) 31. Comenius also describes the expulsion from the Garden of Eden as a process that brought with it the confusion of languages (Wolf Peter Klein, *Am Anfang war das Wort: Theorie- und wissenschaftsgeschichtliche Elemente frühneuzeitlichen Sprachbewußtseins* [Berlin: Akademie Verlag, 1992] 320).

26. Marshall Grossman, *"Authors to Themselves": Milton and the Revelation of History* (Cambridge: CUP, 1987) 14.

27. Christopher Hill, *Milton and the English Revolution* (London: Faber, 1977) 346.

28. See Arthur E. Barker, *Milton and the Puritan Dilemma 1641-1660* (Toronto: UTP, 1942) 167, 176.

29. Colin MacCabe, "'So truth be in the field': Milton's Use of Language," *Teaching the Text*, eds. Susanne Kappeler and Norman Bryson (London: Routledge, 1983) 28. For a much more critical view of the importance of Augustinian semiotics, see Kurt Flasch, *Augustin: Einführung in sein Denken* (1980; Stuttgart: Reclam, 2003) 121-26.

30. MacCabe, "Language, Linguistics, and the Study of Literature," *Modern Criticism and Theory: A Reader*, ed. David Lodge (London: Longman, 1988) 438. For another intriguing interpretation of Milton's intertextual relationship with Saint Augustine, see Thomas Ramey Watson, *Perversions, Originals, and Redemptions in* Paradise Lost: *The Typological Scheme and Sign Theory that Unify Milton's Epic.* Lanham, MD: University Press of America, 2007.

31. MacCabe, "'So truth be in the field': Milton's Use of Language" 28.

32. MacCabe, "Language, Linguistics, and the Study of Literature" 438.

33. See Stanley Fish, *Self-Consuming Artifacts: The Experience of Seventeenth-Century Literature* (Berkeley: U of California P, 1972) 21-43; Barbara Kiefer Lewalski, *Protestant Poetics and the Seventeenth-Century Religious Lyric* (Princeton: Princeton UP, 1979) 73; and Perry Miller, *The New England Mind:The Seventeenth Century* (1939; Cambridge, Mass.: Harvard UP, 1971).

34. See Colish, *The Mirror of Language* 7.

35. Augustine, *The Confessions of St. Augustine*, trans. John K. Ryan (Garden City, N.Y.: Doubleday-Image, 1961) bk. 1, ch. 8 (pp. 50-51).

36. Augustine, *De Doctrina Christiana*, ed. and trans. R.P.H. Green (Oxford: Clarendon, 1995): I.ii.2.4 (p. 13).

37. Augustine, *De Doctrina Christiana* II.I.i.1 (p. 57).

38. *De Doctrina Christiana* II.i.2.2 (p. 57).

39. *De Doctrina Christiana* II.ii.3.3 (p. 57).

40. See Joseph Anthony Mazzeo, "St. Augustine's Rhetoric of Silence: Truth vs. Eloquence and Things vs. Signs," *Journal of the History of Ideas* 23.2 (1962): 178.

41. *De Doctrina Christiana* I.ii.2.4 (pp. 13, 15).

42. Mazzeo, "St. Augustine's Rhetoric of Silence" 179. See Silver, *Imperfect Sense* 59.

43. Mazzeo 179.

44. *De Doctrina Christiana* I.iv.4.8 (p. 15).

45. *De Doctrina Christiana* I.v.5.10. See Mazzeo 187.

46. Tzvetan Todorov, "The Birth of Occidental Semiotics," *The Sign: Semiotics Around the World*, eds. R.W. Bailey, L. Matejka and P. Steiner (Ann Arbor: U of Michigan, 1978) 25.

47. Mazzeo 180-81. See also Milton's definition of sacraments in chapter 28 of the first book of *De Doctrina Christiana*: "In the so-called sacrament, as in most matters where the question of analogy arises, it is to be noted that a certain trope or figure of speech was frequently employed. By this I mean that a thing which in any way illustrates or signifies another thing is mentioned not so much for what it really is as for what it illustrates or signifies. Failure to recognize this figure of speech in the sacraments, where the relationship between the symbol and the thing symbolized is very close, has been a widespread source of error, and still is today" (*CP* VI: 555).

48. *De Doctrina Christiana* I.ii.2.5 (p. 15).

49. Fish, *Self-Consuming Artifacts* 27.

50. *De Doctrina Christiana* II.iv.5.8 (p. 61).

51. Fish, *Self-Consuming Artifacts* 21.

52. *De Doctrina Christiana* III.x.14.33 (p. 147).

53. Mazzeo 181.

54. See Wilhelm Risse, *Die Logik der Neuzeit*, vol. 1: *1500-1640* (Stuttgart-Bad Canstatt: Frommann, 1964) 122. See also Wilbur Samuel Howell, *Logic and Rhetoric in England, 1500-1700* (1956; New York: Russell and Russell, 1961); G.A. Padley, *Grammatical Theory in Western Europe 1500-1700: Trends in Vernacular Grammar I* (Cambridge: CUP, 1985).

55. On Ramism as a logical failure, see Risse 200.

56. See Risse 126. On the relationship between logic and rhetoric in Ramist philosophy, see Walter J. Ong's introduction to Milton's *Logic* in the *Yale Edition* (*CP* VIII: 155).

57. See Howell, *Logic and Rhetoric in England* 211-12.

58. Miller, *The New England Mind* 112.

59. Miller, *The New England Mind* 133.

60. See Walter J. Ong, *The Presence of the Word: Some Prolegomena for Cultural and Religious History* (New Haven: Yale UP, 1967) 64.

61. Francis Bacon, *Works*, eds. James Spedding, Robert L. Ellis and Douglas D. Heath (1858-74; Stuttgart-Bad Canstatt: Frommann, 1963) III: 399.

62. Bacon, *Works* III: 400.

63. Snider, *Origin and Authority* 44.

64. Padley, *Grammatical Theory* 297.

65. Tony Crowley, "John Locke," *Proper English? Readings in Language, History and Cultural Identity* (London: Routledge, 1991) 14.

66. Stevie Davies, *Milton* 22.

67. Bacon, *Works* IV: 60-61.

68. Bacon, *Works* III: 396-97.

69. Snider 42.

70. See Jürgen Kamm, *Der Diskurs des heroischen Dramas: Eine Untersuchung zur Ästhetik dialogischer Kommunikation in der englischen Restaurationszeit* (Trier: WVT, 1996) 111.

71. These terms are translated from Hüllen, *"Their Manner of Discourse"* 56.

72. Kamm, *Der Diskurs des heroischen Dramas* 112 (my translation).

73. Bacon, *Works* III: 222.

74. Snider 43, 32, 51.

75. Kroll, *The Material Word* 144.

76. *CP* IV.1: 80-81.

77. Michael Isermann, *Die Sprachtheorie im Werk von Thomas Hobbes* (Münster: Nodus, 1991) 233 (my translation). See Sharon Achinstein, *Milton and the Revolutionary Reader* (Princeton: Princeton UP, 1994) 96.

78. Samuel I. Mintz, "The Motion of Thought: Intellectual and Philosophical Backgrounds," *The Age of Milton: Backgrounds to Seventeenth-Century Literature*, eds. C.A. Patrides and Raymond B. Waddington (Manchester: Manchester UP; Totowa, NJ: Barnes & Noble, 1980) 162.

79. Kamm 157.

80. See De Grazia 325.

81. Stevie Davies, *Milton* 22.

82. Hobbes, Thomas, *Leviathan. The English Works of Thomas Hobbes*, ed. William Molesworth (1839; London: Bohn; Aalen: Scientia, 1966) III: 23-24.

83. See Richard Foster Jones, "Science and English Prose Style, 1650-75 (1930)" and "Science and Language in England of the Mid-Seventeenth Century (1932)," *Seventeenth-Century Prose: Modern Essays in Criticism*, ed. Stanley Fish (New York: OUP, 1971) 53-89 and 94-111.

84. Kroll, *The Material Word* 1.

85. Hermann J. Flasdieck, *Der Gedanke einer englischen Sprachakademie in Vergangenheit und Gegenwart* (Jena: Frommann, 1928) 18.

86. See Jackson I. Cope and Harold Whitmore Jones, Introduction to Thomas Sprat, *History of the Royal Society*, eds. Cope and Jones (St. Louis: Washington U Studies; London: Routledge, 1959) 65.

87. Hill, *Milton and the English Revolution* 146.

88. Webster, *The Great Instauration* xiv.

89. Critics such as Hüllen (*"Their Manner of Discourse"* 100) point out that the remarks on language are in no way central to the argument of the *History*.

90. Francis Christensen, "John Wilkins and the Royal Society's Reform of Prose Style," *Modern Language Quarterly* 7 (1946): 180.

91. Stanley Fish, *Surprised by Sin: The Reader in* Paradise Lost (London: Macmillan; New York: St. Martin's Press, 1967) 109.

92. Sprat, *History* 42.

93. Christensen 280.

94. See A.C. Howell, "*Res et Verba*: Words and Things," *ELH* 13 (1946): 131-42.

95. Sprat, *History* 113.

96. Sprat, *History* 39, 40, 111.

97. See A.P.R. Howatt, *A History of English Language Teaching* (Oxford: OUP, 1984) 16 and the Introduction to Sprat, *History* xiii.

98. Nicholas von Maltzahn, "Laureate, Republican, Calvinist: An Early Response to Milton and *Paradise Lost* (1667)" 184.

99. See Fish, "Epilogue: The Plain Style Question," *Self-Consuming Artifacts* 374-82.

100. See Morris W. Croll, "Attic Prose: Lipsius, Montaigne, Bacon (1923)," *Seventeenth-Century Prose: Modern Essays in Criticism*, ed. Stanley Fish, who sees Montaigne and Bacon as "the first writers in the vernacular languages who employ a style which renders the process of thought and portrays the picturesque actuality of life with equal effect and constantly relates the one to the other" (8-9).

101. Jones, "Science and English Prose Style, 1650-75" 54; see also Jones, "Science and Language in England of the Mid-Seventeenth Century" 106.

102. See Paul G. Arakelian, "The Myth of a Restoration Style Shift," *The Eighteenth Century* 20/21 (1979): 227-28.

103. Fish, *Self-Consuming Artifacts* 375.

104. Fish, *Self-Consuming Artifacts* 376.

105. N.H. Keeble, *The Literary Culture of Nonconformity in Later Seventeenth-Century England* (Leicester: Leicester UP, 1987) 245.

106. Fish, *Self-Consuming Artifacts* 377.

107. See Robert Markley, *Fallen Languages* 1-2. Contemporary scholars mostly share Fish's critical view of the Jones-Croll debate.

108. Jun Harada, "Self and Language in the Fall," *Milton Studies* 5 (1973): 222.

109. Fish, *Surprised by Sin* 107.

110. Cohen, *Sensible Words* xxv; see Stanley Fish, "Rhetoric," *Doing What Comes Naturally: Change, Rhetoric, and the Practice of Theory in Literary and Legal Studies* (Oxford: Clarendon, 1989) 477.

111. Robert Markley, *Two-Edg'd Weapons: Style and Ideology in the Comedies of Etherege, Wycherley, and Congreve* (Oxford: Clarendon, 1988) 31.

112. Markley, *Fallen Languages* 39.

113. Markley, *Fallen Languages* 63.

114. Cohen, *Sensible Words* 31.

115. John Wilkins, *An Essay Towards a Real Character, And a Philosophical Language* (1668; Menston: Scolar Press, 1968) 2. On Wilkins, see also E.N. da C. Andrade, *A Brief History of the Royal Society* (London: Royal Society, 1960) 3.

116. Rüdiger Schreyer, "Die Tradition der Philosophischen Grammatik in England," *Sprachtheorien der Neuzeit II: Von der "Grammaire de Port-Royal" (1660) zur Konstitution moderner linguistischer Disziplinen*, ed. Peter Schmitter (Tübingen: Narr, 1996) 55 (my translation).

117. Entzminger, *Divine Word* 1.

118. Kroll, *The Material Word* 3.

119. Roy Harris, *Reading Saussure: A Critical Commentary on the* Cours de linguistique générale (London: Duckworth, 1987) 209.

120. John Locke, *An Essay Concerning Human Understanding*, ed. Peter H. Nidditch (Oxford: Clarendon, 1975) 509.

121. Hans Aarsleff, *From Locke to Saussure: Essays on the Study of Language and Intellectual History* (London: Athlone, 1982) 25.

122. Locke 402.

123. Kamm, *Der Diskurs* 160 (my translation).

124. Locke 405.

125. Snider, *Origin and Authority* 130.

126. Kamm 162.

127. Locke 470.

128. See Kamm 162.

129. Kamm 162 (my translation).

130. In the following argument, I will rely mostly on Ferdinand de Saussure's dyadic semiotics and not so much on the triadic system developed by semioticians such as Charles S. Peirce. On differences between the two, see Jürgen Trabant, *Elemente der Semiotik* (Tübingen: Francke, 1996) 45-47.

131. According to Cohen, the term *sematology*, which seems to be an alternative to Locke's *semeiotike* in *An Essay Concerning Human Understanding* (Locke 720), was coined by George Dalgarno in *Didascalocophus; or, The Deaf and Dumb Man's Tutor* (1680): "Sematology is 'a general name for all interpretation by arbitrary signs,' that is, it is the 'art of impressing the conceits of the mind upon sensible and material objects' and thus the basis for any sign system whatsoever" (*Sensible Words* 17).

132. Ferdinand de Saussure, *Course in General Linguistics*, trans. Wade Baskin (London: Peter Owen, 1974) 82.

133. Angela Esterhammer, *Creating States: Studies in the Performative Language of John Milton and William Blake* (Toronto: UTP, 1994) 117; see also William Shullenberger, "Linguistic and Poetic Theory in Milton's *De Doctrina Christiana*," *ELN* 19 (1982): 262-78.

134. Ferdinand de Saussure, *Cours de linguistique générale*, ed. Tullio de Mauro (Paris: Payot, 1991) 97.

135. Harris, *Reading Saussure* 62.

136. Saussure, *Cours* (ed. de Mauro) 97-98.

137. Saussure, *Cours* (ed. Engler) 147.

138. Esterhammer, *Creating States* 47.

139. Robert Scholes, *Semiotics and Interpretation* (New Haven: Yale UP, 1982) 24.

140. Saussure, *Cours* 100 (ed. de Mauro). The only exceptions Saussure admits to the principle of arbitrariness and conventionalism of linguistic signs concern certain cases of onomatopoeia, in which the word imitates a "natural" sound.

141. Snider, *Origin and Authority* 130.

142. See Paul Ricoeur, *The Rule of Metaphor*, trans. Robert Czerny *et al.* (Toronto: UTP, 1981) 65-66 on the necessity of integrating word semantics into the wider frame of a sentence or discourse semantics. See also Mary Louise Pratt, *Toward a Speech Act Theory of Literary Discourse* (Bloomington: Indiana UP, 1977) 7.

143. Harris, *Reading Saussure* 205.

144. Teun A. van Dijk, ed., *Discourse and Literature* (Amsterdam: Benjamins, 1985) 3.

145. See Roland Barthes, *Mythologies, Œuvres complètes*, ed. Éric Marty (Paris: Seuil, 1993) 687.

146. Gérard Genette, "L'envers des signes," *Figures* I (Paris: Seuil, 1966) 193.

147. Cohen, *Sensible Words* 5.

148. Cohen, *Sensible Words* 47; cf. Kroll, who opposes a clear-cut opposition between word-oriented seventeenth-century and sentence-oriented eighteenth-century linguistics (*The Material Word* 184).

3 The Question of Language in Milton's Works

At the beginning of the preceding chapter, I commented on the cultural, philosophical, and scientific background within which Milton developed his ideas concerning the creation and role of language. Before I pay closer attention to his political and literary works, I would like to briefly comment on the ways in which Milton has been treated by the writers of literary history. Hayden White has created the term *emplotment* as a way of pointing out that historiographers often fall back on the use of certain literary models when they narrativize, summarize, and interpret historical developments. The same is of course true of literary historians.

Thus the classification of an author such as Milton depends upon the persuasion of the respective literary historian. A conservative critic's Milton will differ quite a lot from the Milton constructed by a scholar for whom Miltonic ideas still hold a revolutionary potential. Milton analyzed with the help of the traditional instruments of English literary studies looks quite different from Milton deconstructed according to poststructuralist or feminist methodology. On the one hand, Milton has without any doubt always been one of the "great" authors belonging to the canon of English and world literature.[1] On the other hand, he has always been at the centre of criticism. He is not only one of those *strong poets* against whose influence young and ambitious authors have always had to fight in order to find a place for themselves in the field of literature; he also was at the centre of last century's "great controversy which dominated Milton studies until recently" and had to withstand the criticism of *Miltonoclasts* such as T.S. Eliot and William Empson.[2]

Milton poses problems not only for critics but also for literary historians, as he is something like an "erratic bloc" in the seventeenth century, and an epic such as *Paradise Lost* will forever remain a work that can hardly be compared to those of his contemporaries. Is Milton still a representative of the Renaissance, as most literary histories and anthologies suggest? Or does the style of his epic poems make him already part of the Restoration period?

3.1 Prose: From Education to Christian Doctrine, Logic, and Grammar

> I think thus: he who would write worthily of worthy deeds ought to write with no less largeness of spirit and experience of the world than he who did them, so that he can comprehend and judge as an equal even the greatest, and, having comprehended, can narrate them gravely and clearly in plain and temperate language. For I do not insist on ornate language; I ask for a historian, not an orator.
>
> Milton in 1657 (*CP* VII: 501)

The prose works of Milton that I am commenting on here in the more or less chronological order of their production are largely of a political or religious nature, but of course most of Milton's views on language come from theoretical writings on education—such as his pamphlet *Of Education*—or pedagogically motivated works—such as his *Logic* and *Grammar*.

Although Milton's style is of course always an important item in a study of his work, I am primarily interested here in his attitude towards language and in the ideas he holds about its creation and function. It would go far beyond the frame of this study to try to analyze in detail the style of every single one of Milton's prose works, but of course his often idiosyncratic style also gives us certain insights into his attitude towards language. For example, critics have for a long time pointed out the hiatus between prelapsarian and postlapsarian language that is often held to be responsible for the stylistic differences between *Paradise Lost* and *Paradise Regained* or between the first nine and the last three books of *Paradise Lost*. Milton's prose style has also provoked interesting insights, as can be witnessed in reader-response criticism of his prose works.[3]

In general, Milton is often seen as a representative of the rather conservative Ciceronian style against which there was a widespread reaction in the seventeenth century.[4] This classification does not do justice, however, to the early Milton's "wild" and polemical style in his *antiprelatical tracts* in which he seems to be "obsessed with the decorous correspondence between his own sanctified bitterness and the stridency of his literary fruit."[5] That is why some critics prefer to see a pattern of development including "a radical shift" between early and late prose, this stylistic break being also visible in Milton's poetry.[6]

Early Prose

Milton's sensibility about linguistic questions is already obvious in his earliest prose works, even in the *Prolusions* (1628-32) that he wrote as rhetorical exercises when a student at Cambridge in the late 20s and early 30s of the seventeenth century. Here he already criticizes a language that is almost smothered by the useless ballast of *verbiage.* But it is of course very problematic to interpret these academic exercises of a young man as the true opinion of the older Milton, all the more so since the style and occasion of the prolusions do not necessarily encourage their interpretation as serious discussions of the topics concerned. They are rather somewhat reminiscent of the context of a university debating society in our age.[7]

In the first prolusion, Milton addresses his ideal listeners by means of a formula that points ahead to the "fit audience though few" in *Paradise Lost*, although the prolusion was originally composed in Latin, of course:

> The approval of these, few though they be, is more precious to me than that of the countless hosts of the ignorant, who lack all intelligence, reasoning power, and sound judgment, and who pride themselves on the ridiculous effervescing froth of their verbiage. (*Prolusion* I, *CP* I: 220)

Milton sees traditional scholasticism, which is still dominating the teaching in the universities of his age, as the main source of this annoying wordiness. Once again in the third prolusion, "An Attack on the Scholastic Philosophy," he denies any usefulness to such a scholastic "unseemly battle of words": "[T]his contentious duel of words has no power either to teach eloquence or to inculcate wisdom or to incite to noble acts" (*Prolusion* III, *CP* I: 246). He probably wants to replace such old-fashioned methods by those of contemporary philosophers such as Francis Bacon. At least, that is the view of nineteenth-century scholars who were convinced that the prolusions represented Milton's "prepossession in favour of that real or experimental knowledge (Geography, Astronomy, Meteorology, Natural History, Politics, &c.), which it was Bacon's design to recommend in lieu of the scholastic studies."[8]

Milton's ideas during his university years already foreshadow those he will express twenty years later in his concept of educational reform in *Of Education*. Statements about Bacon's influence on Milton have to be analyzed critically, however, since Milton does not seem to have that much in common with most of Baconians such as Bushell, Dymock, Evelyn, Glanvill, Hartlib, Sprat, Sydenham, and Wilkins, and furthermore it would be difficult, if not impossible, to find proof of any contacts with them during Milton's Cambridge years.[9]

In Prolusion VII, "Delivered in the College Chapel in Defence of Learning: An Oration," Milton criticizes the language of the legal profession of his own age, which he calls—in the rather free translation of the *Yale Edition*—"a jargon which one might well take for some Red Indian dialect" (*CP* I: 301).[10] In his *Commonplace* Book, he may be somewhat closer to the historical and linguistic truth by referring to it as "norman gibbrish" (*CP* I: 424).

Some years later, during his travels in Italy (1638-39), more precisely in Florence, Milton again addresses linguistic questions during a meeting with Benedetto Buonmattei, whom the editors of the *Complete Prose Works* call "perhaps the chief authority on the Tuscan tongue" (*CP* I: 328).[11] Although this may be just a compliment, Milton praises Buonmattei not only as a soldier but also as a teacher and regulator of language, "the one who tries to fix by precepts and rules the order and pattern of writing and speaking received from a good age of the nation, and in a sense to enclose it within a wall" (*CP* I: 329). Furthermore, he describes the important task of the language teacher who "with a learned censorship of ears and a light-armed guard of good Authors, undertakes to overcome and drive out Barbarism, that filthy civil enemy of character which attacks the spirits of men" (*CP* I: 329). For Milton, language indicates not only the speaker's level of civilization but also the state of his or her society. Linguistic errors in everyday language point to the negative state of a nation, whereas a nation's pride in its own language rather speaks for its healthy character (see *CP* I: 330).

For an intellectual, especially for an intellectual like Milton, who is later going to become a diplomat, the foremost importance of languages lies of course in the possibilities they offer in the field of communication with the citizens of other countries. For this reason, he asks Buonmattei to add another chapter, "a little something on right pronunciation" (*CP* I: 331), to his new grammar of the Tuscan language, as such an addition would be useful for foreign learners.[12]

The topic of the intonation and pronunciation of foreign languages continues to occupy Milton. For example, in *Of Education* he addresses problems of pronunciation and holds the Italians up as an example to his fellow Englishmen whose "speech is to be fashion'd to a distinct and cleer pronuntiation, as neer as may be to the *Italian*, especially in the vowels":

> For we Englishmen being farre northerly, doe not open our mouthes in the cold air, wide enough to grace a Southern tongue; but are observ'd by all other nations to speak exceeding close and inward: So that to smatter Latin with an english mouth, is as ill a hearing as law French. (*CP* II: 382-833)

The Early Phase of the Revolution

After his youthfully optimistic statements on language, Milton turns to practical political propaganda against the Anglican bishops in the early forties of the seventeenth century, even though he claims that the writings he puts forth are nothing but products of his less gifted left hand. In these pragmatic pamphlets the more theoretical question of language obviously does not hold a prime position. Nevertheless, one may well argue that this very period of political activity and prose writing—the time of his poetic "abstinence" (1641-60)—has a great influence on his attitude towards the written word, as now his political declarations turn into quite powerful means of combating his religious and political adversaries. Stevie Davies claims that this period of transition is "the most important for establishing the status of the written word in his personal and public history." According to Davies, this political tension changes the Renaissance humanist into a highly motivated protagonist of the Puritan Revolution "in expectation of a new world."[13]

In spite of his obvious concentration on political topics, the theme of language still plays an obvious role in the early prose work written at the beginning of the Revolution. In *Of Reformation* (May 1641), for example, his humanist interest in the classical and modern languages—England being "the first *Restorer* of *buried Truth*" (*CP* I: 526)—comes to the fore time and again. In this text, he reminds his readers for example of the influence the Reformation had on cultural life and linguistic concepts. In the age of Reformation, the divine and humanist messages bring forth a kind of cultural re-birth:

> Then was the Sacred BIBLE sought out of the dusty corners where prophane Falshood and Neglect had throwne it, the *Schooles* opened, *Divine* and *Humane Learning* rak't out of the *embers* of *forgotten Tongues*. (*CP* I: 524-25)

The reliability of this biblical message is not really questioned: The general clarity of biblical language, which Milton presupposes almost axiomatically, is only doubtful in the case of some few "Books that remain clouded." On the whole, he contradicts the thesis, however, that the Bible is incomprehensible. Such a theory would have been inspired by the devil and its objective would be to dissuade human beings from reading the Bible. For the first time, Milton here uses the word *ambiguous* in connection with the Bible, but he clearly associates the darkness and negativity associated with this word with worldly human beings:

> We count it no gentlenesse, or fair dealing in a man of Power amongst us, to require strict, and punctual obedience, and yet give out all his commands ambiguous and obscure, we should think he had a plot upon us, certainly such commands were no commands, but snares. The very essence of Truth is plainnesse, and brightnes; the darknes and crookednesse is our own. (*CP* I: 566)

Another context in which Milton uses linguistic arguments is the heated Smectymnuan debate with the Anglican bishop Hall in 1641-42. Here Milton shows great self-confidence as far as his own English language is concerned. On the other hand, it becomes obvious here that Milton, who normally is not overly reticent in praising his own classical knowledge, can be surprisingly flexible if it turns out to be politically advantageous. Instead of admitting that his opponent Hall is right in criticizing a grammatically incorrect inflection in a text written by his Smectymnuan friends, Milton accuses him of being a capricious pedant: His friends do of course have the right of "Englishing" foreign terms; they can even refer to classical models in this strategy:

> if in dealing with an outlandish name they thought it best not to screw the English mouth to a harsh forreigne termination, so they kept the radicall word, they did no

> more than the elegantest Authors among the *Greeks, Romans,* and at this day the
> *Italians* in scorne of such a servility use to doe. (*CP* I: 666-67)

On the other hand, as far as the writings of his opponents are concerned, Milton
is of the opinion that the wrongness of a message can often be deduced from its
outer, linguistic form. For example, he lets his adversary, the "Remonstrant" in
Animadversions (July 1641), know that no "mintmaister of language" would accept
his "odde coinage" (*CP* I: 686).

Milton's growing linguistic patriotism, which had already been visible in *Animadversions* (and in his early poetry), is most obvious in *Reason of Church-
Government* (early 1642), when the poet plans "to fix all the industry and art I could
unite to the adorning of my native tongue" (*CP* I: 811):

> That what the greatest and choycest wits of *Athens, Rome,* or modern *Italy,* and
> those Hebrews of old did for their country, I in my proportion with this over and
> above of being a Christian, might doe for mine: not caring to be once nam'd
> abroad, though perhaps I could attaine to that, but content with these British Ilands
> as my world, whose fortune hath hitherto bin, that if the Athenians, as some say,
> made their small deeds great and renowned by their eloquent writers, *England* hath
> had her noble atchievments made small by the unskilfull handling of monks and
> mechanicks. (*CP* I: 812)

Nevertheless, as Milton himself remarks here in *The Reason of Church-Government*, the high ideal of a completely clear and unambiguous language is not always attainable. He rather soberly has to state that "all corporeal resemblances of
inward holinesse & beauty are now past" (*CP* I: 828).[14] Human beings have lost
their prelapsarian innocence, and Milton therefore seems to be fully aware of the
fact that language is no longer used in ideal contexts of communication but is rather
subject to the imponderabilities of human communication and to the "slippery and
equivocal ways political parties might employ":[15]

> For Truth, I know not how, hath this unhappinesse fatall to her, ere she can come
> to the triall and inspection of the Understanding, being to passe through many little
> wards and limits of the severall Affections and Desires, she cannot shift it, but
> must put on such colours and attire, as those Pathetick handmaids of the soul
> please to lead her in to their Queen. (*CP* I: 830)

In this context, rhetoric obviously plays an important and—in Milton's eyes—not
always positive role.[16]

Milton's rather cynical and acerbic style in his pamphlets is illustrated in *An
Apology Against a Pamphlet* (April 1642). While he is, as he fittingly admits in a litotes, himself well acquainted with the rules of rhetoric, it is only his love of truth
that motivates his political writings:

For me, Readers, although I cannot say that I am utterly untrain'd in those rules
which best Rhetoricians have giv'n, or unacquainted with those examples which
the prime authors of eloquence have written in any learned tongu [sic], yet true
eloquence I find to be none, but the serious and hearty love of truth: And that
whose mind so ever is fully possest with a fervent desire to know good things, and
with the dearest charity to infuse the knowledge of them into others, when such a
man would speak, his words (by what I can expresse) like so many nimble and airy
servitors trip about him at command, and in well order'd files, as he would wish,
fall aptly into their own places. (*CP* I: 948-49)

The view of the word as an active power in the political arena is still held by Milton
when he writes the pamphlet *Of Education* (1644). Language here plays the active
role that according to Colin MacCabe was inherent in Augustinian (and hermetic)
semiotics of the seventeenth century.

But as I pointed out in my interpretation of *The Reason of Church-Government*,
for Milton the existence and/or reconstruction of an "unfallen" ideal language becomes more and more improbable and problematic in his own time. This insight
may well be seen in connection with his unhappy marriage with Mary Powell that
led him to have another (and different) look at the Bible and at what it says about
divorce. Whereas so far he had seen the language of the Bible as clear, transparent
and unambiguous, now—during his search for a way out of his relationship with
Mary Powell—there is a break in his interpretation. Dayton Haskin sees this break
as a "startling discontinuity" and a "return to philology," i.e., to methods of interpretation Milton had so far "rather cavalierly dismissed."[17] The insight that the Bible
often contains contradictory elements waiting to be interpreted—some critics refer
to this process as that of "wresting Christ's own words into a contrary meaning"[18]—
is an important turning point in Milton's work and in his attitude towards language.

In *The Doctrine and Discipline of Divorce*—Milton's attempt to show that,
against first impressions, the Bible does not in fact render divorce almost impossible—he outlines the necessity of "philological" interpretation. Such an act of interpretation, in which one is allowed to revert to the level of figurative meaning if a
text offers difficulties on a literal level, is well known from Augustinian semiotics:

First therfore let us remember as a thing not to be deny'd, that all places of
Scripture wherin just reason of doubt arises from the letter, are to be expounded by
considering upon what occasion every thing is set down: and by comparing other
Texts. (*CP* II: 282)

In the following, Milton points out that Christ himself made use of *ambiguous reasons* (*CP* II: 329), for example in order to irritate the Pharisees. He even goes so far
as to claim that there is hardly any quotation from the Bible that does not have to be
interpreted figuratively in order for its meaning to become clear. Otherwise it might
turn into a repugnant riddle:

Thus at length wee see both by this and by other places, that there is scarse any one saying in the Gospel, but must be read with limitations and distinctions, to be rightly understood; for Christ gives no full comments or continu'd discourses, but as *Demetrius* the Rhetorician phrases it, speaks oft in Monosyllables, like a maister, scattering the heavnly grain of his doctrin like pearle heer and there, which requires a skilfull and laborious gatherer; who must compare the words he finds, with other precepts, with the end of every ordinance, and with the general *analogy* of Evangelick doctrine: otherwise many particular sayings would be but strange repugnant riddles. (*CP* II: 338)

Of Education

Of Education (1644) is "a work much discussed and annotated nigh to death."[19] It has been interpreted as progressively reformed, as medieval-minded, as Baconian, Ramist, Comenian amongst other things, and I do not claim to have any final solution that will once and for all explain away its inherent contradictions. In it, Milton outlines his ideas for a reformed system of education that looks very demanding indeed, if not even utopian, from a contemporary position: "that voluntary *Idea* . . . of a better Education, in extent and comprehension farre more large, and yet of time farre shorter, and of attainment farre more certain, then hath been yet in practice" (*CP* II: 364). It is conceived as an alternative to the traditional school and university system which was still dominated by scholasticism and which Milton had already criticized in his prolusions. In Milton's ideal system of education, the learning of languages and the reform of language teaching hold an important—albeit not the central—position, and the goals of the education process are often seen as twofold, Hebraic and Greek, religious and civic.[20]

Although Milton had become aware of the ambiguities of language—even of biblical language—in his more or less personally motivated study of the biblical texts on divorce, he still seems to have held quite an optimistic opinion concerning the possibility of restoring paradisal language on earth through education. Perhaps this was due to the above-mentioned (but also problematized) influence of Bacon.[21] His optimism becomes most visible in the following famous quotation from *Of Education* (1644):

The end then of learning is to repair the ruins of our first parents by regaining to know God aright, and out of that knowledge to love him, to imitate him, to be like him, as we may the neerest by possessing our souls of true vertue, which being united to the heavenly grace of faith makes up the highest perfection. (*CP* II: 366-67)[22]

For Milton, this sweeping restoration of a world that comes close to the paradisal state here seems to be possible through "earthly" methods, which heretically suggests that there is not too much of a difference between pre- and postlapsarian worlds. Such ideas were quite widespread in the seventeenth century, as Joanna Picciotto points out by referring to the first historian of the Royal Society: "Sprat comes close to elevating the state of nature over the state of grace, daydreaming about a hypothetical humanity that would not require saving and for which religion, as distinct from 'looking into nature,' would not be necessary at all."[23] That is why the John Milton who wrote *Of Education* has been referred to as "himself identifiably prelapsarian."[24] A similar idea of a regenerative process had already been expressed by Milton through the Elder Brother in *Comus*,[25] and the archangel Raphael will promise Adam in Book V.497 of *Paradise Lost* that "Your bodies may at last turn all to Spirit."

The educational process here relies on the materials available on postlapsarian earth, but for Milton these materials still seem to be potentially connected to the world of the lost paradise rather than completely cut off from it.[26] Even if contemporary human beings here on earth feel nothing but "sensible" or "solid things," the Milton of *Of Education* seems to think that the door to paradise is still potentially open, although man may have already moved quite far away from it. The difference between prelapsarian and postlapsarian worlds is still one of gradation rather than of irreconcilable polarities, so that the study of the one will also help pupils to understand the other:

> But because our understanding cannot in this body found it selfe but on sensible things, nor arrive so cleerly to the knowledge of God and things invisible, as by orderly conning over the visible and inferior creature, the same method is necessarily to be follow'd in all discreet teaching. (*CP* II: 367-69)

Concerning the possibility of language providing direct access to the nature of things—the ideal that Milton's contemporaries had thought to be possible (see preceding chapter)—Milton seems to be more sceptical. For him, language no longer gives access to the "form" or essence of things; it rather is only an instrument—and not in itself a central element—of his educational reform project, and *form* anyway means something totally different to the modern Baconian mind than it did to the medieval one, as "the atomistic reinterpretation of form rendered Adam's ability to identify the so-called essence of each creature meaningless."[27] Therefore its teaching has to and can be rationalized as much as possible "so that language is but the instrument conveying to us things useful to be known."[28]

Towards the end of their education, his ideal students are thus given access to logic and poetry, and the readers are confronted with the famous paradox—or *crypsis*[29]—that poetry is on the one hand last in the sequence of subjects to be treated in school while on the other hand—judging by its inherent value—it necessarily holds the first rank:[30]

> And now lastly will be the time to read with them those organic arts which inable men to discourse and write perspicuously, elegantly, and according to the fitted

style of lofty, mean, or lowly. Logic therefore so much as is usefull, is to be re-
ferr'd to this due place withall her well coucht heads and Topics, untill it be time
to open her contracted palm into a gracefull and ornate Rhetorick taught out of the
rule of *Plato, Aristotle, Phalereus, Cicero, Hermogenes, Longinus*. To which
Poetry would be made subsequent, or indeed rather precedent, as being lesse suttle
and fine, but more simple, sensuous and passionate. (*CP* II: 401-03)

Milton's distinction made here between logic and poetry can and should be interpreted as the central dichotomy in *Of Education*. For him, poetry is famously
"more simple, sensuous and passionate," offering "an intuitive, concrete expressive-
ness where 'passion' and meaning are implicit in the images."[31] The language of poetry here is thus "essentialist," almost prelapsarian, resembling the language Milton
is going to describe in the early parts of *Paradise Lost*. In this linguistic realm devised by the young and optimistic Milton, certain acts that the fallen human beings
at the end of *Paradise Lost* can only hope to achieve through and with God's help
are still possible through language.

As Samuel Johnson found out to his chagrin, *Of Education* deals not only with
the humanities but also with the natural sciences. Milton's attitude towards the natural sciences has been treated more adequately ever since Harinder Singh Marjara's
study criticized the views of precursors such as Tillyard, Bush, Svendsen, and Babb,
who over the last few decades had condemned Milton's attitude towards the sciences as medieval or even obscurantist.[32] Marjara stresses Milton's more positive attitude to the latest discoveries of his time and also points out that almost all "scientists" of this era held a somewhat ambivalent position towards traditional, mystical,
and religious views of nature: "There are 'superstitious' elements in the natural philosophy of Kepler, Boyle, and Newton, all of whom have been unstintingly praised
by historians of science for their contributions to the growth of science."[33]

Of Education is thus not a singular phenomenon; it can rather be seen as only
one of a series of works of this era that were all influenced by continental theories of
education and Baconian ideas.[34] It also shows that Milton was part of a pan-
European linguistic discourse as he repeats his criticism of the "barbarization" of the
European languages that he had first voiced in the 1638 letter to Buonmattei quoted
above: "Milton affirmed the importance of maintaining pure and correct speech, arguing that a decadent language indicates a decadent people."[35]

Milton's formulation of his ideas concerning an ideal system of education was
undertaken at the instigation of Samuel Hartlib, the German-born representative of
progressive pedagogical ideas and policies in England. This illustrates the international importance of this kind of educational reform. As mentioned above, Hartlib
was also closely connected to the Moravian educator John Amos Comenius. Milton's deprecating mention of certain *Januas* and *Didactics* may well be seen as a
criticism of Comenius' own *Janua Linguarum Reserata*, but there are many parallels between the Englishman and the Moravian. For example, both stress the precedence of "solid things" in the context of language. Furthermore, Christopher Hill

claims about Milton that "his Baconian vision that learning 'will repair the ruins of our first parents' agrees exactly with Comenius's definition of 'the general aim of the entire education of man' as being 'to restore man to the lost image of God—i.e. to the lost perfection of the free will.'"[36]

Rather than sharing Milton's inductive method, Comenius, the great continental theorist of education, while also claiming to be able to cut down the length of language teaching, starts out from a deductive concept of language and language teaching strongly interested in essences, as we can see in his "description of the development of his plan for an encyclopædia and a great college for scientific research":

> For I remarked that men commonly do not speak, but babble: that is, they transmit not as from mind to mind things or the sense of things, but exchange between themselves words not understood, or little and ill understood. And that not only the common folk do this, but even the half-educated also; and what is more to be grieved at, the well educated themselves for the most part, by reason of the infinite homonymities among words and among things, and again by reason of the almost constant ignorance of their configurations (that is of the inner constitution of each thing). For when in conversation they name God, Angel, Man, Satan, Law, Sin, Virtue, Vice, and the like, yea and in speaking of that which hath body, such as Light, Darkness, Wine, Water, Wind, Cold, Heat, and the Like, and also Hunger, Food, Drink, Digestion, Sleep or Watchfulness, Health or Sickness, they know not what that, which they name, is in essence and how it cometh to be. For which reason whatever language a man may speak, whether rude or cultured, it maketh slight difference, since we are all nought but sounding brass and tinkling cymbals so long as words not things (the husks of words, I say, not the kernels of meanings) be in our mouths.[37]

While Comenius was probably the better educator, also interested in general and vocational training, Milton wanted to expose his elite of students to humane learning.[38]

The traditional opinion on Comenius' and the Comenians' influence on Milton is not in general shared by more recent research. The contemporary tendency is rather to speak about "Milton's real distance, in spite of apparent similarities, from the scientific and educational radicals of the Hartlib group."[39] There is, however, a further parallel between Milton and Comenius, as both rely on Ramist theories: Comenius had been a student of the German Ramist Johann Heinrich Alsted at the university of Herborn, and Milton wrote his own version of Ramus's *Logic*.[40]

Bible and Law, Politics and History

In *Tetrachordon* (1645), one year after Milton's statements in *Of Education*, his position on linguistic ambiguity becomes even clearer than it had been in the earlier writings on divorce.[41] He now sees such an ambiguity as an almost general quality of biblical language. For example, he remarks upon the language of the gospels: "Therefore it is that the most of evangelick precepts are given us in proverbiall formes, to drive us from the letter, though we love ever to be sticking there" (*CP* II: 637). "Driving from the letter" might almost be seen as a poststructuralist, Derridean interpretation that questions the unambiguousness of God's word and forces us to try to reconstruct God's original message on our own. It is no longer the words themselves that are important, but rather the intention lying behind them.

Milton's statement that Christ's language in his communication with the Pharisees was "not so much a teaching, as an intangling" (*CP* II: 642) has itself become almost proverbial among Miltonists. Although seemingly in contrast to the biblical interdiction of lying, the word—even the Word of Christ—is here used not in its original sense but implies an ambiguous, figurative meaning. It turns into a weapon in the sense of a performative speech act: "Much rather then may we thinke that in handling these tempters, he forgot not so to frame his prudent ambiguities and concealements, as was to the troubling of those peremtory disputants most wholsome."[42] In secular as well as religious discussions, it is always helpful to be able to have recourse to some extra arguments if everything else fails: "The Scripture seldome, or never in one place sets down all the reasons of what it grants or commands, especially when it talks to enemies and tempters" (*CP* II: 663).

Milton's politically motivated writings during the civil war and at the beginning of the Puritan Interregnum also deal with linguistic problems, even if these are not of the foremost importance in this context. For example, his discussion of the individual, personal, and honest form of prayer in *Eikonoklastes* (1649), his rejection of Charles I's apology *Eikon Basilike*, deserves special attention in this context. Milton opposes the *set forms* of traditional liturgy and speaks in favour of the individual formulation of prayers: "This is evident, that they *who use no set formes of prayer*, have words from thir affections; while others are to seek affections fit and proportionable to a certain doss of prepar'd words" (*CP* III: 505). He thus underlines the individuality and honesty of human communication with God and points out the dangers of liturgical prayer that potentially loses its original honest and direct character through the act of repetition:

> For in those [voluntary prayers], at least for words & matter, he who prays, must consult first with his heart; which in likelyhood may stir up his affections; in these [set forms], having both words and matter readie made to his lips, which is anough to make up the outward act of prayer, his affections grow lazy, and com not up easilie at the call of words not thir own. (*CP* III: 506-7)

Milton's search for a means of expression in which *words* and *matter* coincide also has an influence on his interpretation of Charles's attitude, as he accuses him of being dishonest. David Loewenstein uses Saussure's concepts of *ambiguity* and of the *signified* and *signifier* in order to paraphrase Milton's position towards *Eikon Basilike* here:

Charles's actions and motives are staged in such a way that they remain highly ambiguous. . . . This disturbing disjunction of image and reality, signifier and signified leads Milton to conclude that the stagework of *Eikon Basilike* is full of "equivocal interpretations" (III, 495).[43]

In his first *Defence of the People of England* (1651), Milton rather pedantically criticizes the language not only of the dead king but also of his posthumous defender, the learned Claude de Saumaise or Salmasius (1588-1653) from Leyden, whom he claims, in spite of "all [his] skill in languages and scanning or scribbling of tomes" to be "but a brute beast at the end."[44]

Pointing ahead to *Paradise Lost*, but probably in the heat of the political debate rather than with any intention of redefining the semiotics underlying his writing, Milton here adopts a position which distinguishes between names and things. Such a position is of course also traditional to a certain extent:

> Shall I answer you thus: "Names give precedence to facts, and it is not our business to worry about names when we have done away with the reality; let those who love kings take care of that; we enjoy our freedom"? That would not be a bad answer for you! (*CP* IV.1: 454-455)

As previously in *Of Education*, Milton's analysis of Salmasius's "fallen" language gives precedence to the "solid things" themselves over their names: "Henceforth you must be aware that names are subordinate to things, not things to names" (*CP* IV.1: 456).

In addition to presenting his attitude to the language of the Bible, Milton's prose works are important first of all for giving us his position towards his own language. English has become the medium expressing the zeal of the English nation and its mission in the world. In his *History of Britain*, language therefore plays an important role: When Milton describes the collapse of the Roman Empire in the fifth century, this decay is equally mirrored in the dismal state of culture and language: "And with the Empire fell also what before in the Western World was chiefly *Roman;* Learning, Valour, Eloquence, History, Civility, and eev'n Language it self, all these together, as it were, with equal pace diminishing, and decaying" (*CP* V.1: 127).

While classical Latin had very positive connotations for Cromwell's Latin Secretary, the same was in no way true for the modern French language that had developed from Latin roots. Milton thus criticizes the assimilation of the English to the culture and civilization of the Norman conquerors in the reign of Edward the Confessor in the eleventh century, and the adoption of French customs and language symbolize for him the abandonment of political autonomy.

All in all, the "Miltonic State Papers" written during the period of his political activity for the Republic show that Milton—in his statements on the biblical justification of the right of divorce as well as in his political propaganda and the diplomatic correspondence with other countries—was quite adept at making use not only of unambiguous straightforward quasi-paradisal semiotics but also of postlapsarian and ambiguous language with all the possibilities and connotations it has to offer the modern politician.

Milton's *Christian Doctrine*

In this chapter, I am not going to join the discussion of whether the text of *De Doctrina Christiana*, only discovered in the nineteenth century, was really written by Milton himself. Such a discussion would go far beyond the frame of this study and would probably not contribute in any way to answering the question of Milton's attitude towards language.[45] So in principle, the name Milton should be seen as set in quotation marks in this chapter whenever I am referring to *De Doctrina*.

In my discussion of *Tetrachordon*, I discussed Milton's attitude towards the possibility of an ambiguity of divine language, of God's "prudent ambiguities," which might be interpreted as an early form—a type, perhaps, in religious terms—of a poststructuralist or deconstructionist reading. In the same way, Maurice Kelley's introduction to Milton's *Christian Doctrine* in the *Yale Edition* seems to invite a further analysis in a Derridean manner, even if such an approach was certainly not at all intended by Kelley. Kelley addresses the question as to whether God's word was seen in Milton's times as primarily spoken or written language. He sees Milton's preference of the spoken word as proof of his conservatism:

> Milton's conservatism appears in such matters as his view of the nature of divine inspiration. Early Reformed theologians, including Calvin, believed that God had originally imparted divine truth orally to certain men, who later wrote it down to form scripture. By the end of the sixteenth century, however, this view had generally given away to the belief that God had dictated the books of the Bible directly to their nominal authors, who were merely amanuenses of God. In chapter xxx, Milton does not discuss this point; but elsewhere his retention of the older view is evident.[46]

Furthermore, Kelley comments on Milton's unorthodox—or even heretical—interpretation of a trinity in which the Son and the Holy Spirit are clearly subordinate to God the Father.[47]

The proof of God's existence in the *Doctrina* once again invites a semiotic or even poststructuralist reading, at least in John Carey's English translation. Although he is "far beyond man's imagination, let alone his understanding" (*CP* VI: 133), God "has left so many signs of himself in the human mind, so many traces of his presence through the whole nature, that no sane person can fail to realise that he exists" (*CP* VI: 130).

As I will argue later on, Milton's role in *De Doctrina* resembles that of the archangel Raphael in *Paradise Lost*. On the one hand, Milton insists on the impossibility of describing divine perfection—which would necessitate the use of the strategy of accommodation in writing about God—and on the other he insists on the importance of seeing God as he presents himself to us. Milton thus relies on "an unusually positive theory of the truth-value of biblical metaphors for God," and from this approach reminiscent of the literal interpretation of biblical texts he develops his "unorthodox and optimistic conception of the materiality of spiritual discourse":[48]

> It is safest for us to form an image of God in our minds which corresponds to his representation and description of himself in the sacred writings. Admittedly, God is always described or outlined not as he really is but in such a way as will make him conceivable to us. Nevertheless, we ought to form just such a mental image of him as he, in bringing himself within the limits of our understanding, wishes us to form. Indeed he has brought himself down to our level expressly to prevent our being carried beyond the reach of human comprehension, and outside the written authority of scripture, into vague subtleties of speculation.
>
> In my opinion, then, theologians do not need to employ anthropopathy, or the ascription of human feelings to God. This is a rhetorical device thought up by grammarians to explain the nonsense poets write about Jove. Sufficient care has been taken, without any doubt, to ensure that the holy scriptures contain nothing unfitting to God or unworthy of him. (*CP* VI: 133-134)

This literal interpretation of the Bible includes a process of "flattening out of biblical language," during which the accommodation of the message for a human audience becomes superfluous: "[I]t no longer makes sense to distinguish between the literal and the figurative, since no literal basis can be specified for any figurative depiction of deity."[49] This process resembles that of the abolishment or questioning of the dichotomy *literal* vs. *figurative* which I will discuss in my interpretation of *Paradise Lost*. Milton briefly summarizes his attitude towards accommodation in the following way:

> Let there be no question about it: they understand best what God is like who adjust their understanding to the word of God, for he has adjusted his word to our understanding, and has shown what kind of an idea of him he wishes us to have. (*CP* VI: 136)

Furthermore, there is a section in the fourteenth chapter of the first book of *De Doctrina* which seems to foreshadow Raphael's negative reaction towards Adam's thirst for knowledge in *Paradise Lost*: "We do not know how it is so, and it is best for us to be ignorant of things which God wishes to remain secret" (*CP* VI: 424).

Equally, "modern" linguistic terminology—and the concept of the ambiguity of the linguistic sign—seem to be foreshadowed here, albeit *ex negativo*, when Milton speaks about the *unambiguous terms* in which God makes himself known: "in terms like these which contain nothing ambiguous or obscure that might mislead his worshippers or leave them in doubt" (*CP* VI: 147). As Milton admits, the Old Testament tends to be somewhat obscure when compared to the clear message of the Gospels (which nevertheless also contain mysterious messages): "On the contrary, the light of the gospel should be used to illuminate the obscurity and the figurative language of the prophets" (*CP* VI: 255).[50]

In the course of *De Doctrina*, Milton develops, on the one hand, a hermeneutics relying firstly on the solid knowledge of language and secondly on the—as we have seen, not always clearly stipulated—separation of literal and figurative meaning of the Bible (*CP* VI: 582); on the other hand, as far as the sacraments and their signification are concerned, he also develops a semiotics that is reminiscent of that of Saint Augustine which I described earlier. For example, he writes in chapter 28 of the first book:

> In the so-called sacrament, as in most matters where the question of analogy arises, it is to be noted that a certain trope or figure of speech was frequently employed. By this I mean that a thing which in any way illustrates or signifies another thing is mentioned not so much for what it really is as for what it illustrates or signifies. Failure to recognize this figure of speech in the sacraments, where the relationship between the symbol and the thing symbolized is very close, has been a widespread source of error, and still is today. (*CP* VI: 555)

In the second book of *De Doctrina* (chapter 13), there is even stronger reliance on a reception-oriented attitude towards language. This is reminiscent of Milton's earlier reference to the *intangling* effect in *Tetrachordon*. Here he touches on questions that he is once again going to deal with in his statement on invented images in his *Logic*, which will be discussed in the following section: Language is primarily judged by its effect on the hearer or reader, not so much by superficial truth values: "parables, hyperboles, fables and the various uses of irony are not falsehoods since they are calculated not to deceive but to instruct" (*CP* VI: 761).

Later Prose, Logic and Grammar

Milton's general attitude towards questions of education seems to have changed from the early optimism in *Of Education* towards a greater and more pessimistic realism at the end of the Puritan Interregnum. Critics often discuss whether there is a difference between early aristocratic attitudes in *Of Education* and more democratic tendencies such as the later demand for a general improvement of education and the establishment of state schools. This new tendency finds its clearest expression in the following excerpt from *The Readie and Easie Way* (1660):

They should have heer also schools and academies at thir own choice, wherin thir children may be bred up in thir own sight to all learning and noble education not in grammar only, but in all liberal arts and exercises. This would soon spread much more knowledge and civilitie, yea religion through all parts of the land, by communicating the natural heat of government and culture more distributively to all extreme parts, which now lie numm and neglected, would soon make the whole nation more industrious, more ingenious at home, more potent, more honorable abroad. (*CP* VII: 460)[51]

As is to be expected, Milton's version of the *Logic* of Petrus Ramus, which was published in 1672 (although we are not sure when he wrote it),[52] offers much linguistic and semiotic material. Like most of his sixteenth-century contemporaries, Ramus imagined language to have been created through a divine act. Even though Ramist logic was not exactly a new development in Milton's times and is generally associated with the preceding century, some of its characteristics seem to be pointing well into the future, as recent critics have shown.[53]

Milton himself seems to have been rather critical towards Ramist ideas, and critics even speak about "Milton's deep-seated, if largely inarticulate, reserve about Ramist logic as it touched, or professed to touch, the more persuasive and fictive uses of language,"[54] but there is clearly a Ramist influence on Milton's linguistic concepts. Even *Accedence Commenc't Grammar*, published about 1669, is clearly influenced by Milton's interest in Ramist logic.[55] Not only one of the most important Cambridge representatives of Ramist logic, Milton is also part of an important tradition of Ramist grammarians that includes such auspicious members as his contemporaries Ben Jonson and John Evelyn.

Whereas Ramus himself had still defined logic as *ars bene disserendi* and thus—in spite of his clear separation of rhetoric and logic—had seen the latter as "art of discourse" within the framework of interpersonal communication, Milton interprets logic as nothing but the "art of reasoning well" or *ars bene ratiocinandi*.[56] Nevertheless, as is obvious in works such as *Comus*, *Samson Agonistes*, *Paradise Lost* and *Paradise Regained*, Milton was of course a master rhetorician himself. Walter J. Ong, who calls Milton's logic "a rhetorical logic," shows in his introduction in the *Yale Edition* that for the seventeenth century there existed a much stronger and much more complex hierarchy of rhetorical devices than for us today.[57]

Even though I have shown in my theory chapter that seventeenth-century theories of language hardly ever went beyond the word as the unit of linguistic analysis, the structure of Milton's *Logic* (as well as that of his *Grammar*) naturally shows a clear awareness of the levels of the sentence as a unit of analysis. The first part of the *Logic*, a wide-ranging strategy for the classification of what Milton calls arguments, is entitled *Inventio*, whereas the second bears the title *Dispositio* and deals with the combination of the elements thus classified.

In the preface to his *Logic*, Milton declares that "the form and end of logic" is "not so much the orderly arrangement as it is simply discoursing well" (*CP* VIII:

214). In the first chapter he then gives the better-known definition already quoted above: "Logic is the art of reasoning well" (*CP* VIII: 217). In the second chapter, he insists on aspects which will be of supreme importance in the course of this study: "whenever words must be used they be distinct and thus unambiguous, and not inappropriate" (*CP* VIII: 221).

Another distinction that will also be very important for my interpretation of *Paradise Lost* is that between *artificial* and *inartificial arguments*, although Milton's definition of *argument* as "*that which is suited to the arguing of something*" (*CP* VIII: 220) is not necessarily very helpful:[58]

> An argument is either artificial or inartificial. . . . Cicero divides arguments into *innate* and *assumptive*. But an argument is called artificial not because it is discovered by art more than is the inartificial, but because it argues by itself, that is, by an innate and proper force. (*CP* VIII: 221)[59]

As Milton later defines in Ramus' words, an *inartificial argument* is "one which argues not by its own nature but by a force derived from some artificial argument" (*CP* VIII: 318). Among such *inartificial arguments* is the form of "testimony; namely, as Cicero says in the *Topics*, 'something taken from an external thing to produce conviction'":

> it is the bare attestation of someone concerning a thing, or an affirmation or denial of the person attesting. But neither do things exist because of an affirmation nor fail to exist because of a denial: testimony, therefore, does not argue anything of itself and by its nature *but rather by the assumed force of some artificial argument.* But this force is the authority of the person giving testimony, on which the reliability of the testimony totally depends. (*CP* VIII: 318)

There are human and divine variants of *testimony*, of which the divine one leads to faith: "And divine testimony does indeed affirm or deny that a thing is so, and it makes me believe; it does not prove, it does not teach, it does not make me know or understand why it is so, unless it also adds reasons" (*CP* VIII: 319).

As in the following parts of this study, especially of course in my interpretation of *Paradise Lost*, I will be dealing with the propriety and reliability of comparisons in the context of strategies of accommodation—with the possibility of comparing earthly and heavenly spheres—chapters 18 to 22 are of special interest here. In chapter 18, "On Equals," Milton addresses the presuppositions that make a comparison possible:

> Although by the very nature of comparison comparatives are equally well known, nevertheless one of them must be better known and more evident to some one than the other. . . . But to one with whom we debate, a comparative used as an argument should, by its nature and before the comparison is made, be better known and more evident than that which is argued; for something equally obscure would

argue nothing. From this the remarkable utility of comparatives becomes clear; by their use it comes about that an unequal knowledge of things is made equal by virtue of a comparison.

Milton does not even exclude the use of invented comparisons: "But comparatives, even fictitious ones, not indeed by their own nature, but in virtue of the comparison, do argue real objects and produce conviction" (*CP* VIII: 271).

In chapter 21, "On the Similar," Milton warns, however, "that similar things . . . should not be pushed beyond that quality which the person making the comparison intended to show to be the same in both things." Milton's disquisition on the use of comparisons may not seem as interesting here as the archangel Raphael's display of his theory of accommodation at the beginning of his visit to paradise, "but the handbook does reveal both the extent of Milton's familiarity with current and fashionable theory regarding the similitude and some signs of his own independence from Ramist method and even Ramist assumptions."[60] Towards the end of this chapter, Milton remarks upon *similes* resembling those used by Raphael in *Paradise Lost*: "A fictitious similarity has the same force as those mentioned above, and in this explicated similarity the fables of Aesop especially excell."

Regarding *notation*—or etymology, as we call it today—Milton aligns himself with a nominalist tradition that dates back beyond Cicero to ancient Greece:

> NOTATION (notatio) is the interpretation of a name, that is, a reason given why a thing is named as it is. . . . "Notation," says Cicero in the Topics [8.35], "is called by the Greeks etymology, which means, in its own derivation, true-speaking: but we, avoiding the novelty of a word not sufficiently fitting, call this genus notation, since words are the signs (notæ) of things."

At the beginning of the second part of his *Logic*, the *Dispositio*, Milton then remarks upon the structure of his work, stating that

> Just as the first part of grammar is about single words and the second part about their syntax, so the first part of logic was about the invention of arguments and the second is about their disposition, that is, it is the part which teaches how to arrange arguments correctly. Thus, disposition is as it were a certain syntax of arguments, but not merely with a view to judging well, as Ramus holds, for this is too narrow, but with a view to reasoning well, which is the general end of logic. (*CP* VIII: 323)

In this second part, Milton comments on the ways in which the arguments that have been discovered through the process of *inventio* can be joined together. As was to be expected from the dichotomous hierarchy of the *Logic*, here we also have a subdivision into two classes of arguments: axiomatic vs. dianoetic. Axiomatic arguments are immediate and easy to understand, as "For Aristotle an axiom often means a proposition or affirmation which is so clear that it is as it were worthy of being assented to for its own sake" (*CP* VIII: 325). About the more complex, dianoetic form of *dispositio*, Milton writes: "The Greek word διάνοια signifies a discourse of mind and reason, which occurs chiefly when one statement is by reasoning deduced from another" (*CP* VIII: 350).

Milton then proceeds to distinguish between two kinds of dianoetic *dispositio*: *syllogism* and *method*. *Syllogism* means the logical way of conclusion well known to us, and in a statement reminiscent of the unfortunately lost paradisal state Milton comments on the unfortunate necessity of such a kind of argument in the fallen world of today:

> Indeed, this gathering or deducing has arisen from the weakness of the human intellect, which weakness, being unable by an immediate intuition to see in an axiom the truth and falsity of things, turns to the syllogism, in which it can judge whether they follow or do not follow. (*CP* VIII: 350)

Of course, in the fallen world there are not only logical conclusions but also *paralogisms*, which are rejected by Milton (and his predecessor Ramus). Among these we find *homonymy* or *equivocation* and ambiguity:

> Ambiguity in the thing itself, which is also called *improper exposition*, occurs when the attribute of a thing in the assumption is not the same as the one in the proposition, whereas if the attribute is changed the argument is changed. (*CP* VIII: 354)

Method, the second kind of dianoetic *dispositio*, is a way of describing situations that once again corresponds to the dichotomous hierarchy of Ramist philosophy:

> Method is a dianoetic disposition of various homogeneous axioms ordered according to the clarity of their nature, from which the mutual agreement of all of them is judged and embraced by the memory. (CP VIII: 390)

An interesting detail lies in the fact that Ramus (and with him, Milton) refers to a process of naming:

> Certainly names are the signs of things, and every name, whether derived or compound, if the name was indeed bestowed by means of a true notation, can be accounted for from some primary argument.
> *For example, homo (man) from humus (earth)*. Here the notation is from the matter. (*CP* VIII: 294)[61]

Although Milton argues that all languages, including those arising in the Tower of Babel episode, are God-given,[62] the recreation of an original, paradisal language, which still seemed debatable in *Of Education*,[63] seems to be hardly possible any more:

But languages, both the first one which Adam received in Eden, and those various ones, perhaps derived from the first, which the builders of the tower of Babel suddenly received, were without doubt divinely given; hence it is not strange if the meaning of primitive words is not known. But as for words which are derived or compound, either their origins are to be sought in other ancient and now obsolete languages, or because of their age or the usually corrupt pronunciation of the lower classes they are so changed and from the practice of incorrect writing are as it were so far obliterated that a true notation of words is very rarely to be had. (*CP* VIII: 294)

Interestingly enough, Milton's "reserve about Ramist logic" becomes most visible towards the end of his *Logic*. First of all, he condenses four chapters of Ramus's into a single one, and then he makes it

unambiguously clear—more unambiguously than Ramus certainly—that Ramist method applies only to handing on or teaching already processed knowledge (knowledge typically organized in a "methodized" Ramist art, which moves relentlessly from general to particular or special).[64]

Furthermore, like Ramus, Milton here leaves a last alternative rhetorical route open to himself should strictly logical interpretation fail: I am speaking about *crypsis* (*CP* VIII: 395), which Ramus had also referred to as *methodus prudentiae* in earlier versions of his *Dialectics*.[65] Milton thus feels in no way bound to follow Ramist prescriptions, neither as politician, nor as poet or prophet: "But to orators and poets should be left their own account of method, or at least to those who teach the art of oratory and poetry" (*CP* VIII: 395).

The Theme of Language in Milton's Prose: A Summary

As early as in the *Prolusions* written in his youth, Milton proves to be not only a linguistic patriot proud of the language of his home country but also student sensitive to questions of language and critical of the use of empty verbal phrases. For him, language still seems to have the ability to mirror reality directly and unproblematically.

Even in the early writings of the Puritan revolution, Milton still believes in the clarity of biblical language. In *Of Education*, he still seems to speak out in favour of (the re-creation of) a quasi-prelapsarian language in which speakers always mean what they say and by means of which the injustices of the world can be repaired.

Probably for personal reasons, Milton soon has to realize, however, the necessity of a "philological" approach to texts, even to biblical texts. Looking for a justification of divorce and regicide he finds a justification to interpret even God's word instead of accepting the divine message literally.

In his *Christian Doctrine*, Milton seems to level the distinction between the literal and figurative meaning of God's message, which may also be interpreted as a questioning of the existence of a difference between prelapsarian and postlapsarian language. As in Milton's *Logic*, language is now judged by its effect and no longer by its formal truth value.

In addition, Milton's Ramist *Logic*, with its strong rhetorical slant, shows in detail to what purpose one can and may use verbal images and comparisons or similes. Milton makes an important distinction between *artificial* and *inartificial arguments*, the latter of which carry a special weight in the form of *divine testimony*. Still, Ramus and Milton generally prefer a logical syllogism to axiomatic *testimony*.

3.2 Poetry: The Early Works, *Comus* and *Samson Agonistes*

As quoted above, Milton himself claimed in *Of Education* that poetry is "more simple, sensuous and passionate" than prose. That he himself valued his literary work more highly than his political prose appears to be obvious from his statement, in the introduction to the second book of *The Reason of Church Government*, that in writing his political tracts he had "the use, as I may account it, but of my left hand" (*CP* I: 808). Therefore it is not surprising that this part of my study—concentrating on Milton's attitude towards language in his poetical works—is much longer than the corresponding part on his prose works. It is self-explanatory that he spent more time and a greater effort on the literary texts which therefore turn out to be more complex than the satirical (and often only aggressive) pamphlets or the diplomatic correspondence Milton had to write under all kinds of pressure; still, critics such as Stanley Fish have been able to show that Milton's prose also offers perspectives for analyses going well beyond the seventeenth-century political and historical background.

Once again, at first sight this part of my study appears rather unbalanced as its subdivisions considerably differ in length. But the sheer quantitative relation between *Paradise Lost* and *Paradise Regained* on the one hand and the rest of Milton's poetic work on the other shows a similar disproportion, and furthermore language becomes more and more important in Milton's later and central works. This is especially the case in *Samson Agonistes*, *Paradise Lost* and *Paradise Regained*, and these works will therefore be at the centre of my attention. If some of Milton's most famous poems—such as "Lycidas," "L'Allegro," "Il Penseroso" or the sonnets—are not covered here, this is not because of a lack of artistic merit but rather because the theme of language does not play as important a role in them as it does in the texts I am going to focus on.

"At a Vacation Exercise"

One of the earliest texts in which Milton deals with language is the poem "At a Vacation Exercise" written in 1628. It was originally part of one of the prolusions that Milton wrote as a student in Cambridge.[66] He presents the first part of Prolusion VI, on sports and philosophical studies, in a rather carnivalistic mood celebrating the beginning of the summer holidays. But in spite, or because, of the carnivalistic mood, he speaks in Latin, the official language of learning. Latin had also so far, with few exceptions, been the language he had used in his early poetry.[67] As Hanford remarks, in his second year at Cambridge, Milton seems to have put away his early experiments in English verse and—"as a result of the humanistic tendency to undervalue the vernacular as a source of serious culture"—to have turned towards the learned medium, i.e. Latin.[68] Now, however, Milton returns to his mother tongue, greets it vigorously, and promises to use it to serve up the "daintiest dishes" at the end (*CSP* 76, ll. 1-14).

As Milton remarks some lines later, in addressing the English language, that "I had rather, if I were to choose, / Thy service in some graver subject use" (ll. 29-30), this poem certainly is not meant to be an utterly serious statement.[69] Nevertheless, one may read this invocation of the muse of the English language as an indication that even at the beginning of his literary career Milton sees language as more than just the tool for the acquisition of knowledge for which many readers of his pamphlet *Of Education* (1644) would have taken it. Furthermore, the invocation may already indicate a certain linguistic patriotism[70] of the young writer who knows that the English language is also the medium in which to describe "some graver subject." On the other hand, there are certainly good reasons not to over-interpret such an early poem addressed to an audience of "[c]onvivial, callow students with no thoughts beyond the coming vacation."[71]

"At a Solemn Music," "Ad Patrem" and Sonnet 13

In the first lines of Milton's early poem "At a Solemn Music" (1633), he seems to distinguish between medium (form) and content of his writing when he invokes the "Blest pair of sirens, pledges of heaven's joy, / Sphere-borne harmonious sisters, Voice, and Verse" (*CSP* 162, ll. 1-2). Interestingly enough, the originally unproblematic consonance of the two can no longer be taken for granted in the "fallen" world of today. Ever since the "disproportioned sin" (*CSP* 164, l. 19) of the Fall and the ensuing "jarring" (l. 20) of the original melodious sound of "first obedience" (l.

24), human beings no longer have a direct access to God. This event will be described in detail thirty years later in *Paradise Lost*, but here there is still hope that the loss may be easily compensated:

> O may we soon again renew that song,
> And keep in tune with heaven, till God ere long
> To his celestial consort us unite,
> To live with him, and sing in endless morn of light.
> (*CSP* 165, ll. 25-28)[72]

In his Latin poem "Ad Patrem" (written in 1637, according to Hughes),[73] Milton states about music and text, which he had referred to as "harmonious sisters" in "At a Solemn Music," that linguistic form without a corresponding message is absurd: "And after all, what use is the voice if it merely hums an inane tune, without words, meaning or the rhythm of speech?" (*CSP* 151, ll. 50-51).

Even though he becomes more and more convinced of the possibilities of the English language, Milton still thanks his father for having made him study "the beauties of Latin and the high-sounding words of the sublime Greeks" and for having encouraged him to learn the modern foreign languages Italian and French as well as "those mysteries which the prophet of Palestine utters" (CSP 154). Although Milton may have largely seen the study of foreign languages as nothing more than the way of accessing the message they transport, the characteristics that he attributes to some of these foreign languages indicate that he sees them as more than just instruments for the propagation of knowledge.

He again addresses the theme of his English mother tongue in Sonnet 13 addressed to Henry Lawes, the composer of the musical score of his masque *Comus*. He praises Lawes' music for giving precedence to the lyrics over musical harmony so that the music does not hide the sense of a song.[74]

Comus

The *Masque Presented at Ludlow Castle* (1634, generally known as *Comus*), Milton's somewhat surprising contribution to the then very popular genre of the court masque, seems to be a juvenile work that can only with difficulty be integrated into a coherent interpretation of the Miltonic canon. I would like to argue that its theme is not only the chastity of the Lady who withstands Comus's temptations and "a verbal trap,"[75] but also that of language.[76] Furthermore, as I will show in a later section, the masque presents an early example of a plot structure or technique that Milton is going to put to even greater and more momentous effect in *Paradise Lost*. The Lady's simple style in her refutation of all of Comus's entreaties furthermore points ahead to the simple style that the Son uses in his refutation of the Satanic temptations.[77]

In his speech, Comus, the evil and sensuous spirit, "a forceful rhetorician and a first-rate poet,"[78] deviates from the truth in order to goad his victims into drinking "this cordial julep here" (*Comus* 671) which will then turn them into animal-like beings giving in to their licentious desires in his company. The Lady, whom he has captured with a spell, refutes his offer to taste the drink even though he claims— thus resembling his "successor" Satan in paradise—that its powers will easily restore liberty and joy of life to "those dainty limbs which Nature lent / For gentle usage, and soft delicacy" (*Comus* 679-80). She resists the temptation and correctly analyzes her "foul deceiver's" (*Comus* 695) semiotic strategy: "'Twill not restore the truth and honesty / That thou hast banished from thy tongue with lies" (*Comus* 690-91).

The lady is enraged by the impudence underlying Comus's suggestion to "be not coy, and be not cozened / With that same vaunted name virginity" (*Comus* 736-37), and she expresses her disgust at his rhetoric. Although she "had not thought to have unlocked [her] lips / In this unhallowed air" (*Comus* 755-56), she has to react because she hates "when vice can bolt her arguments, / And virtue has no tongue to check her pride" (*Comus* 759-60). After almost twenty lines of justified indignation, she finally asks, "Shall I go on? / Or have I said enough?" (*Comus* 778-79), only to then continue for another twenty lines or so in the same style, condemning "him that dares / Arm his profane tongue with contemptuous words / Against the sun-clad power of chastity" (*Comus* 779-81).

Comus cannot recognize the true value of chastity. His "dear wit" and "gay rhetoric" are not worth the effort of lashing out against, although this is exactly what the Lady is doing rather vehemently. If nothing else, Comus is impressed by her righteous indignation and her "sacred vehemence"—"a combination of Orphean harmony and the apocalyptic voice of the judging Redeemer."[79] Her words seem to be what Northrop Frye calls "words with power,"[80] so that Comus fears that they are "set off by some superior power" (*Comus* 800).

That is why he reverts to even stronger strategies of persuasion in his last attack on her, from which she is fortunately saved by her Brothers and the Attendant Spirit: "I must dissemble, / And try her yet more strongly" (*Comus* 804-05). In spite of his art of dissemblance, Comus's attempts are not crowned with success, so that the Attendant Spirit can proclaim the victory of virtue in his rhyming couplets:

Mortals that would follow me,
Love Virtue, she alone is free,
She can teach ye how to climb
Higher than the sphery chime;
Or if Virtue feeble were,
Heaven itself would stoop to her.
(*Comus* 1017-22)

One of the main topics of this study, the problematic relationship between sign and referent in language here comes to the fore in the contrast between the superficial meaning of Comus's words addressed to the Lady and his real intention. As Maryann Cale McGuire states, "The first two characters to appear [in the masque], the Attendant Spirit and Comus, embody the contrast between proper and improper rhetoric."[81] Angus Fletcher realizes that "the failure of the villain results from his literalist belief . . . in demonic magic" and that the "Attendant Spirit can spiritualize the magic that must govern the world of the Lady because he knows the illusionistic conditions of the action itself."[82] The Lady, giving an example of the ideal "Miltonic paradigm"[83] of behaviour, can finally withstand Comus through her insistence on "truth and honesty," but she can only withstand him by relying on the support of others.

Samson Agonistes

At first sight, *Samson Agonistes*, the story of a hero who generally impresses us through active warfare rather than words, seems to be even less interesting from a linguistic point of view than *Comus*. At least, one may get this impression by looking at one of the recent monographs on *Samson Agonistes*, Joseph Wittreich's *Interpreting* Samson Agonistes. For Wittreich, "the crucial question concerning the meaning of Milton's poem" is that of Samson's religious status: "[I]s Milton's Samson the Samson of his twentieth-century critics—a regenerate Samson; or is he instead the Samson of pre- and post-revolutionary England, the vengeful Samson of Spenser and Shakespeare, of Andrew Marvell and of many poets and biblical commentators during, and after, Marvell's and Milton's own time?"[84] However, just like *Comus, Samson Agonistes* also centres on the topic of seduction, on a type of seduction which is only superficially concerned with eroticism and largely depends on the well-planned use of words.

As Heather Asals shows, in the course of the play, Samson is confronted with three important applications of rhetoric represented by Manoa, Dalila, and Harapha. Manoa plays the role of the "deliberative orator" in his attempts to admonish his son and to persuade him to surrender; as a "forensic orator," Dalila is occupied with justice and injustice; and Harapha as an "epideictic" speaker deals with "the noble and disgraceful."[85]

Samson's doubts about the reliability of the words that Dalila speaks when she visits him—he calls them "feigned religion, smooth hypocrisy" (*SA* 872)—are typical of the seventeenth-century attitude towards the trustworthiness of language: "Like many of Milton's contemporaries, Samson has come to distrust language, to seek to insulate himself from the capacity of words for ambiguity and deception."[86] If Samson had not trusted Dalila and given in to her, he would not have been captured and would not have lost his eyesight. This negative experience explains Samson's growing scepticism towards verbal messages that clearly contrasts with his earlier self-confident reliance on linguistic manipulations and wordplay: "Though he had once exploited the capacity of language for ambiguity and figurative meaning, he now views its polysemous quality with suspicion, requiring the Chorus to speak with a precision that admits no misconstructions."[87] Therefore, in his discussion with Dalila, Samson falls back on a "terse, rational style favored by Restoration linguists."[88]

According to folk clichés, Samson's blindness should have heightened his sensitivity towards linguistic phenomena. Yet at the beginning of the drama, his loss of vision is such an overwhelming experience for him that he tends to underestimate the truly original and primary power at the base of the "first-created beam" (*SA* 83), the Word. Samson is also made aware of the limits of his acoustic abilities right at the beginning when he can "hear the sound of words," but "their sense the air / Dissolves unjointed ere it reach my ear" (*SA* 176-77). The chorus also conclude their answer to Samson's insight by a quasi-linguistic statement we may interpret as a somewhat more consolatory expression of the power of language:

> Counsel or consolation we may bring,
> Salve to thy sores; apt words have power to 'suage
> The tumours of a troubled mind,
> And are as balm to festered wounds. (*SA* 183-86)

So contrary to first impressions readers may have had of *Samson Agonistes*, language is in fact a very important topic in the drama. Marcia Landy even writes that "Milton's primary technique for embodying his situation is his exploration of the nature of language, the tool whereby man attempts to apprehend and fix reality."[89] What comes to the fore again here too, though, is the limitation of language, "the fact that the actual contemplation and experience of a transcendent reality can only be dimly approximated in words."[90] Dalila defeated Samson's "fort of silence" (*SA* 236)—and he blames himself for this—not by means of the Word but rather "with a peal of words" (*SA* 235), i.e., in the field of oral-aural communication. Samson also remembers that he had been betrayed in a similar way by his first Philistine wife (*SA* 384-87). But he has learned very little from his earlier experience and marries Dalila, another Philistine. His bitter question regarding her faithfulness (*SA* 387-88) turns out to be nothing but rhetorical.

As the reader soon realizes, *Samson Agonistes* is a work in which linguistic behaviour is thematized all the time. Especially Dalila's act of unfaithfulness towards her husband can be shown to be first of all a linguistic problem:

> Thrice she assayed with flattering prayers and sighs,
> And amorous reproaches to win from me
> My capital secret. (*SA* 392-94)

And while Samson had so far been the foremost jester whose verbal traps and riddles confused the others (see *SA* 1016), he now has to realize that his "riddling days" (*SA* 1064) are over, as he is overpowered by Dalila's "foul effeminacy" and becomes her "bond-slave" (*SA* 410, 411). He had been able to delude her three times, but the fourth time he succumbs to her "blandished parleys, feminine assaults" (*SA* 403).

The Chorus, even though not necessarily a reliable source of information, also provide a "linguistic" commentary on the action. When Samson, who has once again rejected Dalila's peace offer, is approached by the giant Harapha, the Chorus warn that Samson should not expect any "enchanting voice" or "honeyed words" from the latter (*SA* 1065, 1066).

Towards the end of the drama, however, Samson regains his former power so that he can confidently assert that "I begin to feel / Some rousing motions in me which dispose / To something extraordinary my thoughts" (*SA* 1381-83). One may wonder if this can be interpreted as a sign of Samson's regeneration. His relationship towards language has changed, too: once again, his verbal statements have the power, known from his earlier riddles, of bringing together words and things that do not seem to have anything to do with each other. Similarly, his hair, supposedly the source of his power, turns out to be nothing but an "arbitrary" sign imposed by God, a sign of the same order—as I am going to show later—as the tree of the knowledge of good and evil in *Paradise Lost*.

At the beginning of the drama, Samson seems to have given up all linguistic games and wordplay he had earlier on used to ridicule his opponents in his rudely ironic jests and riddles. As Robert Entzminger points out, "his effort to abjure verbal play is . . . a reversal of his previous attitude, for prior to his humiliation the biblical Samson is a bully who plays crude practical jokes and takes an unmerited pride in his verbal dexterity."[91] Nevertheless, one can also detect a regenerative development in *Samson Agonistes* by means of which he once again—and with God's permission—uses ambiguous language. As Entzminger puts it, "he acquires the opportunity to fulfill God's promise not by renouncing words but by recovering his ability to exploit verbal ambiguity." In contrast to his earlier use of irony, however, now "he adopts a metaphoric, ironic language that expresses both self-deprecation and faith in God."[92] He regains his trust in the power of language. The situation in which he ends up by accepting Harapha's challenge will prove fatal for himself, but ironically it will also prove fatal for his enemies. It points ahead (or, if one accepts the theory that *Samson Agonistes* is one of Milton's late works, it points back) to Jesus' precarious situation on top of the battlements of the temple in *Paradise Regained*, a situation which I will later interpret as the final point or *telos* of the "linguistic development" in Milton's work.[93] Preceding Jesus, Samson can solve the paradox of the human situation through a metaphor that is supported by God, even though he has to give his life for this solution. Falling back on such a distinction between metaphor and paradox, Robert Entzminger describes Samson's regained trust in his own language: "Samson's spiritual recovery depends in part upon his renewed ability to interpret metaphorically circumstances he has previously regarded as paradoxical." Through his faith, Samson succeeds in turning metaphorical language into literal language in a truly Miltonic manner:

> By the end of the poem we are led to realize that language is capable of expressing meanings confined neither to the speaker's intentions nor to the understanding of his auditors. Yet while at the outset Samson takes this polysemous quality of language as a cause for distrust, his development finally reaffirms the metaphoric potential of language as the only means of expressing truths otherwise too complex and apparently contradictory to be apprehended.[94]

The Theme of Language in the Early and Shorter Works: A Summary

Except for *Comus* and *Samson Agonistes*, Milton's shorter works do not provide much explicit material regarding language. The Prolusions and the poem "At a Vacation Exercise," both written during Milton's studies at Cambridge, mirror his youthfully optimistic linguistic patriotism. Milton's gift for languages and his interest in them are witnessed and illustrated by his Italian sonnets addressed to the mysterious Emilia. "At a Solemn Music" provides the first instance of his distinction between prelapsarian and postlapsarian communication, albeit in the field of music. Interestingly enough, the restitution of the ideal prelapsarian state still seems to be possible.

In his masque *Comus*, Milton finally describes a seducer who uses lies and rhetorical tricks in order to seduce his victims. But he also introduces the figure of a god-like, albeit somewhat reserved teacher figure who watches over his pupils without denying their own responsibility for their actions. The seducers in *Samson Agonistes*, first of all Dalila, also use lies and rhetoric, and even Samson himself has in the past, marked by his bodily and military strength, deviated from a clear and simple language. At the end of the drama, though only for a short time, he regains his old bodily and linguistic power, a power which even permits him to literalize metaphors.

3.3 *Paradise Lost* and *Paradise Regained*

Since the mid-1980s, there have been numerous attempts to study Milton's *magnum opus* from a linguistic point of view. But of course many earlier studies focused on the language—although not necessarily on the attitude towards language—in *Paradise Lost*. In fact, as early as in the seventeenth century, the language of Milton's epic was one of the main reasons for which he was accorded an eminent position in English literature.[95]

Still, among Milton's contemporaries there were also critical voices about the language and style of *Paradise Lost*. Charles Gildon, for example, felt it was necessary to defend Milton against such criticism and calls Milton "a perfect, unimitable *Master of Language*."[96] And in the early eighteenth century, Joseph Addison claims that Milton "has carried our Language to a greater height than any of the *English* Poets have ever done before or after him, and made the Sublimity of his Stile equal to that of his Sentiments."[97]

Twenty years later, Jonathan Richardson grudgingly admits that Milton's language is English,

> but 'tis Milton's English; 'tis Latin, 'tis Greek English; not only the words, the phraseology, the transpositions, but the ancient idiom is seen in all he writes, so that a learned foreigner will think Milton the easiest to be understood of all the English writers. This peculiar English is most conspicuously seen in *Paradise Lost*, for this is the work which he long before intended should enrich and adorn his native tongue.[98]

Even more critical is Leonard Welstead's reaction to Milton's style in 1724, when he calls Milton's language an "uncouth unnatural jargon . . . which is a second Babel or confusion of all languages."[99] Samuel Johnson's negative judgment of Milton's language is of course well-known. He writes not only the hardly flattering lines that *Paradise Lost* is "one of the books which the reader admires and lays down, and forgets to take up again," but also remarks about Milton that

> Of him, at last, may be said what Jonson says of Spenser, that 'he wrote no language', but has formed what Butler calls 'a Babylonish Dialect', in itself harsh and barbarous, but made by exalted genius and extensive learning the vehicle of so much instruction and so much pleasure that, like other lovers, we find grace in its deformity.[100]

Still, the opinion that Milton wrote in an archaic and overly Latinate style seems to be a prejudice, albeit a widespread one. Lalia Phipps Boone, for example, states that there "are many more linguistic innovations than there are so-called archaisms" and that Milton „is a linguistic innovator, not an adopter of antiquated words."[101]

In the middle of the twentieth century, Milton's work as a whole, and of course also his language, is at the centre of a „great controversy which dominated Milton studies until recently."[102] While his use of imagery, especially his similes, still had the reputation of being relatively clear-cut and easy to decipher in the 1930s,[103] more than twenty years later the *Miltonic simile* is rather seen as the expression of a technique that finally (in *Paradise Regained*) turns into an "iconography of renunciation" which relies on "the disparity as much as the similitude of the comparison."[104]

T.S. Eliot had earlier, in his essay on the Metaphysical Poets, condemned Milton's style as an expression of the infamous "dissociation of sensibility" that he located in the seventeenth century and from which, he claimed, English poetry never recovered.[105] One may argue that today Milton's reputation is still suffering from this attack in the same way that, according to Eliot, English poetry still shows the after-effects of seventeenth-century "dissociation of sensibility." Within the wider context of Eliot's criticism of Milton, Terry Eagleton even speaks about a "contrived dislocation of the unified sign, the sonorous excess of language over meaning." Milton's language, according to Eagleton, is basically different from the language of the Metaphysical Poets, who are much more in tune with Eliot's ideas: "Nothing could be further from the swift fusion of the Metaphysical conceit than the calculated self-conscious unfurling of the epic simile, with all its whirring machinery of production on show."[106]

In the 1960s and 70s, Milton criticism brought forth important and basic work on Miltonic language, focusing on themes such as the quality and idiosyncrasy of Milton's literary style, but also on the logical and philosophical significance language had for him and his contemporaries. For example, Milton's epic can be and has been interpreted as the dramatization of seventeenth and eighteenth-century concepts of language that see the Fall as bringing about "a corruption of mankind's speech."[107] According to some of these interpretations of *Paradise Lost*, Milton leaves behind the equation of words and things put forth by contemporaries such as Wilkins and rather tends towards the position held by such philosophers of language as Locke: "Milton . . . uses language as language. His words are not substitutes for stuff but signs for ideas."[108]

Poststructuralists of the 1980s, such as Herman Rapaport, also claim that "Milton makes language into something abstract, stylish, and rhetorical and thereby violates the relationship between word (signifier) and meaning (signified), a relationship ideally preserved in ordinary speech, according to Eliot."[109] In the course of the 1990s, more and more Milton critics make use of linguistic and semiotic approaches influenced by structuralist and poststructuralist theories. In 1991, Stevie Davies describes Milton's linguistic strategy as that of "fabricat[ing] a language of men and of angels in its original purity and chart[ing] the fall of that language into a linguistic field of ambiguity, *double entendre*, pun, innuendo, self-deception and rancorous abuse."[110] Angela Esterhammer claims "that some of the assumptions behind Milton's use of the inspired and creative Word are most accessible by way of twentieth-century theories of difference, performance, and the autonomy of linguistic systems."[111]

While Christopher Ricks remarks as early as 1963 that in *Paradise Lost*, the Fall of humankind coincides with the Fall of language,[112] Robert Entzminger in 1985 goes so far as to state that the Fall of the language of Adam and Eve in paradise and human attempts to reverse it in order to regain a "redeemed speech" are the main themes of all seduction poems by Milton:

> The Lady in *Comus* and the Christ of *Paradise Regained* reveal the spiritual condition upon which redeemed speech is predicated, and the narrator of *Paradise Lost* demonstrates its practice. But it is in *Samson Agonistes* that we find the complete pattern, the spiritual renewal together with the verbal redemption, most fully articulated.[113]

We can see here that even in the works Milton wrote before *Paradise Lost* and *Paradise Regained*, there is—as I have claimed above—a general concern with language, although it does not always take the central position in his argument.

As I have shown earlier, Stanley Fish (in *Surprised by Sin*) thinks that the concept of a perfect language—with a clear and unambiguous relationship between word and thing, sign and referent—was irrevocably a thing of a prelapsarian and prehistoric past for Milton's contemporaries. Fish claims that the postlapsarian readers of *Paradise Lost* are no longer capable of limiting their act of reading to the literal and original meaning of the biblical words describing paradise. This inability attests to Milton's scepticism and, according to Fish, to "the speciousness of a programme that offers salvation in the guise of linguistic reform."[114] Seventeenth-century linguistic and educational reforms—such as those envisaged by Hartlib and Comenius—alone are not sufficient to re-establish paradise. One certainly cannot accuse Milton of naively trying to restore paradise through mere linguistic manipulation, but—as I have shown above—such thoughts may have been held by some radical representatives of the Puritan Revolution.

Milton himself was probably aware of the utopian ideas held by the linguistic reformers among his contemporaries, but in his later writings he seems to have regarded the ideal language that they aimed at as a thing of the irretrievable past about which one might assume "that Adam spoke a perfect non-conventional language in which word and referent corresponded, that he knew their essential natures and names issued forth of their own accord, that preternaturally appropriate designations virtually assigned themselves."[115] Dayton Haskin, on the other hand, thinks "that Milton did not share the view that all language is arbitrarily established by custom and convention."[116] Although he believes that Milton was fully aware of the insights of the secular philosophers of language of his time, he also assumes that for him human language still held an important role in God's plan and "although tainted since the Fall, might still operate as a vehicle for joining humans and God, just as the Scriptures, though corrupted over the course of the history of their transmission, would nonetheless serve as the means for reconstructing the Word of God."[117]

As several critics of *Paradise Lost* indicate, a deviation from the original and ideal non-arbitrary relationship between referent and sign (as, according to Haskin, it was conceived by Milton) is possible and even necessary in the biblical and historical development of language: It is even possible and necessary, I would claim, in Adam's prelapsarian language. According to the traditional interpretation, such a problematization of the complete and unambiguous coordination of referent and sign, of thing and word, was not possible until briefly before Satan's temptation of Adam and Eve, thus making it possible for the serpent to seduce Eve. But one may follow modern linguistics in arguing that the "loss" of unambiguous relationships between words and things is not necessarily a consequence of the Fall (or its preparation): "Of course, neither reference nor representation is ever—save in the most limited, quasi-arithmetical cases—rigorously exact or closed, nor is the correspondence of signifieds in different minds perfect."[118]

In our—and Milton's—times, the description of the prelapsarian world and language is not possible in any but our own "fallen" language that is geared to our fallen sensibilities. However, this fallen linguistic sensibility also opens up a whole range of creative and artistic possibilities of using language, and *Paradise Lost* itself depends on the limitations and possibilities of fallen language.[119]

In addition to the influential Augustinian interpretation of the Fall, emphasizing Adam and Eve's sinfulness, there are also other readings that do not necessarily see such a large and unnegotiable gap between the pre- and postlapsarian worlds. Among the seventeenth-century alternatives to the Augustinian dogma there is for example the position of the Arminians, for whom the Fall was "largely a relative term"[120] and who were consequently accused of "draw[ing] down our first parents . . . into the same condition wherein we are ingaged by reason of corrupted nature."[121] One can also argue that certain contradictions and tensions exist even within a prelapsarian world and a prelapsarian language, especially if one interprets the Edenic state not as a situation in which our first parents were completely sheltered from temptation but rather as a state of "fallible perfection."[122]

Nevertheless, a linguistic interpretation of *Paradise Lost* encourages me to assume that at least some of Milton's narrators in the epic—not necessarily Milton himself—are not as far removed from Wilkins' ideas of a "paradisal language" as for example Stanley Fish takes them to be. Milton at first seems to be quite in favour of at least some of the optimistic linguistic theories underlying the philosophy of language of his century, although he also appears to support the linguistic restrictions that the archangel Raphael introduces into the Garden of Eden. By introducing the figure of the archangel who insists on the necessity of a superhuman instance of moderation and translation (i.e., Raphael himself) in the communication between God and human beings, Milton can on the one hand pass judgment on the linguistic optimism of his contemporaries.[123] On the other hand, he is the author of what

Stanley Fish calls a *self-consuming artifact*, in which he undermines the very message of his own epic and questions the statements that it seems to make about language. In opposition to the archangel Raphael, the narrative voice and Adam still seem to uphold a *word-thing language* that would make a *divine interpreter* redundant in the communication between heavenly and earthly beings. Perhaps we here come pretty close, after all, to discovering the aporia the existence of which Annabel Patterson considered to be rather improbable in *Paradise Lost*.

In a seemingly deconstructionist manner, Raphael's message of the necessity of translation (or accommodation) undermines itself when the archangel inadvertently hints at the possibility that the "Fall" of language may have become a reality on earth, but that its theological and linguistic explanation and justification are only one half of the truth and that the separation of earthly and heavenly spheres based on it may not have been necessary after all. [124]

My discussion of the different narrators in *Paradise Lost* and of their possible unreliability shows that the linguistic and social consequences of the Fall concern not only the description of the Fall itself but also—and above all—the sometimes rather complicated and complex "narrative situation" of the epic such as the question of who tells what to whom at what time, not to mention even the question of what previous knowledge of his audience he can and does count on. [125]

Paradise Lost: The Linguistic "Primal Scene"

This interpretation of *Paradise Lost* analyzes Milton's view of Adam and Eve's first use of language in the Garden of Eden as it becomes visible, for example, in Adam's naming of the animals. It partly relies on the structuralist model of the linguistic sign first designed by the Swiss linguist Ferdinand de Saussure and further developed by contemporary linguists and theorists of literature. [126] At first sight the use of such a modern model seems to be very anachronistic in connection with a seventeenth-century epic, but as I have pointed out above, there are striking parallels between the ideas about language held by Milton's contemporaries and those of contemporary linguists.

This linguistically motivated interpretation based on the linguistic "primal scene" of using language in the Garden of Eden then will be extended to the epic as a whole. In my analysis I am going to deviate from Milton's rather complex plot every now and then and rather follow the "true" chronology of the events that add up to Milton's *story*. [127] This will make it easier to follow the development of language, but the reader still has to keep an eye on the various and complex narrative perspectives of the episodes narrated in the epic.

The most important narrative voice in *Paradise Lost* is of course Milton's "omniscient" narrator who guides the reader by means of his "interpretive statements." Even though one may have detected certain signs indicating that this narrator is not always reliable and may even be "devilishly misleading" sometimes,[128] his statements should on no account be disqualified as "superfluities, irrelevancies, or just clumsy mistakes."[129] Other narrative perspectives that sometimes differ quite distinctly from that of the omniscient narrator are for example rendered in the "minor restricted voices" of Adam or Eve or in the "major restricted voices" of the archangels Raphael or Michael.[130]

Furthermore—following Stanley Fish's phenomenological insight that Milton's readership is *surprised by sin*—we should not forget that we as readers always depend on the information that Milton gives us through the construction of his plot. Thus the following analysis is a constant hermeneutic process in which the reader has to negotiate between the different levels of Milton's version of the creation account and his narrators' reports of the events taking place in the Garden of Eden before and after creation.

When Adam remembers his first days on earth in his conversation with Raphael in Book VIII, he sees the acts of speaking and of naming the animals as an expression of divine inspiration. This corresponds to the theories current in the seventeenth century described above: "to speak I tried, and forthwith spake, / My tongue obeyed and readily could name / What e'er I saw" (*PL* VIII.271-73). One should keep in mind that, at the time of this rather sudden and intuitive act of naming, Adam was still relatively inexperienced in his new environment, but that he was not necessarily childish and ignorant.[131]

Adam's naming of the animals (and possibly also Eve's naming of the flowers in Book XI.277) seems to depend on a close connection between the "superficial" act of naming and a deeper insight into the underlying character of the animals named. This becomes even more obvious a little later when Adam remembers that he followed a *sudden apprehension*, an intuition, to give names to all the animals (*PL* VIII.354). Here, relating to "earthly" objects and animals, Adam's names or signs still mirror their referents in a clear and unambiguous one-to-one relationship. One may even go as far as claiming that "[t]he poem's implicit linguistic premise is that word and thing were one in prelapsarian language."[132]

The corresponding prelapsarian language with its solid coordination of names and things represents "a universe constructed on the principles of analogy and hierarchy" in which language "is an expression of order."[133] Every animal named by Adam has one name only, and this name refers to only this one animal. In this respect, the language of paradise does not share the general characteristics that one normally ascribes to a natural language, for it is difficult to imagine that the logical principle of an unambiguous one-to-one relationship would apply to natural languages: ideally, a paradisal language would imply the existence of a single word for every single object, and every word would only be permitted to have one single meaning.[134] In such a paradisal language there would at first be no distinction between what modern linguistic semantics calls reference and denotation, and thus it would be difficult in such a linguistic environment to make the step from relating to a single and definite object (reference) to that of relating to a whole class of similar objects (denotation) or a "semantic prototype."[135]

In Adam's language, reference and denotation are at first identical: "true name for true nature is unfailingly given."[136] Connotations, which over time are added to the denotative meanings, are signs of the speakers' awareness of the historical contingency of language. Prelapsarian Adam naturally did not have such knowledge, for within the framework of *Paradise Lost* it can only be gained either from the meta-level of divine knowledge or from the rear-view mirror perspective of the postlapsarian reader:

> only for those participants in the cosmic drama who are blessed with foresight beyond the immediate present—specifically, God, the narrator, the angels and the reader himself—do words like "fruit," "grace," "taste," and "Fall," which the unfallen Adam and Eve use and understand only in a literal denotative sense, acquire their later fallen connotations.[137]

In this sense, the language of paradise has certain disadvantages in comparison with our fallen language. Even if it seems to give speakers direct and intuitive access to the topics in question, it cannot express certain other levels of meaning that we have grown used to.

Some critics would trace the direct and intuitive access of prelapsarian language to the essence of things, the total coincidence of name or sign with the things signified, back to a kind of non-linguistic direct communication between God and human beings through a *dream vision* or *epiphany*.[138] In such a dream the names are, however, not yet used in a "real" act of communication, at least they are not communicated through a truly linguistic channel.

One can equally argue, however, that even the paradisal coordination of sign and referent is in itself only a conventional and not necessarily essential coordination, even though it is inspired by God and even though Adam holds it to be essential.[139] This linguistic state of an "absolute signatory system,"[140] which however does not necessarily represent the perfect and unique truth, is consequently questioned and shown to be of limited value by Adam himself and—later on—by Raphael. Adam, confronted with his linguistic inability to name his creator, wonders "by what name" he may adore him who "Surpassest far my naming" (*PL* VIII.357, 359): according to Michael Lieb "a question that, Milton suggests, borders upon presumption."[141]

Although in the process of naming the animals Adam has access to "direct revelation as the supplement to the Book of Nature," his linguistic abilities fail when he sees God, so that he is "unable to name that which transcends his nature."[142] As Robert Entzminger puts it, "If, as God explains (VIII.343-45), the naming of the animals seals Adam's lordship over the rest of Creation, then his fruitless search for a name when he encounters God indicates his own subordination to the beings higher on the Great Chain."[143]

At this point, where the coordination of names and things is of central importance, we are confronted with aspects of semiotics that were already known to the Presocratics but which are of special significance in Ferdinand de Saussure's theory of signs and which are today generally—and this may well be an over-generalization—associated with his name.[144] Like many linguists of the nineteenth and early twentieth centuries who deal with the nature of the linguistic sign, Saussure makes use of the principle of the arbitrary coordination of sign(ifier) and referent.[145] Even though it may appear to be anachronistic in connection with linguistic theories of the seventeenth century, the concept of the arbitrariness of the linguistic sign—which has its obvious precursors in the nominalist theories of language of that era—proves very helpful in the analysis of *Paradise Lost*, and it sheds light on the attempts of Milton's contemporaries to create a "transparent" language.[146]

In his theory Saussure rejects the possibility of the existence of a monolithic prelapsarian language which, for many philosophers of language of the seventeenth century, represented the model case of a non-arbitrary relationship between words and things. Many Miltonists claim that—corresponding to these ideas—the prelapsarian words in *Paradise Lost* are "not arbitrary labels assigned to things but sounds that are themselves intimately bound with the things' natures or essences,"[147] but one may of course argue that even in such a prelapsarian language the relationship between names and things is either a convention created by Adam in an arbitrary manner while he was inspired by God, or a convention first created by God in an arbitrary manner and then communicated to Adam in the form of an inspiration or a dream vision.[148]

In general, one assumes that in God's language there is no deviation from a complete symmetry between word and deed or names and things; for this reason, Georgia Christopher has called God's language concrete poetry.[149] But the non-existence of a "gap" between word and deed does not imply that the two are one and the same thing, and a one-to-one relation is obviously not limited to the relation of equality. Only as long as Adam and Eve employ words in exactly the way authorized by God, as long, that is, as reference and denotation remain identical, does the unity of name and thing remain unchallenged. Of course the act of naming also implies a position of power for Adam and Eve:

> While divine naming creates the elements of God's universe, human naming makes them into significant elements of Adam's world. God's naming and Adam's both confirm the paradigm inherent in an ex Deo theology of creation: that creative effort is equivalent to the fundamentally linguistic process of imposing a differential system on pre-existent matter, such as chaos or chaotic sound.[150]

That the divinely inspired act of naming relies on an "arbitrary" divine act may also be deduced from the fact that the fallen angels lose their originally God-given names after their rebellion and Fall—"of their names in heavenly records now / Be no memorial blotted out and razed / By their rebellion" (*PL* I.362-64); at least one can thus interpret the situation in Book I in which the fallen angels remain nameless for a time: "Nor had they yet among the sons of Eve / Got them new names" (*PL* I.364-65). For example, the "postlapsarian" name Lucifer is only bestowed upon Satan in Book X through an act of allusion (or, in today's terminology, metonymy): "Lucifer, so by allusion called, / Of that bright star to Satan paragoned" (*PL* X.425-26). The new names that the fallen angels have "among the sons of Eve" thus are no longer sanctioned by God so that human readers have the chance to follow their etymological derivation in the act of reading.

From the Act of Naming to Theorizing Verbal Communication

The underlying pattern of naming that was created in the "primal scene" just described will also have to be applied outside of paradise—without the possibility of divine inspiration, of course. Even in prelapsarian times, Adam discovers, however, that words like those of Eve "mixed with love / And sweet compliance" (*PL* VIII.602-03) gain additional layers of meaning in the communication between human beings and are thus no longer restricted to the nominal meaning they had had originally. If a word is to be useful in human communication, it must be applicable in situations other than the one in which it was used for the first time.

Furthermore, as long as Adam only gives names to the animals, he restricts himself to the level of the word as the basic unit of language. In principle, he uses words only as signs standing for those animals that are present at the very moment of naming them and not as signs that might also refer to other members of the same species. As long as the use of words is restricted to this situation, we may use a simple Saussurean model in order to describe the act of naming, although one has to admit that for Saussure the terms *signifiant* (signifier) and *signifié* (signified) are idealized psychological units that are not identical with the actual referent and the actual sound pattern.[151]

But as soon as God talks to Adam about animals in general, these "psychological units"—or rather, the words corresponding to them—must be integrated into the context of discourse.[152] Somewhat later, the names "invented" by Adam are also used in his communication with Eve, and, keeping the story of the Fall in mind, we can trace the development from an—as Jun Harada calls it—original honest monolithic language to an ambiguous language in the course of *Paradise Lost*:

> As Edenic innocence degenerates into ignorance, which worked in Eve's fall, so the concept of oneness is deprived of its paradisiacal content and becomes an emptied name which functions as a fatal trap to deceive Adam into a oneness of destruction. The reader sees throughout these episodes the monolithic honest quality of Edenic language changing into the hypocritically ambiguous quality of our fallen language.[153]

One may also interpret this process as that of a growing linguistic "arbitrarization," as the switch from prelapsarian linguistics to another linguistic system that offers a necessary but not necessarily sufficient explanation of Adam and Eve's "Fall." In this context, and this is one of the main points of my argument, the archangel Raphael plays a more important role than has generally been accorded to him. We are dealing here with a linguistic process in the course of which the original identity of denotation and reference can no longer be upheld so that it now becomes possible to use linguistic signs for a whole class of animals or objects rather than for only a single animal or a single object.

The "primal" linguistic scene in Book VIII of *Paradise Lost* represents Adam's human version of the creation story as he relates it to the archangel Raphael. At this time Adam is still unfallen and thus can freely communicate with the angel. In the epic, however, this scene is displayed to the postlapsarian reader who is also able to understand it. Is the postlapsarian reader's insight due to an act of accommodation and narrative simplification on the part of Raphael? The "fallen" reader is part of a system of communication constructed by the epic narrator, "Milton," at the beginning of Book I. Literary convention renders the narrative voice omniscient, but it is of course also a postlapsarian voice aiming to "assert eternal providence, / And justify the ways of God to men" (*PL* I.25-26).

As Edward Le Comte shows, these lines can be interpreted as being ambiguous. Their ambiguity depends on the somewhat fuzzy status of the phrase *to men*: Does it refer, as an indirect object, to *justify*—as in *to justify to a human audience what God has done*—or is it a complement to *the ways of God*—as in *to justify the ways in which God has treated human beings*?[154] If one interprets line 26 in the first, traditional fashion, the whole epic enterprise turns into a general process of accommodation through which the entire universe is rendered intelligible to a human audience. If one, however, interprets the line to be the justification of the way in which God has treated mankind, then it is not so much an accommodation for a human audience as the commentary of a voice that seems to claim the same level of authority as the one whose actions it justifies. As R.A. Shoaf argues,

> For if Milton seeks 'to justify the ways of God to men,' to re-establish equity between the Creator and his creature in the dimension of understanding, he must presume, necessarily, that God's ways are intelligible to man, that man can understand them. No justification is possible without prior understanding. Man must still possess, then, some basic likeness to the Divine, on account of which and through which he can perceive and understand the ways of the Divine, because of which he is still dual with God. This basic likeness, we recall, is the ruins of the image of God in man after the Fall (Gen. 1:26).[155]

On the other hand, the commentator, although he sees himself as a prophet, has to formulate his message in such a way that normal postlapsarian human beings can understand it.

As I will show, linguistic ambiguity is of supreme importance not only in these lines but also in the epic as a whole; or, as Alastair Fowler puts it in his edition of the epic: "If the Latinisms in *Paradise Lost* have been overestimated, it is quite the reverse with the ambiguities and ironies" (*PL* 15). From the perspective of an interpretation of *Paradise Lost* in which linguistic ambiguity plays a central role, it is thus of major significance that right at the start of his epic (but of course not only there) Milton makes use of verbal and syntactical ambiguities which have a decisive influence on our reading of the position and attitude of his narrative voice.

For example, one wonders in the course of the epic why Milton himself admits in his invocation at the beginning of Book VII that his readership is a "fit audience . . . though few" (*PL* VII.31). Does Milton see his own role of the epic narrator as that of a quasi-divine instance that can only be understood by a few *illuminati*, or does he indicate—in the same way as in the ambiguous formulation at the beginning of the epic—that the divine message is after all and foremost a human one that can be understood by simple human beings? The second possibility might indicate that in the end the difference between divine and human beings is not as profound as first assumed and not insurmountable.

God's Ambiguous Language in Paradise: *Divine Irony*

In her interpretation of *Paradise Lost*, Stevie Davies assumes that a linguistic "Fall" occurs during the construction of the Tower of Babel, and that as its result the one heavenly language, "God's creating Word," is replaced by numerous fallen human languages, "shadowy, riddling guides to truth, a corporate fabrication enshrining our ignorant assumptions, sophistical devices and our wish to oppress one another."[156]

I would agree with Davies that there must be something like a "linguistic Fall" somewhere in *Paradise Lost*. But there are alternative possibilities to the implied identification of this Fall with the construction of the Tower of Babel. One may claim that the "sophistical devices" and "riddling guides to the truth" she mentions have—at least in *Paradise Lost*—existed long before the Tower of Babel, perhaps even before the Fall in the Garden of Eden. For it was God himself who, soon after having created Adam, introduced him to the dual character of the linguistic sign and to the dialectical processes of communication when the two discussed Adam's wish for a companion.[157]

Does this mean that God himself deviated from unambiguous paradisal language and thus laid the ground for the Fall of language that often is identified with the Fall in paradise or with the events surrounding the construction of the Tower of Babel? There are some indications that the linguistic Fall takes place earlier than critics and theologians normally think: one may even imagine that it happens before the serpent's seduction of Eve and Adam by means of the infamous fruit. For example, as mentioned above, one may here point to the episode of the discussion that

God and Adam have about a companion. This scene, in which God uses an ironical strategy of argumentation is described by Adam himself in *Paradise Lost* and thus does not depend upon mediation or accommodation through an angel such as Raphael or Michael. While critics claim that God abstains from political rhetoric before the revolt of the rebel angels in heaven,[158] Miltonists have for a long time pointed out his "divine irony,"[159] and often this irony is even praised as "one of the few human qualities Milton allows God the Father in *Paradise Lost*."[160]

Like the description of the creation of language, this scene is part of Adam's account of his first days in paradise. It follows directly after his inquiry regarding God's name, and Adam now appeals to God's sympathy with a lonesome human being who has no fit partner: "In solitude / What happiness, who can enjoy alone, / Or all enjoying, what contentment find?" (*PL* VIII.364-66) This appeal, which Adam himself later calls "presumptuous" (*PL* VIII.367), causes the "vision," as which he perceives God, to smile benevolently and thus not to reject his wish immediately. In this prelapsarian world, he is still able to communicate directly with God or the Son, who first of all encourages him to associate with the other living beings in paradise, with whom Adam also seems to be able to communicate without any problem (*PL* VIII.369-75). Adam's ensuing words in the report he gives to Raphael—"So spake the universal Lord, and *seemed* / So ordering" (*PL* VIII.376-77, my italics)—show that, looking back at the encounter, he no longer interprets God's words as a simple rejection but that he is aware of God's irony. God here seems to deviate from the one-to-one relationship between words and things that he had introduced himself: he says one thing and means something quite different;[161] he rejects Adam's plea for a companion only to admit later, after having provoked Adam to come forward with a convincing argument, that his uncooperative behaviour had been nothing but a pedagogical strategy: "God *wanted* to be contradicted in precisely this way"[162] and had only played the role of the Socratic *eiron* trying to elicit a certain behaviour from his pupil.

God's negative response had thus only been a test "for trial only brought, / To see how thou couldst judge of fit and meet" (*PL* VIII.447-48), a test, by the way, which Adam passes with flying colours so that God is "not displeased" (*PL* VIII.398).[163] The first human being thus proves that he can communicate with his creator, that he is even capable of "disambiguating" the latter's deviations from the principle of monolithic language. Although aware of his own limitations, he sees himself as part of a continuum that does not contain insurmountable differences but only gradual differences between human and divine beings. While "Thou in thy self art perfect, and in thee / Is no deficience found; not so is man, / But in degree" (*PL* VIII.415-17).[164] I see the words "But in degree" as an indication that mankind and divinity are not that different. The unusual syntax of the sentence at first invites (or tempts) us to read the words "But in degree" as a complement to the preceding line rather than relating them to the following phrase: "the cause of his desire / By conversation with his like to help, / Or solace his defects" (*PL* VIII. 417-19). As the reader realizes, *surprised by sin,* this is probably even the primary sense of the lines. As a human being, Adam has to admit, however, that communication with a divine being is a stressful and tiring experience.

As Milton critics have known for a long time and as Michael Bryson has pointed out again recently,[165] such a discussion between God and human beings as Adam's questioning of God's will is based upon biblical patterns, for example on Abraham's and Moses' successful attempts to pacify God and to convince him that an all too harsh action against the Sodomites (Gen. 18) or against the Israelites would damage his reputation as a good god. John E. Parish interprets the scene in which Adam asks for a partner as a reflection of these biblical discussions in which God even encourages Adam to disobey him: "Here, for once, the sense of humor which Milton attributes to God is appealing. Adam is emboldened to argue because the smile on God's face tells him that God is merely teasing him! And the episode is material from the simple Old Testament disputes with God, transfigured by gener-ous interpretation."[166]

This case of God's ironical deviation from an unambiguous language—Michael Bryson claims: "The Father, in short, *lies*"[167]—is not the only one to be found in the prelapsarian world: in Milton's paradise we find also other situations in which the use of monolithic language comes under pressure. As Entzminger points out, "In his presentation of unfallen language, Milton offers metaphor and pun where the lin-guists expect mathematical precision, opulent redundancy where they imagine terse-ness."[168] One may of course argue that Raphael here gives Adam and Eve a full and comprehensive insight into the relationship between verbal and natural signs and their referents. One may, however, also assume that Raphael's reliance on the prin-ciple of the arbitrariness of the coordination of sign and referent has quite far-reaching consequences on language in paradise (and beyond), whereas God's first "deviation" from a monolithic language had been intended to be nothing but a peda-gogical strategy that in no way been was meant to undermine the basic underlying relationship between word and thing. Raphael's theory of translation and accommo-dation deserves a closer study.

Eve's Dream

While Raphael's visit to the Garden of Eden—which I will focus on in the following sections of this study—takes place in Book V, Eve is still haunted by a dream she had the night before and which, as shown in Book IV, had been inspired by Satan. The latter had sat "Squat like a toad, close at the ear of Eve" (*PL* IV.800), trying to instil illusory dreams and wishes or "At least distempered, discontented thoughts, / Vain hopes, vain aims, inordinate desires / Blown up with high conceits engendering pride" (*PL* IV.807-09).

Eve describes her dream to Adam as one "of offence and trouble, which my mind / Knew never till this irksome night" (*PL* V.34-35). This description by Eve herself cannot—at least according to some critics—make the same claims to authenticity as those by the narrative voice, which ostensibly has access to divine insight. As Mary Nyquist remarks, "Far from having any kind of status as an event, the dream-temptation is therefore produced by *Paradise Lost*'s complexly articulated narrative discourse as, precisely, a non-event."[169] In this dream, Eve discovers the "tree of interdicted knowledge" and there meets an angel-like figure who praises the beneficent effect of the fruit of this tree and wonders why knowledge is "so despised" (*PL* V.60). He does not even hesitate to pluck and taste the fruit.

In her dream, Eve is shocked at "such bold words vouched with a deed so bold," but the angel claims that even human beings can become God-like by eating the fruit, that it is "able to make gods of men." In this case, God would not be "impaired," but even "honoured more" (*PL* V.65, 70, 73). The angel thus offers Eve the fruit as well as the possibility of becoming "Thy self a goddess"; he even suggests that access to heaven is "by merit thine," which comes as a slight surprise as Eve has not yet been on earth for any length of time (*PL* V.78, 80). Eve cannot resist temptation and dreams that the angel takes her with him to heaven from where she looks down on earth. Still, in the end she is glad "To find this but a dream" (*PL* V.93).

Some critics interpret this dream as a first step of Eve's Fall, as a step, that is, without which evil could not have taken hold of her soul.[170] Others, however, hold that the temptation and "evil motions" alone do not yet mean that Eve has fallen.[171] This is also Adam's attitude when Eve tells him about the dream: he is upset but does not believe that she herself can "harbour" evil as she is "Created pure" (*PL* V.99, 100). He describes in detail how evil may arise in her dreams while she is asleep, as sleep is a phase in which reason tends to lose control so that "lesser faculties" such as fancy can produce "Ill matching words and deeds long past or late" (*PL* V.113).

These "ill matching words and deeds" are once again an example of the problematic relationship between words and deeds, names and things. And this instance takes place even before the archangel Raphael comes down to earth in order to warn Adam and Eve of Satan, the "Artificer of fraud" and "the first / That practised falsehood under saintly show" (*PL* IV.121-22). Eve, too, points out the rather unusual coordination of "such bold words" and "a deed so bold" (*PL* V.66). However, the non-identity of word and deed here is of a different quality than the other cases of linguistic disparity discussed so far in as much as here the words no longer refer to a true core of meaning that is meant to be discovered (as, for example, in God's ironic statements in his communication with Adam). Reference and denotation are no longer identical; they do not even overlap in the most essential aspects any more.

Adam does not see an imminent danger in the evil that has found its way into Eve's thoughts. While later critics such as Tillyard interpret the dream as an earlier stage of the Fall—"Are we to believe, with Tillyard, that Eve, already anxious and troubled, is no longer innocent?" asks Fowler (*PL* 263)—Adam still holds that "Evil into the mind of god or man / May come and go, so unapproved, and leave / No spot or blame behind" (*PL* V.117-19).

Raphael's Mission and the Need for Accommodation

The first event in the chronology of *Paradise Lost*, i.e., the event on which the whole action of the epic is based, is "[t]he first exaltation of the Son of God who is pronounced head of the angelic hierarchies."[172] This event described in Book V causes the resentment and envy of Satan, who is ambitious and interested in "political machination, court intrigue, and 'old-style' heroism,"[173] so that the "reform" of the heavenly hierarchies leads to the rebel angels' open rebellion and finally to their expulsion from heaven.[174]

It is the archangel Raphael who relates the account of the Son's exaltation to Adam and Eve in paradise. Following God's command, the archangel has come down to earth in order to warn the human beings of Satan's revenge for his banishment from heaven. In this situation, Raphael thus addresses the first two human beings before they fall, that is, before they move from a prelapsarian to a postlapsarian state. Although, as I will show later, Adam has so far been able to communicate with God (or the Son) without any recourse to the rhetorical strategy of accommodation, Raphael assumes that his mission now includes the task of accommodating his divine message to Adam's limited human capacities, of—in other words—translating it.

Even though it is doubtful whether prelapsarian Adam's mental capacities were so limited as to necessitate Raphael's strategy of accommodation, one may of course argue that Milton's postlapsarian readers certainly need all the angelic help they can get. Of course, such a postlapsarian limitation would also affect Milton himself and his epic voice (unless one is willing to grant him prophetic powers).

As I have shown above, the question of narrative authority addressed here affects the epic right from the start when Milton (or his narrator) states in the first invocation of the muse in Book I that his aim is "to justify the ways of God to men." The parallel arising between the narrative positions of the archangel Raphael and the epic narrator "Milton" opens up exciting and important questions for Milton critics, such as the possibility of reading *Paradise Lost* as a *self-consuming artifact* or as an aporia.[175]

Eve's dream in which an angel tells her to disobey the divine command has of course a negative effect on her and Adam's belief in a reliable and unambiguous language, all the more since they now have come across a case in which language can and must also convey an untruth. Either God's command or the angelic message in Eve's dream must be wrong. In this situation Raphael, "the sociable spirit" (*PL* V.221), appears sent by God, the omniscient Father, who knows Satan's plans regarding Adam and Eve—"how he designs / In them at once to ruin all mankind" (*PL* V.227-28)—as he tells Raphael and the other angels in heaven. Raphael's mission is to warn Adam and Eve. As described above, the two have already been confronted with the concept of deceit and lies in Eve's dream, and perhaps they have already been "infected" by it, but they are not yet aware of the full range of verbal untruthfulness.

For this reason, God tells Raphael to converse with Adam "as friend with friend." Raphael is to use any kind of *discourse* that "may advise [Adam] of his happy state" which is soon to be under siege; he is to inform him of the importance of "his own free will" and responsibility in the confrontation with evil, "Lest wilfully transgressing he pretend / Surprisal, unadmonished, unforewarned" (*PL* V.229, 234, 236, 244-45). Raphael's message is repeated once again—and more directly—after the somewhat prudish archangel has recovered from Adam's rather indiscreet question regarding bodily love in heaven: Adam is to "stand fast" as he is self-sufficient and able to rely on his "own arbitrament" (*PL* VIII. 640, 641).

As God remarks, Raphael has to leave it to Adam's and Eve's own free will whether they follow his advice. His reliance on the concept of free will in the human beings' obedience to God's advice and in their belief in his message is the central point which makes it possible for Milton to depict God as a good God in spite of all the arguments to the contrary brought forth by a line of critics ranging from Blake to Empson and beyond. Such a "good God"[176] cannot be held responsible for the Fall of his creatures: he has created them in a way that would have enabled them to withstand temptation; they have been warned, and if they fall and give in to temptation, they have only themselves to blame. As Milton (or "Milton") writes in the third chapter of the first book of *Doctrina Christiana*:

> The matter or object of the divine plan was that angels and men alike should be endowed with free will, so that they could either fall or not fall. Doubtless God's actual decree bore a close resemblance to this, so that all the evils which have since happened as a result of the fall could either happen or not: if you stand firm, you will stay; if you do not, you will be thrown out: if you do not eat, you will live; if you do, you will die. (*WJM* XIV: 80)

Raphael's mission, a "mission of complexity and subtlety,"[177] confronts him with the challenge of communicating with the newly created human beings about whom and whose mental capacities he does not know very much.[178] The archangel does not yet know a lot about Adam and Eve, about their creation and their ability to communicate "as friend with friend" with superhuman beings, all the more so since Raphael was not present at the time of Adam's creation as he belonged to the group of angels whom God had sent on the unsuccessful mission ostensibly meant to prevent Satan from escaping from Hell and to save the earth from his threat. Still, Raphael's response to Adam's invitation "in yonder shady bower / To rest, and what the garden choicest bears / To sit and taste, till this meridian heat / Be over, and the sun more cool decline" (*PL* V.367-70) is quite friendly—or perhaps, taking his somewhat indirect style into account, not unfriendly. Raphael's "mild" answer does not exclude the possibility of equality and communication of human beings and angels, but it is, stylistically and didactically speaking, less than straightforward through its use of double negation. One wonders if communication "as friend with friend" really has to sound as complicated as the following "compliment":

> Adam, I therefore came, nor art thou such
> Created, or such place hast here to dwell,
> As may not oft invite, though spirits of heaven
> To visit thee. (*PL* V.372-75)

While Raphael's style and syntax still are quite reserved here, the archangel's following statements quite often leave the reader with the impression that the differences between earthly and heavenly spheres may rather be of an only gradual kind and indicate a "consistency of creation."[179] Earthly food, for example, which Adam first thinks might be "unsavoury food perhaps / to spiritual natures" (*PL* V.401-02), meets with the angel's appreciation.[180] Furthermore, the meal shared by angels and human beings is a form of communion and communication between God's creatures that no longer exists in this form after the Fall.[181] Even though man in paradise may be only "in part / Spiritual," he still is to a certain extent spiritual so that earthly food "may of purest spirits be found / No ingrateful food." In short: "whatever was created, needs / To be sustained and fed" (*PL* V.405-06, 406-07, 414-15).

The impression that heavenly and earthly spheres are similar and comparable is also supported by Raphael's admission about the Garden of Eden: that "God hath here / Varied his bounty so with new delights, / As may compare with heaven" (*PL* V.430-32), all the more so since the angel here does not hide behind theological reservations but rather eats "with keen despatch / Of real hunger" (*PL* V.436-37). Even though some critics disqualify the question regarding the shared meal of human beings and angel as "rather puerile,"[182] one may detect a certain ontological connection between heavenly and earthly spheres, between spirit and body, between Raphael's and Milton's strategies of narration.[183] The inhabitants of heaven and earth are comparable at least to some extent, so that some critics even go so far as to interpret Raphael's words as meaning that the relationship between heaven and earth is "not allegorical or merely metaphoric, but analogical," that there is "a relationship between earth and heaven, between the physical and the spiritual, which is inherent in the nature of things."[184]

Raphael also indicates (perhaps even suggests) that not only the spheres of heaven and earth but also their inhabitants are comparable in their relationship towards God and capable of "upward" development. There is "one almighty . . . from whom / All things proceed, and up to him return, / If not depraved from good" (*PL* V.469-71). For Raphael, and probably also for Milton, here all living beings are part of one *Great Chain of Being* which one may interpret as an indication of Milton's original monism:

> All that exists, from angels to earth, is composed of one living, corporeal substance. An understanding of this monism is necessary for Adam if he is to grasp his place in Milton's universe; the same understanding is necessary for us if we are to grasp much of the action of *Paradise Lost* as well as the poem's participation in a seminal debate in early modern thought.[185]

As this chain represents a gradual process, there is, I feel, no missing link in it:[186] bodily and spiritual, heavenly and earthly, animate and inanimate, intuitive and discursive spheres are interconnected, "Differing but in degree, of kind the same" (*PL* V.490). Or, as Margaret Olofson Thickstun puts it, "Most of the time [the angels] must muddle forward just as humans do."[187]

Human beings can even hope to one day live together with the angels ("participate," *PL* V.494) and become wholly spiritual beings so that heaven and earth may become exchangeable. Adam draws the same conclusion from Raphael's speech that Milton himself had formulated as early as 1644 in *Of Education* concerning the repair of the "ruins of our parents":[188] that "In contemplation of created things / By steps we may ascend to God" (*PL* V.511-12). However, there is a large *if*, even though it does not appear that large in connection with Raphael's prophesy of a possible equality of humans and angels: "If ye be found obedient" (*PL* V.501). The rise to quasi-divine status thus depends upon Adam and Eve's obedience. It is probably this *if* that marks the difference between the originally envisaged "improvement" of unfallen mankind to a purely spiritual existence as angelic beings and the later, postlapsarian "repair" of the "ruins of our first parents" in *Of Education*.[189]

Adam immediately wonders about this condition: "Can we want obedience then . . . ?" (*PL* V.514). This condition is the real core of Raphael's mission in the Garden of Eden: it is Adam and Eve's own responsibility, their own free will, on which they have to rely in their fight against temptation: "that thou art happy, owe to God; / That thou continuest such, owe to thyself" (*PL* V. 520-21).

When Adam asks for more information about the background of the archangel's mission and about the events in heaven, Raphael decides to base his narrative of the politics of heaven on a semiotic strategy of accommodation, on a "universal metaphor."[190] Still, one might argue that Raphael goes too far in his accommodational eagerness. As Thomas F. Merrill points out, "The fact is that Raphael curiously accommodates all the hexameral material to Adam when there seems no apparent reason to accommodate at all."[191] When asked by Adam to describe politics in heaven, Raphael wonders: "how shall I relate / To human sense the invisible exploits / Of warring spirits; . . . / . . . how last unfold / The secrets of another world, perhaps / Not lawful to reveal?" (*PL* V.564-66, 568-70). His solution is the following:

> . . . what surmounts the reach
> Of human sense, I shall delineate so,
> By likening spiritual to corporal forms,
> As may express them best.
> (*PL* V.571-74)

Raphael's strategy here is one of accommodation: "When Raphael tells Adam of heavenly events, of angelic motives and of heavenly war, Adam is to believe literally what is not literally true but is as near the truth as his limited understanding can come."[192] It becomes very difficult to distinguish between literal and figurative meaning in this context.[193] The decision to accommodate is, as Lobsien puts it, possible (because the earth is a reflection of heaven) and problematic (because it encourages inadmissible anthropomorphism) at the same time.[194] Such a strategy of accommodation and its insistence on the necessity of distinguishing between the divine and human spheres would have been supported by at least some of Milton's contemporaries.[195]

Raphael's accommodation implies the process of interpretation described above in my discussion of Augustinian semiotics: It entails a switch from the concrete literal level over to that of figurative meaning. The archangel uses—or at least thinks he uses—the following method: He makes use of concrete earthly things (*res*), whose everyday literal meaning is well-known to his audience, as signs (*signa*) standing for a supposedly higher heavenly truth. In this context, the relationship between these signs and the truths they stand for is arbitrarily and idiosyncratically established by Raphael himself. He thus deviates from the original intrinsic and natural naming of heavenly objects and relationships which he assumes human beings would not be able to comprehend without his mediation. Although Raphael thinks that this action is authorized by the Father, there are indications that this may not exactly be the case.

Through Raphael's semiotic strategy, heavenly objects suddenly are referred to by earthly names: an originally "natural" sign—i.e., a sign that had been linked to an earthly referent with God's permission and through his inspiration—now is used in order to refer to a heavenly referent, and thus the originally clear and unambiguous one-to-one relationship between sign and referent is destroyed. Instead, the sign becomes ambiguous. Language that had once provided a "monolithic" image of reality can now be used in a figurative sense, but this gain in expressivity has its price: language moves away from an erstwhile transparency towards ambiguity and convention, towards a coordination of signs and referents that can be arbitrarily influenced, at least by archangels.

The Consequences of the Decision in Favour of Accommodation

The visit of the archangel Raphael on earth and his strategy of accommodation in his communication with Adam have grave consequences for Adam and Eve's linguistic self-consciousness. Although some critics call his visit in paradise "a wonderful model of civilised social discourse between courteous angel-teacher and unfallen man-pupil," others immediately qualify such a positive judgment by skeptically stating that: "Adam is left only mildly persuaded of the danger which awaits him."[196]

Before Raphael's pedagogically motivated visit in the Garden of Eden, Adam and Eve are not yet aware of the possibility that they use a nominalist and conventional rather than an "essentialist" language. But as early as in Book IV, when we meet Adam and Eve for the first time, it is God himself—rather than the possibly fallible archangel Raphael—who introduces a non-monolithic kind of semiotic relationship between signified and signifier in the Garden. For it is God himself who makes use of the tree of knowledge as more than just a fruit bearing tree by turning it into a sign (albeit not a linguistic one at first) of human obedience.[197] As Adam tells his wife, it is "The only sign of our obedience left / Among so many signs of power and rule / Conferred upon us" (*PL* IV.428-30).[198] The "real" tree referred to by Adam is still the same tree in the Garden of Eden, and thus the denotation (according to Lyons) is identical, but there are now two possibilities of talking about it: on the one hand, as an apple tree within the context of paradisal vegetation, or, on the other hand, as the "tree of knowledge" in the context of God's commandments.[199]

Once the apple tree has left the original semantic sphere of unambiguous one-to-one relationships between sign and referent, it becomes easier for Satan to insinuate to Eve that it has another meaning that she does not know about yet: eating the fruit will, according to Satan, provide human beings with divine insights.[200]

After Ferdinand de Saussure, another—and even more contemporary—semiotician, Umberto Eco, offers an enlightening interpretation of the linguistic situation in paradise that makes use of modern linguistic concepts. In his essay "On the Possibility of Generating Aesthetic Messages in an Edenic Language," Eco, who recently also wrote an important study of the history of the search for the ideal language, describes the prelapsarian state of language: "Words thus equal things (or rather the sensations which Adam and Eve are aware of) and things equal words."[201] But then the interdiction to eat the apple threatens the balance of the recently acquired semiotic system:

> Adam and Eve have only just settled down in the Garden of Eden. They have learned to find their way around with the help of language—when out comes God, who pronounces the first factual judgment. The general sense of what God is trying to tell them is as follows: "You two probably imagine that the apple belongs

to the class of good, edible things, because it happens to be red. Well, I've got news for you. The apple is not to be considered edible because it is bad."

God's decision that apples are off limits for human beings cannot be explained easily within the confines of the original language; it is a message that Adam and Eve cannot understand: "This constitutes a factual judgment, as it affords a notion which is as yet unfamiliar to those God has addressed; for God is both referent and source of the referent—his pronouncements are a court of reference."[202]

In addition, a new and more complex semiotic system is created as God's decision "posits a new type of connotative pairing between semantic units which had previously been coupled together differently." Eco argues, however, that God's decision to make changes to the semiotic system was a grave error: "In an effort to elaborate a prohibition which would put his creatures to the test, God provides the fundamental example of a subversion in the presumed natural order of things." All this because of an "ambiguously phrased prohibition."[203]

After mentioning the tree of knowledge as a "sign of obedience," Adam also mentions other objects that have become "signs of power" (*PL* IV.429) in addition to their everyday function. He himself is aware of—and already uses—ambiguous signs that serve as *inartificial arguments* by pointing beyond themselves to other contexs, (as, according to Milton's . Unexpectedly, it is the archangel Raphael who points out this equivalent of the Saussurean concept of arbitrariness in the relationship between signs and referents by indicating that he uses a strategy of accommodation in order to render the Father's message comprehensible for Adam and Eve.[204] Although it corresponds to theories current in the seventeenth century, his strategy of accommodation destroys the original union and/or coordination of signs and things with which Adam and Eve had been familiar.

There is, however, also a way of seeing the archangel's linguistic error in a more positive light, as his accommodational "misuse" of signs renders language more flexible after all:

> Raphael's accommodations, then, must be seen as introducing human concepts and coining new words, or at least employing theoretically existent but still unused words for mundane objects and phenomena. And so, in this regard, Adam's linguistic and conceptual experience is perforce enlarged by this discussion.[205]

Although Raphael's questioning of the integrity of the linguistic sign of course takes place within the context of a conversation, i.e., of spoken discourse consisting of phrases and sentences, this discussion and its important repercussions focus primarily on the "basic" level of communication that was generally still at the centre of seventeenth-century linguistic discussion: that of the word. An example of the no longer unambiguous coordination of names and things—and also, of course, of the rhetorical opportunities this can offer in a wider context—is provided by the situation in the postlapsarian Book X, when Adam ruefully remembers Eve's seductive "soft words" (*PL* X.865) and refers to her as "thou serpent" (*PL* X.867), as he thinks that "that name best / Befits thee with him leagued, thy self as false / And hateful" (*PL* X.867-69).[206] Here we no longer have the case of an unambiguous coordination of the concepts of woman and serpent. Language has fallen, and words no longer have a clear and unambiguous meaning. The word *serpent* has acquired connotations that Adam can use not only in order to refer to but also to hurt his female companion.

Miltonists are far from united in their view of the reliability of Miltonic narrators such as the archangel Raphael: Some assume that his position as an archangel alone makes him "even more authoritative than the epic narrator."[207] Others cannot help showing a certain cynicism in their comments on the scene just quoted.[208] On the other hand, one has to keep in mind that the Father himself does not mention the necessity of employing a strategy of accommodation when he sends Raphael on his mission to paradise.[209] Either God thinks that the need for such a strategy of accommodation is obvious or he does not regard the differences between heaven and earth to be important enough to justify such a strategy. As it is, he seems to have granted Raphael "artistic license in devising appropriate forms of discourse."[210]

Raphael seems to assume that God holds the use of accommodation to be an adequate strategy of communication, and thus he develops his own method of granting human beings insight into the politics of heaven, especially so in his description of the War in heaven (Book VI). The most important aspect of his "semiotics" consists in "likening" spiritual and bodily forms to each other. Repeatedly he points out the difficulties that arise in the telling heavenly history in earthly terminology. His— and especially of course God's—speech has to undergo a semiotic procedure in order to be intelligible on earth as his message "to human ears / Cannot without process of speech be told, / So told as earthly notion can receive" (*PL* VII.177-79). So far we cannot tell whether such a "process of speech" rendering the divine message intelligible for mankind is a semiotic one-way street, whether it only presents a simplified version of divine truth that does not really permit them to see and understand more than just a glimpse of the true heavenly state.[211]

In addition to the application of—admittedly anachronistic—structuralist linguistic theories to Raphael's semiotics, which is nevertheless based on clearly existing parallels between seventeenth- and twentieth-century ideas of language, one might even consider using a poststructuralist approach to Milton's work that would interpret the "great gulf fixed between all signification and the Divine Referent" as evidence of his being a deconstructionist *avant la lettre*: Milton could be seen as an intellectual addressing in his work the same problems of language and communication that still occupy contemporary literary theorists.[212] In today's postlapsarian society, words are always already fraught with historical connotations and always already fallen, even though we think we can fix their meanings by writing them down.

There is a clear step in *Paradise Lost* from the linguistic situation in Book IV, where there is still "truth in images"—"all things seen bespeak their true meaning directly and immediately"—to that of Books V and VI, for here "the image" turns into "a multifaceted analogue of the truth."[213] Seen from a somewhat naive linguistic point of view, the general "loosening" of the connection between signified and signifier, i.e., the growing awareness of the arbitrariness of their coordination, makes it possible that more than just one sign can stand for a single referent, whether this be in the positive context of a sacrament in religious language or in the negative context of a lie. Similarly, several signifiers can be related to one object or concept. Theoretically, such a linguistic state might lead to a situation in which a homogenous language splits up into different dialects or even new languages, and such a concept even has found its way into certain theories of language development. The speakers of these new languages would sooner or later have to depend upon interpreters in order to be able to communicate. Raphael may even have had such a possibility in mind when in his report to Adam he makes reference to the "palace of great Lucifer" which supposedly only bears this name "in the dialect of men / Interpreted" (*PL* V.760-62), and—interestingly enough—Adam calls the archangel a "Divine interpreter" (*PL* VII.72).

Milton here uses the verb *interpret*, which according to the *OED* could have the meaning 'translate' in the seventeenth century, and the meaning of *interpreter* as 'oral translator' is current in today's world of international communication. It is thus tempting first of all to see Raphael's strategy of accommodation as an act of translation.[214] An admittedly simplistic theory of translation that sees language as a nomenclature—a possibility which, as we have seen, Saussure rejected in his *Cours de linguistique générale*—would be the following: in the act of translation, referents, which remain the same in the source and target language contexts, are connected to new signs that represent them in the foreign language; the sign in the source language is replaced by an equivalent sign in the target language.[215]

Raphael's strategy of accommodation works differently, though: the archangel makes use of traditional signs that habitually are related to an earthly referent and then applies them to a heavenly referent that is new to Adam and Eve. So the signs remain the same while the referents change. Instead of his using dissimilar words in order to refer to similar contexts, here a seemingly dissimilar context is referred to by similar words.

As far as the "fallen language" is concerned, which does not yet exist at this stage of *Paradise Lost*, its loss of a solid coordination between sign and referent is not only a loss, as it will increase linguistic flexibility: "As a gift of God, postlapsarian language consists of division not precision of names but complementarily also of a means for bridging the gap between name and thing or name and meaning and a process for translating one language into another."[216]

Is Accommodation Necessary?

While he is engaged in the process of accommodation and translation in the Garden of Eden, the archangel Raphael more or less inadvertently gives the reader many hints indicating that his insistence on splitting language up into arbitrarily coordinated signs and referents may not have been necessary after all. Especially, there are indications in Raphael's speech that the spheres of heaven and earth may after all be so similar that the whole process of accommodation is superfluous.[217] Some of his marginal comments indicate that for Milton (or perhaps rather for Milton's narrator) the relationship between heaven and earth can be expressed not only through arbitrary but also through analogous signs, even though Raphael may not even be aware of it: as an angel he, too, is not omniscient, and of course his limitations can also be explained as a narrative technique on Milton's part.[218]

Several of Raphael's speeches in *Paradise Lost* allow the reader to question his position as a reliable translator, giving them the impression that he does not tell (or know) the whole truth.[219] Unexpectedly, Raphael also undermines his own position right from the start and encourages readers to suspect "that heaven may not be categorically 'other' after all":[220] although he claims to describe "what surmounts the reach / Of human sense" by comparing "spiritual to corporal forms," he later questions his own use of "extended metaphors." One may even assume that here his own opinion shines through, as "for a moment the anxiety is great enough to force the poet into speaking *in propria persona*":[221]

> . . . though what if earth
> Be but the shadow of heaven, and things therein
> Each to other like, more than on earth is thought?
> (*PL* V.574-76)

Arnold Stein explains this "enigmatic questioning of the metaphor" by arguing that the metaphor here is not discredited but rather extended or "further qualified,"[222] but many other examples show that the relationship between heavenly referent and earthly sign is possibly completely different from the more or less arbitrary metonymy that Raphael otherwise uses in his accommodational strategies.[223] Furthermore, Raphael's statement that earthly and heavenly objects are more alike "than on earth is thought" obviously (and against his will) indicates a gradual difference that would not justify a lengthy explanation, interpretation or even translation. heaven and earth can almost be measured by using the same scale and terminology, although heaven is of course much larger.[224]

Often Raphael even goes so far as to (inadvertently?) downplay this difference between the heavenly and earthly spheres by trying to express it by means of numbers and relations that are well-known to Adam and Eve. Even when he formulates his "ambivalent"[225] semiotic theory in V.573ff. that more or less invites further in-

quiries on Adam's part and when he proclaims that it is his aim to unveil "the invisible exploits / Of warring spirits" (*PL* V.565-66) and the "secrets of another
world, perhaps / Not lawful to reveal" (*PL* V.569-70), he has to admit that purely
spiritual beings such as angels have a lot in common with only partially spiritual beings such as man and woman.[226] In this respect, Milton's display of the "continuity
of nature"[227] seems to contradict almost all the spiritual authorities of his time.

More recent studies of Milton's monism and materialism conclude that Milton
represents a "monist materialism in which bodies can spiritualize and spirits can
corporealize because there is simply no ontological divide to cross."[228] A look at the
young Milton's *Commonplace Book* supports this view, as Milton here states that

> A good man by some reckoning seems to surpass even the angels to the extent
> that, enclosed in a weak and earthly body and always struggling with his
> passions, he nevertheless aspires to lead a life like that of the inhabitants of
> heaven. ("Of the Good Man," *Commonplace Book, CP* I: 364)[229]

In Book VI, Raphael shows once again that heavenly regions can be described
using an earthly scale—"measuring things in heaven by things on earth" (*PL*
VI.893)—when he states that "darkness there might well / Seem twilight here" (*PL*
VI.11-12). That heavenly space can still be measured by human beings despite all
its supposedly immeasurable size is shown in Raphael's description of the heavenly
army, its formation being "many a province wide / Tenfold the length of this ter-
rene" (*PL* VI.77-78). Celestial soil bears the same or similar treasures in its "hidden
veins" of "mineral and stone" (*PL* VI.516-17) as the earth (and, if we remember
Book II.270ff., the underground of Satan's realm). Satan himself expresses his
"bursting passion" when he finds the lost pleasures of heaven down on earth which
is "like to heaven, if not preferred / More justly, seat worthier of gods, as built /
With second thoughts, reforming what was old!" (*PL* IX.99-101).

Raphael's Insistence

Not only recently, but more often nowadays than in earlier times, critics have
pointed out the similarity of earthly and heavenly realms in *Paradise Lost*.[230] Nevertheless, Raphael as a faithful servant seems to insist on the distinction between
heaven and earth and answers Adam's wish for knowledge only "within bounds"
(*PL* VII.120), although God had not mentioned any such limits when he sent the
archangel on his mission. Even though he may as an angel partake in divine intelligence to a certain degree, Raphael cannot prohibit the Fall officially predicted by
the Father in III.95-97. One might even say that he chooses the easy way out by ad-
vising Adam simply not to question certain laws and rules "To none communicable
in earth or heaven" (*PL* VII.124) rather than trying to understand them.

Raphael tries to avoid "abstruse" (*PL* VIII.40) questions about astronomy, questions that are "ambitious to the point of being presumptive"[231] and might be difficult to answer even for himself as an angel who has accepted and internalized the limitations of his position. This goes so far that he does not try (or dare) to understand all the "wondrous works" in the "book of God" some of which "From man or angel the great architect / Did wisely to conceal" (*PL* VIII.72-73). Some things should be admired rather than understood: "Solicit not thy thoughts with matters hid, / Leave them to God above, him serve and fear" (*PL* VIII.167-68).[232] His appeal to "be lowly wise" (*PL* VIII.173) is thus addressed not only to Adam but also to the angels, who were shown as early as in the War in Heaven that their power is limited and that the victory over the rebel angels would not have been possible without the Son's omnipotence (*PL* VI.684).[233]

Raphael now applies the angelic principle of absolute obedience, self-restriction and self-humiliation to Adam and his world. The good angels, above all Abdiel, Michael, and Gabriel (and of course Raphael himself), have proved their obedience in the War in Heaven by following God's command to attack Satan's army although they must have been aware that the fallen angels were "Equal in their creation [...] / Whence in perpetual fight they needs must last / Endless, and no solution will be found" (*PL* VI.690, 693-94). Nevertheless the angels were obedient and followed God's command to the letter. The angels' faith and obedience vindicated God's "ironic" command which had seemed paradoxical at first. Interpreting it as a test of their absolute obedience, they disambiguated the command and thus re-translated it into a monolithic language.[234] For this reason, the Son praises the angels: "Faithful hath been your warfare, and of God / Accepted, fearless in his righteous cause" (*PL* VI.803-04).

God's command challenges the angels in a similar way as Adam is challenged when God seems to deny him a human partner. In both cases the ironical language is disambiguated in the end, and the identity of what is said and what is meant is reaffirmed. But in the case of the angels this happens through their unquestioning obedience to God's will. In Adam's case, however, this congruity is achieved through Adam's intelligent reaction to the divine challenge.

After his first positive experience regarding obedience towards God's commands, Raphael of course does not see any reason to question God's further commands even though they may seem to be very demanding and even paradoxical. His knowledge about the implicit dangers of human disobedience in the light of Satan's plans encourages his him to insist even more strongly on such an automatic and unquestioning obedience. The archangel cannot see that his own position may appear as paradoxical and contradictory as many of Christ's statements and parables in the Bible seem to be at first sight. Neither can he imagine that his mission may be yet another test of Adam's ability to understand God's irony, that Adam after all may be expected not to be absolutely obedient for a change.

Raphael's acceptance and internalization of the hierarchical structure of heaven leads him to assume that the relationship between heaven and earth is equally hierarchical in its structure and that the communication between human beings and God depends upon a mediator (i.e., himself).[235] In order to render his message comprehensible for his human audience, he thinks he has to loosen the formerly solid connection between signs and referents which Adam had so far assumed to be God-given and natural. Therefore the archangel follows seventeenth-century tradition and neoplatonically "splits" man into spirit and body (*PL* V.478), although he himself, a supposedly purely spiritual being, willingly admits that he is not above enjoying bodily pleasures (*PL* VIII.618-29).

Can we interpret this contradiction as another indication of the possibility that the differences between human beings and angels—on the importance of which Raphael insists—are not that important after all? Even if one interprets God's pleasure about Adam's questioning of the structure of creation as contentment with his creature's ability to see through—and disambiguate—divine irony, one has to admit that neither the teacher Raphael nor his pupil Adam recognizes the parallelism between Raphael's educational role and that of the Father.[236] This parallelism has its limits, though, as—without being aware of it—the teacher Raphael is himself only a tool in God's didactic plan. He does not understand that Adam is permitted—and even supposed—to see through and question him and his message in the same way in which Adam had been permitted to doubt God's decision not to grant him a human companion in paradise.

Raphael's acceptance of the heavenly hierarchy and his conviction that God's commands are always unambiguous and should never be questioned keep him from realizing that according to God's plan he is—and is supposed to be—a "pedagogical failure."[237] According to John Rumrich, his angelic nature and experience would "render him incapable of comprehending the full significance of Adam's crucial questions or of answering them with much sensitivity, tact, or understanding."[238]

Raphael uses earthly language in order to communicate messages about heaven, but after all, his perspective of heavenly politics may itself be of rather limited validity. The conclusions that he has drawn from his experience during the War in Heaven and the successful strategy of obedience indicate that—in spite of all his benevolence and intelligence—he as an angel is incapable of understanding the full range of God's plans: by means of various theoretical constructions, Raphael tries to keep men and angels as well as things and signs apart from each other. On the other hand, however, in his description of creation, he himself quotes the Father to the effect that all the different categories will be reunited in the end, and this view seems to be confirmed by God in Book X.638-39.[239]

In Book VII, the Father tells the unfallen angels that he will create "another world" in order to "repair" the loss of the rebel angels. Out of "one man" he will create a race that will finally "by degrees of merit raised / [. . .] open to themselves at length the way / Up hither, under long obedience tried" (*PL* VII.157-59). Finally, then earth and heaven will become exchangeable, "joy and union without end" (*PL* VII.161). As we have seen, this new kingdom created by the Father at first still partakes of heavenly language, even though the process is related to us in postlapsarian speech.[240] The readers have overheard the narrator's account of the original discussion in heaven in Book III. After the Son has asked the Father to be merciful to mankind, the Father tells him that

> . . . thy humiliation shall exalt
> With thee thy manhood also to this throne,
> Here shalt thou sit incarnate, here shalt reign
> Both God and man, Son both of God and man,
> Anointed universal king. (*PL* III.313-17)

As a consequence of the Son's action, the distance between God and his creation disappears, and through the Son, man is united with God: "The distance between God and man vanishes at this point, and God at last becomes 'All in All.'"[241]

It is highly questionable, though, whether, after the envisaged reunification of heavenly and earthly realms planned by God, men and angels will once again be able to communicate in the *word-thing language* which Wilkins and his fellow scholars assume to have existed in the prelapsarian past and which they try to reestablish through their research. If it is at all possible to bridge the gulf between human and divine language, then it will probably be overcome through the performative aspect of God's Word rather than through the linguistic experiments of the Royal Society. While we are waiting for the ideal and probably utopian case of this reunification, only faith in God's Word can make us accept the coordination of sign and referent (or signified and signifier) as a solid and motivated convention that makes language appear as a monolithic and "solid" base of human communication.

Raphael, who has been trained to be obedient, brings Adam the message of obedience and faith, but by postulating that there is an unbridgeable difference between human and divine language and knowledge, he endangers the growth of an ideal faith based on scientific evidence which Milton advocates in *Of Education*. Therefore I see Raphael's message as yet another example of God's irony challenging both angels and human beings, an irony that God has already used during the War in Heaven and during the discussion about a partner for Adam. Ironically, Raphael himself is not aware of being the bearer of God's irony when he claims that human and divine language are essentially different, and he himself does not know that the separation of sign and referent that he introduces may after all be nothing but a further test of Adam's ability to recognize and disambiguate God's irony.

While Raphael proves that he is able to make use of complex semiotic theories, his message proclaims certain features of seventeenth-century philosophy of language which does not treat of the rhetorical and syntactic use of linguistic signs. At least he is not very good at deciphering God's ironic strategies in his communication with mankind and angels. This lack of sophistication is shared by other angels such as the archangel Gabriel, who in Book IV.990-1013 does not recognize the ambiguity of another one of God's signs (the scales in which Satan is weighed and found wanting).[242] While Raphael—like Gabriel and the other faithful angels—is saved by his own faith in the War in Heaven, he cannot rely on this faith in his attempt to judge and understand Adam's behaviour.

Irony and the First Lie: Communication and War in Heaven

The account of history that Raphael gives in Book III relates God's reaction to Satan's plan to attack paradise and mankind, although of course the word *reaction* seems inadequate in connection with an omniscient being that observes world history from a perspective of "passionless logic."[243] From God's perspective past, present, and future coexist simultaneously. Although he points out that he created Adam "just and right / Sufficient to have stood, though free to fall" (*PL* III.98-99), God is willing to grant postlapsarian Adam and Eve a certain advantage over those rebel angels who had fallen in heaven: through their rebellion they have lost any chance of being shown God's mercy. Whereas "The first sort by their own suggestion fell, / Self-tempted, self-depraved," "man falls deceived / By the other first," so that "man therefore shall find grace / The other none" (*PL* III.129-32).

While the Son thanks the Father for his merciful treatment of Adam and Eve, the Father reinforces his intention to "renew" the "lapsed powers" of mankind (*PL* III.175-76). But as God is a just God, Adam and Eve's sin, their striving for "Godhead" (*PL* III.206) has to be paid for either by Adam or by someone else:

> Die he or justice must; unless for him
> Some other able, and as willing, pay
> The rigid satisfaction, death for death.
> (*PL* III.210-12)

This other one is of course the Son, so that God can save "the whole race lost" (*PL* III.280) through the—temporary—loss and "humiliation" (*PL* III.313) of his Son.

The interpretation of the archangel Raphael's role as a victim of God's dramatic irony[244] or as the somewhat naive pawn in God's intricate game of chess seems to do injustice to God's faithful servant, and, in addition, it seems to neglect the much greater threat that Satan represents to mankind. After all, Satan was the original reason for Raphael's visit in the Garden of Eden.

In this context, we see once again—as in *Samson Agonistes*—that the language of the epic is adroitly manipulated by the author John Milton who is manifestly different from the narrator "John Milton." In general, the Fall is seen to be a consequence of Eve's seduction by Satan, who himself is a master of ambiguous irony and/or hypocrisy or even of Derridean deconstruction that neither man nor angel can detect (*PL* III.682-83).[245] As readers, we are no doubt surprised when we first find out that there are false angels, even a "false archangel" (*PL* V.694) in heaven, while evil has not yet found its way into the Garden of Eden.[246] The lines in which "the false archangel" uses "Ambiguous words and jealousies, to sound / Or taint integrity" (*PL* V.694, 703-04) have been called the "most overt comment in the poem on the destructive power of Satanic language."[247]

While for me it is the Father who is responsible for the (not only negatively connotated) ambiguity of language that is part of his education of Adam and Eve, others interpret the consequences of the "linguistic Fall" as completely negative and blame it on Satan alone. The fallen archangel, by the way, is the first among the characters that appear in the text (as opposed to the reconstructed chronology of events) of *Paradise Lost* to make use of "the concept of empty words" in Book I.528-29.

Whereas so far there had been congruity between words and deeds, Satan has now thrown the linguistic system off balance and ironically even goes so far as to comment on this imbalance. In addition, it is now he who criticizes others of making use of the ambiguity of language, although he himself is the most adept practitioner of this strategy in his lies, hypocrisies, and flattery. He is an "Artificer of fraud," even, as the text claims, "the first / That practised falsehood under saintly show, / Deep malice to conceal, couched with revenge" (*PL* IV.121-23).

Satan undermines the balance of the linguistic system by denying a solid connection between words and things: "By assuming the proposition that words and their referents have no necessary connection, Satan establishes the basis for recasting language to suit his purposes."[248] Unfortunately, his interlocutors do not always have Ithuriel's spear ready at hand, which would enable them to immediately test the validity of his statements.[249]

Even though Georgia B. Christopher insists that it would be a great mistake to assume that God and Satan speak the same language,[250] there are obvious parallels in their rhetoric, although these parallels are of course based on quite different motives: even before Satan exploits the ambiguities of human language by persuading Eve to eat the fruit from the tree of knowledge, God himself has used ironic (and thus non-monolithic) language in heaven and in the Garden of Eden, and Adam and Eve have learned to understand and interpret it.[251]

The distinction between prelapsarian and postlapsarian mankind and language has also been questioned for quite some time.[252] Recent criticism often has a more egalitarian tendency of interpreting the status of human and divine beings in *Paradise Lost*, pointing out "that even in prelapsarian Eden, matters like domestic relations, gender, all the evidences of hierarchy—indeed including corporeality itself—are fluid and quite possibly temporary (Milton's more disquieting word is 'mutable')."[253] Critics argue that even before the Fall, Adam and Eve did not or not only lead an unproblematic paradisal life; otherwise their fateful discussion about the distribution of work that leads to the temptation scene would hardly have been necessary. In Milton's version of the Garden of Eden, Adam and Eve obviously had to carry their "burden of interpretation."[254]

The general insecurity of the seventeenth-century population looking for an original authority has already become visible in the search for a reliable language that I described in my first chapter, but we see that the solid foundation one was looking for does not even exist in Milton's paradise any longer.[255] Rather than being the product of the Fall in paradise, linguistic ambiguity existed (at least potentially) even before this event.[256]

Linguistically inspired theories of the ambiguity of language in *Paradise Lost* thus support the interpretation that it is not so much Adam and Eve as individuals who are "always already fallen" but rather that the language that God provides for them is "always already ambiguous"—or at least characterized by binary oppositions. These binary oppositions then would, for example, enable or even invite speakers to make use of irony. And no critic of *Paradise Lost* would any longer seriously deny that irony plays an important part in the epic.[257]

Recent Milton criticism thus sees a "programmatic rhetorical ambivalence" at the centre of even the prelapsarian world.[258] The potential root of the Fall of language thus already exists in the prelapsarian world, perhaps even before the creation of this world. Robert Entzminger, who states in the first sentence of his study *Divine Word* that "[w]hen Adam falls in *Paradise Lost*, so does his language," comments on the insufficiency of language that exists already in paradise. For him, Milton shows "that even in Eden the signs of God in Nature are insufficient without supplementary revelation."[259] One has to point out, though, that Entzminger's statements refer to Adam's and Eve's linguistic abilities and limitations after Satan's first intervention in Eve's dream. In the same way, Raphael's message with its probably inadvertent allusions to the similarity or dissimilarity of heaven and earth may have reinforced Adam and Eve's linguistic doubts that were originally aroused by the dream.[260]

Satan's loosening of the coordination of sign and referent (or signified and signifier) here lays the foundation of the later misunderstanding. With regard to the two elements of the Saussurean sign, William Myers expresses this in a highly Miltonic metaphor: "It follows that signifieds are really only the shadows cast by signifiers."[261] Robert Entzminger illustrates how Eve is seduced by Satan: "Despite what Raphael has taught, she too quickly infers reason from speech and thus becomes an accessory to her own undoing, assenting to Satan's detachment of words from their referents and then adopting his tactics as she presents the case to Adam."[262] Raphael may have warned Adam and Eve of Satan's evil intentions, but as far as his statements about divine and human language are concerned, he is a most puzzling teacher.

If we see the Raphael's attempts at accommodation—which the well-intentioned archangel thought he was undertaking on God's behest and which can be seen as one of the reasons leading to the Fall—then we can see the dialogue between

Father and Son in Book III as the beginning of the restorative process through which God's irony is disambiguated and at the end of which there is a "language of grace."[263] This act of disambiguation then ideally leads to the reinstitution of the incarnation of the Word, to the reunification of word and thing, to the identity of signifier and signified,[264] until God or the Word will be "All in All."[265]

The pedagogical strategy here used by the Father to convince the Son to accept his role as mediator and saviour is irony. Even here in heaven there is always already—even before Satan's rebellion—a pedagogically motivated deviation from the principle of a monolithic language. The only one who understands this deviation from monolithic language and who disambiguates it through an act of "literalization"[266] is the Son, while other angels—such as Satan—misunderstand it. In this, as in other cases of ironical use of language quoted above, the "examinees"—whether they are of divine, angelic or human nature—have to decide whether they want to simply obey God's commands or whether they want to question them in order to explore the roots of divine irony and thus overcome the rift between what God says and what he means. In this sense, God's irony can be seen as a kind of barrier that God erects between himself and his creatures and which they can only overcome by making use of the free will and intelligence that God has provided. The rift between God and mankind, creator and creature, can thus only be breached by means of an act of free will (for Adam)—or faith (for postlapsarian mankind).

In postlapsarian times, only an act of faith and obedience can reintroduce such a unified state and thus disambiguate the language that Raphael has brought down to earth. Only an act of faith can retranslate the postlapsarian word that has lost "the extraliterary properties that God's 'word' was presumed to have in Milton's religious tradition"[267] into God's Word. The effect of the "heartfelt words" then would not be sorcery, as some of Milton's contemporaries argued, but rather a religious speech act.[268]

From the archangel Michael's words addressed to Adam in Book XI one may conclude that there is a reason for such a faith that attributes words a meaning far beyond their mere referential function and that turns them into "words with power"[269] or "sacred metaphor(s)"[270] so that they become part of a poetic and hieratic or (according to Vico) even hieroglyphic language.[271] Michael, "with regard benign," tells Adam that "in valley and in plain / God is as here, and will be found alike / Present" and that "of his presence many a sign" is still visible, such as "of his steps the track divine" (*PL* XI.334, 349-51, 354).[272]

Here we can clearly distinguish between "two different modes of knowing God": on the one hand direct prelapsarian communication "face to face," which Adam had known at the beginning of his existence in paradise, and on the other the postlapsarian "metaphorical" knowledge of God that is dependent upon signs.[273] The signs that Michael mentions here are of course not linguistic signs, but those, too, play an important—if not the most important—role in the postlapsarian and often only indirect communication between mankind and God. In the poetical and metaphorical language which, according to Northrop Frye, is the only kind of language, through which the Christian doctrine can be expressed for us, the crux of ambiguity, the "disjunction between God's word and Reason"[274] is always already inherent:

> The sense in Christianity of a faith beyond reason, which must continue to affirm even after reason gives up, is closely connected with the linguistic fact that many of the central doctrines of traditional Christianity can be grammatically expressed only in the form of metaphor.[275]

According to Marshall Grossman, such metaphors bring together the "prelapsarian and monistic" and "postlapsarian and dualistic" views of human life,[276] so that one can interpret the linguistic Fall as the passage from a monist to a dualist epistemology. In recent years, critics have repeatedly and convincingly shown that Milton is the representative of a monist world view—"Milton's marvelous monism."[277] Such an interpretation is complementary to the theory of a linguistic Fall from a seemingly monolithic and monist language—with an arbitrary but still unambiguous coordination of signified and signifier—to a dualistic language with an arbitrary and no longer unambiguous coordination of its components.[278]

As mentioned above in my chapter on the linguistic theories of the seventeenth century, one can also see the translation of *logos* as *sermo* as the basis for an interpretation that takes the whole act of communication into account and goes beyond the analysis of single words.[279] Through a reading that is aware of the connotation that the word *logos* has in common with the Hebrew *davhar*, "which was understood to unite speaker and speech to hearer in one mighty deed,"[280] we arrive at a view of God's actions as a "unity of divine deed":

> This unity of deed makes the puritan esthetic, as it were, a "syntactical" esthetic. Spiritual mystery resided, not in *being*, but in grasping, via words, the *relation* between beings: Luther held that God was to be encountered, not in his substance, which was unknowable and terrifying, but "in the category of relation" (. . .). In Milton's tradition, the Spirit clings, not to bodies, but to language itself and skips like Ariel along the tucks and gaps in the syntactical chain forming metaphor, metonymy, and other tropes.[281]

In spite of this "unity of divine deed," especially the written word (which, because of the duality of written vs. spoken language, is less liable to inspire a "prelapsarian" impression of a unity of word and thing) also bears the danger of being misused: It is "at once the only pure record of Christ's ministry, yet subject to corruptions."[282] The archangel Michael indicates already in Book XII that the reliability of messages formulated in postlapsarian language sometimes has to be doubted even if used by the clergy. For example, he speaks of the "grievous wolves" who will turn "all the sacred mysteries of heaven / To their own vile advantages" and taint "the truth / With superstitions and traditions" (*PL* XII.508, 509-10, 511-12).[283]

So far I have discussed the role of language within the plot of *Paradise Lost*, but—as André Verbart impressively shows in *Fellowship in* Paradise Lost: *Vergil, Milton, Wordsworth*—Milton's narrator also addresses the topic of language and its ambiguity on the metalinguistic and metadiegetic level of his own discourse. This is especially the case in his invocations, for example in Book VII, when he somewhat insecurely or ironically addresses Urania, "by that name / If rightly thou art called" (*PL* VII.1-2). In whatever way one may want to interpret this invocation of the "traditional patroness of astronomy,"[284] the postlapsarian narrator, although he himself has quasi-prophetic aspirations, no longer believes in the unambiguous character of names and has to admit that it is the "meaning, not the name" that he calls (*PL* VII.5).

"Fallen" Language in Hell and on Earth

At least the higher ranks of the fallen angels who are expelled from heaven after their rebellion and who reunite in hell are very well aware of the rhetorical possibilities offered by a fallen language in which the coordination of signs and referents can be manipulated according to the needs of the ruling class. This is proved in Book II during the discussion in Pandaemonium, the parody of a parliament, but as early as in Book I, while the fallen angels are still suffering "with looks / Down cast and damp" (*PL* I.522-23), Satan starts to use political rhetoric in order to rally his battalions once again. He does this "with high words, that bore / Semblance of worth, not substance," but he succeeds in "gently rais[ing] / Their fainting courage" (*PL* I.528-29, 529-30). Although Milton insists that Satan's impressive rhetoric is lacking in substance and healing power, his gifts as an actor and propagandist are beyond doubt, for "thrice in spite of scorn, / Tears such as angels weep, burst forth" until "at last / Words interwove with sighs found out their way" (*PL* I.619-21).[285]

In Book II, during the debate in Pandaemonium, the fallen angels openly discuss the possibility of regaining their place in heaven, "our just inheritance of old" (*PL* II.38), through "covert guile" (*PL* II.41), i.e., with words that are no longer grounded in facts. A classic example of such a "fallen" rhetorician is Belial, who had already shown his tendencies towards an ironic use of language during the War in Heaven (Book VI.620-27) and now symbolizes the great difference between semblance—"A fairer person lost not heaven; he seemed / For dignity composed and high exploit" (*PL* II.110-11)—and reality:

> . . . all was false and hollow; though his tongue
> Dropt manna, and could make the worse appear
> The better reason, to perplex and dash
> Maturest counsels: for his thoughts were low;
> To vice industrious, but to nobler deeds

Timorous and slothful, yet he pleased the ear.
(*PL* II.112-17)

As he is well aware of God's omniscience and omnipotence, Belial speaks out against any kind of warfare against God and suggests to somehow make the best of the hellish *status quo*. Milton's narrator, however, judges this argument, which may seem rather reasonable at first sight, to be dishonest and dishonourable as "Belial with words clothed in reason's garb / Counselled ignoble ease, and peaceful sloth, / Not peace" (*PL* II.226-28).

It is Beelzebub's task to present "his devilish counsel, first devised / By Satan," (*PL* II.379-80) to the others. In the hierarchy of hell, which to quite some extent seems to be a mirror image of the heavenly hierarchy, only the highest-ranking members know what actions are undertaken and what speeches are given for exactly what purpose. With respect to his attitude towards his subjects, Satan pulling the strings in the background is not that different from the Father who tells his messenger Raphael only little more than what he absolutely has to know in order to conscientiously fulfil his task.

Planning to fight on his own and without the help of any of the other fallen angels—"this enterprise / None shall partake with me" (*PL* II.465-66)—Satan intends to attack the earth, "(If ancient and prophetic fame in heaven / Err not) another world" (*PL* II.346-47), which is an easier target than well-defended heaven. His rhetoric that says one thing while it means something completely different shows here, too: although "some new race called Man" (*PL* II.348) is attacked, the real target is he "who rules above" (*PL* II.351), God himself.

While Adam in Book VIII still had talked about direct communication with God and had still been able to communicate with a divine being such as the archangel Raphael, the theme in Book IX is more tragic. After the success of Satan's plan, i.e., Adam and Eve's eating the fruit of the tree of knowledge, communication between God (or angel) and man becomes more difficult. Now one can hardly speak of a conversation "as friend with friend" that Raphael had initially been asked to have with Adam. It is only the archangel Michael's later hint at the possibility of a "Paradise within" that rekindles fallen man's hope again, but most critics see postlapsarian communication as hardly comparable to its prelapsarian state.[286] That is why Milton's narrative voice reports instead of Adam's or Raphael's that there will be "No more of talk where God or angel guest / With man, as with his friend, familiar used / To sit indulgent" (*PL* IX.1-3): Rather, "I now must change / Those notes to tragic" (*PL* IX.6).

As mentioned above, even before Raphael's visit, Satan had penetrated into the Garden of Eden and had inspired Eve's dream, which I claim is a linguistic influence leading to the loosening of the connection between sign and referent. Now, for his decisive attack, Satan chooses the form of the serpent, "subtlest beast of all the field." Milton calls the serpent a "fit vessel" (*PL* IX.89) filled with a dangerous content that does not correspond to its outer appearance. The coordination of names and characters, signs and things, to which Adam had paid attention or which he had himself established (with God's authorization) is now impaired, and one might argue that the principle of the arbitrariness of the linguistic sign is introduced into the Garden of Eden by Satan. As I have also shown, however, the use of arbitrary signs had already been established in paradise by God himself, although not many critics would join William Empson in assuming that it is based on the latter's evil intentions. While arbitrary signs are not new in paradise, arbitrary signs used with an evil intention certainly are.

On the other hand, in the discussion about the division of labour which leads more or less directly to the seduction scene, Eve mentions a kind of language that hardly serves the purpose of true communication any more and that for this reason appears rather suspect to her—and to Milton's Puritan ethic. For when she suggests to Adam that they should shoulder the burden of the growing amount of work by going separate ways so that they would not distract each other, she mentions the dangers of "casual discourse" (PL IX.223) that lie in its threatening to interrupt the work process without giving the interlocutors the benefit of any important information. Although Adam thinks that smiles and talk are grounded in human reason so that talk may well be called *food of the mind* and that "smiles from reason flow, / To brute denied" (PL IX.239-40), he eventually cannot reject Eve's arguments, all the more so, since she accuses him of doubting her firmness in opposing Satan's "fraud" (PL IX.287).[287]

Although Adam responds to her reproach with "healing words," it becomes obvious that the words of both of Milton's protagonists are already qualified by rhetorical connotations. Eve's reaction to the "matrimonial love" of "domestic Adam" is the use of an "accent sweet" (PL IX.319, 318, 321). Finally she even repeats Milton's own argument from *Areopagitica*: "And what is faith, love, virtue unassayed / Alone, without exterior help sustained?" (PL IX.335-36) Adam finally gives in to her entreaties, not, however, without having warned her about possible rhetorical tricks that her reason and free will may perhaps not—or not yet—be able to resist,

Lest by some fair appearing good surprised
She dictate false, and misinform the will
To do what God expressly hath forbid. (PL IX.354-56)

When the serpent finally addresses Eve in his "pseudo-plainness,"[288] he makes use of a similar theme as the one that Raphael had employed—intentionally or not—in order to justify his theory of accommodation: he tries to please Eve by claiming that she should "be seen / A goddess among gods, adored and served / By angels numberless, thy daily train" (PL IX.546-48). Interestingly enough, this statement by the "tempter" mirrors almost exactly Satan's own reaction on first seeing the newly created earth: "O earth, how like to heaven, if not preferred" (PL IX.99). It thus becomes obvious that the intention of the respective speaker plays an important role in the interpretation of any speech act and that even here in paradise the meaning of a sentence depends not only on the linguistic signs of which it is composed but also on their pragmatic context. Although Eve is of course flattered by the serpent's message, the unexpected combination of message and messenger also strikes her as somewhat peculiar so that—once again in a curiously negative way of putting it—she is "not unamazed" (*PL* IX.549-57) and "thus in answer spake":

> What may this mean? Language of man pronounced
> By tongue of brute, and human sense expressed?
> The first at least of these I thought denied
> To beasts, whom God on their creation-day
> Created mute to all articulate sound.
> (*PL* IX.552-57)

Although Eve wonders about the serpent's ability to speak and to speak even in a way comprehensible to mankind, one has to point out that God himself had pointed Adam in the way of the animals when the latter had first asked him for a human companion. At least for Adam in his prelapsarian state such a communication with animals would not necessarily have been so remarkable. What is striking, though, is Satan's rhetorical aptitude that is compared to that of the great rhetoricians of Greek and Roman antiquity (*PL* IX.671). It is thus all the less surprising that later on Jesus in *Paradise Regained* is not overly impressed with classical elocution and education.

The serpent (or Satan) refers to the tree of knowledge as the "mother of science" and ascribes to it the effect of giving human beings the ability "to trace the ways / Of highest agents, deemed however wise" (*PL* IX.682-83). He denies any possibility of danger connected to the eating of the fruit of this tree and encourages Eve to use a shortcut to profit even earlier from the positive effects that Raphael had promised to Adam anyway, i.e., that eventually "ye shall be as gods, / Knowing both good and evil as they know" (*PL* IX.708-09). In this sense, the fact that Raphael is willing and able to enjoy earthly food is interpreted as meaning not only that beings higher up on the scale of development (i.e., angels) can adapt to the mode of existence of those who are at a lower stage (i.e., human beings), but that the reverse is true, too: "And what are gods that man may not become / As they, participating god-like food?" (*PL* IX.716-17).

The conclusion drawn by the serpent—"God therefore cannot hurt ye, and be just; / Not just, not God" (*PL* IX.700-01)—paraphrases the problem of theodicy that has occupied Milton criticism for centuries and that the Father within the epic solves by having recourse to the free will of sinful mankind. But of course, these words uttered by Satan are once again "replete with guile," i.e., with rhetorical connotations. In spite, or because, of this, they easily find "into her heart too easy entrance" (*PL* IX.733, 734). To Eve's ears they are "persuasive words, impregned / With reason, to her seeming, and with truth" (*PL* IX.737-38).

After the serpent has encouraged her to doubt God's interdiction to eat the fruit growing on the tree of knowledge, Eve starts to question the general character of the sign "tree of knowledge." As mentioned above, this tree is one of the first signs on earth that God created in an obviously arbitrary manner, resembling an *inartificial argument*, so that its meaning was not originally and immediately apparent to Adam and Eve. In this respect, the word *tree of knowledge* does not correspond to the traditions and conventions of naming that apply to those names that Adam gave to the animals. While animals and plants were generally named by Adam and Eve (both being endowed with or following divine guidance), the tree of knowledge was named by God "naming thee the tree / Of knowledge, knowledge both of good and evil" (*PL* IX.751-52).

Eve, who gives in to the temptation, regrets this mistake almost immediately and now is afraid of losing Adam, perhaps even of losing him to "another Eve" (*PL* IX.828), who may be more than willing to help him forget the loss of his first wife. In addition, and somewhat surprisingly in the context of jealousy just described, she affirms that "So dear I love him, that with him all deaths / I could endure, without him live no life" (*PL* IX.832-33). Fowler fittingly qualifies this sentence as "the first explicit expression of love from Eve—and the first false expression" (*PL* 487). One may really wonder if Eve herself is convinced of the truth of her statement.

She certainly is not convinced of the truth of the words she uses in order to try to persuade Adam to also taste the forbidden fruit. She claims that the tree is not— as God claimed—"a tree / Of danger tasted" but rather "of divine effect" (*PL* IX.863-64, 865). As she pretends to have attained—and to be unable to give up— divine status, she encourages him to follow her example. Obviously, she does not seem to have learned much from the example of Raphael, who, she knows, has no problem communicating with human beings. Adam tries to understand her argumentation and thinks that a "proportional ascent" of human beings to the status of angels or demigods may be possible (*PL* IX.936). Fowler calls his train of thought "Satanic reasoning" (*PL* 493), but it may also be seen to be in keeping with Raphael's statements that make a transition from the human to the divine realm seem possible.[289] As is to be expected, Adam makes use of his free will and commits the crime of eating the fruit. One may blame Adam's fall in the numerologically fascinating line 999 of Book XI, however, not so much the serpent as on his wife's charms, as he fell "Against his better knowledge, not deceived, / But fondly overcome with female charm" (*PL* IX.998-99).

When he, eventually and retrospectively, demands that she should have "hearkened to my words, and stayed / With me" (*PL* IX.1134-35), it is too late. His first reaction after the Fall is to refrain from any further intellectual activity, from any challenging of visible reality or godly commands, although it had been God himself who had at first encouraged him to use his critical intellect. Whereas Adam had been able to see through God's irony earlier on, Satan's strategy now appears to be too opaque to be recognized as what it is; he is even assured that "thou couldst not have discerned / Fraud in the serpent" (*PL* IX.1149-50). His words now seem to be pointing forward to Michael's later advice to be "lowly wise" when he decides to no longer "seek needless cause to approve / The faith" he owes: Human beings' earnest seeking for "such proof" would only imply that "they then begin to fail" (*PL* IX.1140-41, 1142).

As far as absolute commands and interdictions are concerned, Eve suggests that Adam should have "absolutely" forbidden her to go to work on her own, but this would of course have limited her free will. A further discussion of this question would lead to the theme of Milton and women's rights, a theme that exceeds the frame of this study. Such a discussion would probably end in a similar way as Book IX:

> Thus they in mutual accusation spent
> The fruitless hours, but neither self-condemning,
> And of their vain contest appeared no end.
> (*PL* IX.1187-89)

After the Fall, to which nature reacts twice with a groan or a sigh, Eve already seems to be speaking a postlapsarian language characterized by lies. Does this mean that the fall of language coincides with the Fall? An answer to this question is difficult, since my study has so far shown that rhetorical deviations from a language relying on an unambiguous relationship between words and things were already possible before the Fall and were in fact employed by both God and Satan. In addition, the other consequences of the Fall do not become effective until after God's (or rather the Son's) visit in paradise. During this visit, communication between Adam and the Son is still possible, although Adam feels ashamed of his nudity as well as of having broken God's commands and thus hides. In his rhetorical question, the Son wonders:

> My voice thou oft hast heard, and hast not feared,
> But still rejoiced, how is it now become
> So dreadful to thee? (*PL* X.119-21)

In *Paradise Lost* as well as in the Bible, God does not formulate the punishment of the serpent in clear and unambiguous terms but rather in oracular fashion, "in mysterious terms, judged as then best" (*PL* X.173). Even though Fowler glosses *mysterious* as "mystical" (*PL* 516), this does not necessarily clarify the situation: the serpent's condemnation to forthwith move "upon thy belly grovelling" (*PL* X.177) and to eat dust is complemented by the really mysterious sentence implying that God will "put / Enmity" between the serpent and Eve and that "Her seed shall bruise thy head, thou bruise his heel" (*PL* X.179-81). A few lines later, the mysterious character of these lines is explained typologically as pointing forward to the situation Milton will describe at the end of *Paradise Regained*.

While soon after this judgment Satan's allies and incestuous relatives, Sin and Death, find their way into paradise, the time of idyllic vegetarianism is over so that "Beast now with beast gan war, and fowl with fowl, / And fish with fish," and man is estranged from the rest of creation that now "fled him, or with countenance grim / Glared on him passing" (*PL* X.710-11, 713-14). Within the context of human communication, the tendency that had started immediately after (if not even before) the Fall continues: words carry more and more connotations and thus are less and less reliable signs of what they were originally meant to express, even though Adam's characterization of Eve as a serpent—"that name best / Befits thee with him leagued, thy self as false / And hateful" (*PL* X.867-69)—may be relatively comprehensible as a consequence of his "fierce passion." For Adam thus any coordination of signifier and signified, of word and thing, of form and content has become suspect to start with. One almost has the impression that he wants to withdraw from any kind of communication, and Eve states that "by sad experiment" she knows

> How little weight my words with thee can find
> Found so erroneous, thence by just event
> Found so unfortunate. (*PL* X.967-70)

On the other hand, her plan to escape her punishment by either having no children or committing suicide does not vouch for her strength of character (and might once again be blamed on Milton's supposed misogyny). One has to admit, though, that Adam also points out to Eve at the "grand moment toward which *Paradise Lost* is moving"—"the moment when the gates of Paradise swing open to Adam and he *hears* the promise in the *protevangelium* (X.1026-37)"[290]—that it is her task to fulfil an important and positive role in God's plan: "that thy seed shall bruise / The serpent's head" (*PL* X.1031-32). Both thereupon decide to face God again, to admit their guilt, and to ask him to forgive them. Through this act of contrition another ideal kind of honest (albeit non-verbal) sign is to be created: a "sign / Of sorrow unfeigned" (*PL* X.91-92).

Through their remorse and God's "prevenient grace" (*PL* XI.3) that helped to remove "the stony from their hearts" (*PL* XI.4), a sort of communication is reestablished between Adam and Eve and God. In addition, the Son adopts the role of a mediating and translating instance which had not been necessary in prelapsarian times. The Son refers to himself as "thy priest" (*PL* XI.25) and is willing to act as an "interpreter" and "advocate" (*PL* XI.33) on behalf of mankind whom he holds to be "Unskilful with what words to pray" (*PL* XI.32). Still, even the Son's taking their part cannot prevent Adam and Eve's expulsion from the Garden of Eden, although the archangel Michael's message is not only a negative one but also promises that God's covenant will be "in the woman's seed renewed" (*PL* XI.116).

In Michael's message, names and language thus at first regain some of the positive strength they had had earlier on. Michael calls Eve the "Mother of all Mankind" (*PL* XI.159) and emphasizes that this name is justified "since by thee / Man is to live, and all things live for man" (*PL* XI.160-61). Eve is well aware that, as the originator of the Fall, she might have deserved a much harsher punishment and "far other name" (*PL* XI.171). But her freshly aroused optimism is soon to be frustrated somewhat when she finds out that she and Adam will have to leave paradise and that there are clear "signs" (*PL* XI.182) in nature that indicate a major change in world order.[291] Adam, too, realizes that "some further change awaits us nigh, / Which heaven by these mute signs in nature shows" (*PL* XI.193-94).

He is waiting for the archangel Michael, who approaches him "as man / Clad to meet man" (*PL* XI.239-40). While Eve takes leave of the flowers which she had named, as we learn (*PL* XI.277), Adam comes to terms with the fact that the time of direct—visual and verbal—communication is over, at least in the form he had known so far: "This most afflicts me, that departing hence, / As from his face I shall be hid, deprived / His blessed countenance" (*PL* XI.315-17). Michael points out to him, however, that the omnipresent God will also be present outside of the Garden of Eden, leaving—as mentioned above—"many a sign" of his presence and "the track divine" of his steps (*PL* XI.351, 354). The archangel illustrates this by means of a visual and didactic overview of world history as seen from the hill in the Garden of Eden, a hill which is typologically linked to the mountain in *Paradise Regained* on which Satan tempts Christ, the "second Adam" (*PL* XI.383).

After Book XI has described the history of mankind up to the end of the great flood and to God's new covenant with Noah, Book XII continues the prophetic view of future history up to Milton's present. Here, too, one can detect the process in which language is further and further alienated from its prelapsarian origins. While he had so far presented the future of the world visually, Michael now joins the narrator in pointing out that the confrontation with divine images may easily overtax human eyes, and thus he switches over to narrative as he perceives "Thy mortal sight to fail; objects divine / Must needs impair and weary human sense" (*PL* XII.9-10).

What follows is the story that is traditionally seen as the start of linguistic diversity: the story of the construction of the tower of Babel. God himself comes down to earth in order to inspect the town built in the plains "wherein a black bituminous gurge / Boils out from under ground, the mouth of hell" (*PL* XII.41-42) and where a tower is constructed "whose top may reach to heaven" (*PL* XII.44). One can interpret Milton's view of this plan from a linguistic point of view (i.e., with regard to the activity of naming), too, although of course Nimrod and his crew see the act of naming from a perspective that is completely different from Adam's: as a way of getting

> themselves a name, lest far dispersed
> In foreign lands their memory be lost
> Regardless whether good or evil fame.
> (*PL* XII.45-47)

The words of Nimrod's language thus lack a clear and unambiguous relationship to the facts that they are used to describe.[292]

It is true that the names of those who built the tower of Babel have not been forgotten, but their fame is based on totally arbitrary naming and ridiculous linguistic confusion. God succeeds "to raze / Quite out their native language" and to replace it with "a jangling noise of words unknown" (*PL* XII.53-55).

Future history is first of all the history of "one peculiar nation" (*PL* XII.111) chosen by God, and in spite of all the stylistic parallels to the references to England in Milton's prose, this nation is obviously Israel. Like (though less problematically than) Raphael earlier on in paradise, the archangel Michael now has to make use of a strategy of translation that compares two different phases of postlapsarian history (and not, as in Raphael's case, by comparing prelapsarian and postlapsarian stages): "Things by their names I call, though yet unnamed" (*PL* XII.140). Michael also points out, however, how fallen and imperfect law and language can be re-translated into a coherent regenerative language:

> So law appears imperfect, and but given
> With purpose to resign them in full time
> Up to a better Covenant, disciplined
> From shadowy types to truth, from flesh to spirit,
> From imposition of strict laws, to free
> Acceptance of large grace, from servile fear
> To filial, works of law to works of faith.
> (*PL* XII.300-06)

This "typological" prophecy will then be fulfilled by Christ through whom heavenly and earthly spheres will be reunited so that finally, as Adam ecstatically exclaims, "God with man unites" (*PL* XII.382). This union after the Second Coming will extinguish the distinction between heaven and earth through "this world's dissolution" (*PL* XII.459),

> . . . for then the earth
> Shall all be Paradise far happier place
> Than this of Eden, and far happier days.
> (*PL* XII.463-65)

The linguistic means employed by Christianity to rein in the Babylonian confusion are illustrated by the missionary concept by which the apostles are sent out "to evangelize the nations" and by the experience of Pentecost that "shall them with wondrous gifts endue / To speak all tongues" (*PL* XII.499-501). Outside the field of religion, however, language is powerless, according to Michael, and he holds it to be a fruitless waste of time to try to identify the names of phenomena unknown or incomprehensible to us. In the same way as Raphael, he advocates an attitude of modesty and self-denial: "to obey is best" (*PL* XII.561), he states. Like Raphael, he uses the example of astronomy: "hope no higher, though all the stars / Thou knew'st by name" (*PL* XII.576-77). He can, however, offer Adam something to make up for the loss of paradise—the hope for "A Paradise within thee, happier far" (*PL* XII.587)—so that the ending of the epic, when the whole world lies open in front of the two exiles from paradise, is not without hope for the future of mankind. As Mary Ann Radzinowicz writes, "The openness of the epic's conclusion, with the world all before Adam and Eve, offers to Milton's own time the resumption of the challenge to read correctly the easily abused linguistic sign."[293]

Paradise Regained

In many of Milton's texts that I have dealt with in detail so far, the theme of the ambiguity of language and the question of whether language users are aware of this ambiguity play an important role. The most important example so far has been Milton's *magnum opus*, the epic *Paradise Lost.* It is also to be expected, however, that the role of a clear and unambiguous language also plays a central role in the reestablishment of a paradisal state promised in the title of *Paradise Regained*, even though generations of readers have been disappointed by the style of the later epic, which is "usually said to be flat, colorless, and austere in comparison with that of *Paradise Lost.*"[294]

There are, on the other hand, also more positive views of *Paradise Regained*, stretching from structural and stylistic analyses to linguistic and deconstructionist interpretations. Northrop Frye, for example, points out Milton's unequalled construction of "a double argument on the same words, each highly plausible and yet as different as light from darkness,"[295] whereas William E. McCarron draws our attention to the importance of rhetorical strategies in the supposedly unadorned text.[296] John Carey emphasizes not only Satan's "professional interest in ambiguity" but also the fact that "the poem culminates in Christ's ambiguous 'Tempt not the Lord thy God', which Satan at any rate . . . seems to interpret as a revelation of Christ's own godhead, whether Christ meant it like that or not."[297] Leonard Mustazza studies to what extent the epic conflict has repercussions on "the nature and uses of language itself."[298] Stevie Davies also sees *Paradise Regained* as "perhaps the most extraordinary linguistic experiment of this limitlessly self-extending poet who changed every literary genre he touched and who touched every available genre." She reads the short epic as "a profound critique of language itself," comparing the older Milton's "harsher poetic affiliation" in *Paradise Regained*—so "severe on the richly ambiguous language which actively encourages such a plurality of suggestion"— with his former youthful enthusiasm: "The poem presents a critique of language which may be read alongside Hobbes' attack on metaphor on the one hand, and alongside the Puritan search for a plain style on the other."[299]

Right at the start, Milton's narrator—"I who erewhile the happy garden sung, / By one man's disobedience lost" (*PR* I.1-2)—counters the linguistic "wiles" of Satan with a profoundly non-linguistic action, "one man's firm obedience" (*PR* I.4), which in the end manifests itself in "deeds / Above heroic" (*PR* I.14-15).[300] Regarding speech acts and their effects, which go beyond a purely linguistic aspect, an important scene takes place at the beginning of Book I of *Paradise Regained*, when St. John the Baptist recognizes Jesus and "the Father's voice / From heaven pronounced him his beloved Son" (*PR* I.18-32). The words of the Father clearly impress Satan so that "[h]is distress at the divine proclamation is visible."[301] One might even go so far as to say that here (as in *Paradise Lost*), it is God himself who uses a linguistically ambiguous formulation—ambiguous to Satan at least. As in *Paradise Lost*, Satan feels provoked by this ambiguity and thus is the first to speak.[302]

God's word here in *Paradise Regained* is once again clearly a "word with power" which leaves Satan "with envy fraught and rage" (*PR* I.38). As in *Comus* and *Samson Agonistes*, linguistic questions arise in *Paradise Regained* with regard to the criminal (ab)use of language. Thus Satan's reaction to the events just described and the plan he draws up in front of his council are based on linguistic ambiguity or, in other words, lies: "Not force, but well-couched fraud, well-woven snares" (*PR* I.97).

Stevie Davies interprets the first temptation scene—after Christ's forty days of fasting in the desert—from a linguistic and psychological perspective: "Language loses its basis in the material world and the words dance before his famished eye like nearly meaningless counters" so that "words lose stable meaning in relation to one another as well as to their referents."[303] Interestingly, the Son responds to Satan's urge to demonstrate his divine powers and turn stones into bread by referring to the written rather than the spoken word, and he also indicates that he is well aware that he is dealing with a master of verbal ambiguity who wants to shatter his faith and sow distrust (*PR* I.355). Here, as in the other temptation scenes, the Son "constantly proposes prudent theological concepts and often substitutes metaphorical for literal meanings in Satan's mundane offers."[304]

While Satan indicates to the Son that, despite his banishment from heaven, he is often able to leave his "dolorous prison" (*PR* I.364), readers of *Paradise Lost* know that he could only escape from hell with God's permission and as an instrument in God's greater plan. From God's and the reader's perspective, his proud view of himself is soon identified as nothing but dramatic irony. In this context, the ways in which he presents himself as a "copartner" and advisor of mankind "by presages and signs, / And answers, oracles, portents and dreams" (*PR* I.394-96) seem pathetic, and the Son is not impressed, but rather calls Satan a liar: "The other service was thy chosen task, / To be a liar in four hundred mouths; / For lying is thy sustenance, thy food" (*PR* I.427-29).

At the beginning of Book III, after the Son has rejected money and power in Book II, Satan is even ready to admit to him with "soothing words" (*PR* III.6) that

"Thy actions to they words accord, thy words / To thy large heart give utterance due, thy heart / Contains of good, wise, just, the perfect shape" (*PR* III.9-11). On the other hand, he immediately downgrades the Son's position by comparing it to that of a former Jewish oracle (*PR* III.12-15).

While the Son's general quietness automatically highlights every single word he utters, Satan's verbosity produces a "new train of words" (*PR* III. 266) whenever he opens his mouth. Possibly he is not even any longer aware of the ambiguity of his statements.[305] For example, he mentions "Babylon, the wonder of all tongues" (*PR* III. 280) without realizing that he is not only describing the architectural beauties of the city but rather placing himself in the tradition of the story of the Tower of Babel and its repercussions on the state of language. At the beginning of Book IV, Satan seems to realize that he cannot impress the Son with traditional rhetoric so that

> Perplexed and troubled at his bad success
> The tempter stood, nor had what to reply,
> Discovered in his fraud. (*PR* IV.1-3) [306]

Thus it is not to be expected that either the worldly power of Rome or Athenian eloquence, "the temptation of learning," will impress the Son.[307] He prefers the prophets of his homeland—"men divinely taught, and better teaching / The solid rules of civil government / In their majestic unaffected style" (*PR* IV.357-59) to "all the oratory of Greece and Rome" (*PR* IV.360). While the son praises their message as being plain and easy, Satan points out the ambiguity lying in the Son's status as "Son of God":

> The Son of God I also am, or was,
> And if I was, I am; relation stands;
> All men are Sons of God; yet thee I thought
> In some respect far higher so declared.
> (*PR* IV.518-21)

While Satan tries to find an answer to his question by placing the Son on the highest pinnacle of the temple and by challenging him to show his power, several critics reject Satan's question as inadequate as they claim that he is well aware of being confronted with *the* Son rather than just *a* son of God. For example, Walter MacKellar concludes from the Son's question in I.355-56—"Why dost thou then suggest to me distrust, / Knowing who I am, as I know who thou art?"—that "[a]fter these most unequivocal words Satan can have no slightest reason to doubt Christ's identity, nor Christ to conceal it."[308] The Son adroitly evades the challenge by referring to God's (written) word: "Also it is written, / Tempt not the Lord thy God" (*PR* IV.560-61), so that "Satan smitten with amazement fell." (*PR* IV.562).

Satan—who supposedly was looking for a clear and unambiguous language that he as an ironist never used himself—falls because he is beaten with his own weapon:

language.[309] A problem resembling the contradiction between the concept of the Christian trinity and the principle of a monolithic language surfaces here once again: the Son's statement that "Also it is written, / Tempt not the Lord thy God" (*PR* IV.560-561) can be interpreted as a case of non-monolithic and ambiguous use of language, for "his quotation of the biblical injunction assumes a double meaning in this context, for the Lord, he and Satan now realize, is not simply God the Father but also the Son."[310] Satan seems to be incapable of understanding the linguistic complexity of the Son's "divine duplicity."[311] The Son, however, succeeds in solving his problem through one of the numerous paradoxes for which his teaching is known. A disambiguating act of faith that we have already met in Adam and Eve's "redeemed speech" at the end of *Paradise Lost* is also of central importance here in *Paradise Regained*.[312] As Victoria Silver puts it, the Son "express[es] his belief that there is another meaning potential in his predicament than his own guilt or God's abandonment."[313]

One might, however, also use Milton's "apparent grammatical slip"[314] in line 583 of Book IV as the starting point of a blasphemous deconstructionist reading of the epic and see the fallen angel as being rescued by the other, unfallen angels:

> So Satan fell and straight a fiery globe
> Of angels on full sail of wing flew nigh,
> Who on their plumy vans received him soft
> From his uneasy station. (*PR* IV.581-84)

Such an interpretation would exaggerate the grounds for a deconstruction of Milton's short epic, however, even though this lapse might of course be seen as a quasi-Freudian proof of Blake's statement that "he was a true poet, and of the Devil's party without knowing it."[315]

The Theme of Language in the Epic Poems: A Summary

For obvious reasons, the part of this study dealing with *Paradise Lost* and *Paradise Regained* has to be much longer than the preceding chapters, not only because these works are undoubtedly Milton's most important literary productions, but also because language plays a central role in them. It starts by looking at the discussion of Milton's language and style in *Paradise Lost* from the seventeenth century up to postmodern and poststructuralist interpretations in the present, and it ends with a re-interpretation of the role of the archangel Raphael and of his rhetoric.

Interpretations of *Paradise Lost* are always complicated by the fact that Milton does not give us the epic events in a chronological fashion and that he makes use of different narrators ranging from Adam through Raphael and Michael to his "own" narrative voice. The reliability of these voices is of course open to discussion. The focus is first of all on the scene in which language is first used on earth, the scene in which God inspires Adam, who had so far communicated intuitively with him, to make use of words in order to name the elements of his environment. Adam experiences the act of naming as a divine inspiration, and that is why the names he gives to objects and animals bear divine authorization. The coordination of signifying name and signified object is still clear and unambiguous here, but it is of course conventional in spite of being divinely authorized. As far as arbitrariness and conventionality of linguistic signs are concerned, Milton's semiotics corresponds to theories of seventeenth-century nominalism as well as to certain aspects of modern structuralism.

Adam and Eve's—as well as the readers'—trust in the unambiguous character of the coordination of word and thing is destroyed in *Paradise Lost*. In his prose works, Milton himself had pointed out the ambiguity of some of Christ's words that were meant to confuse the Pharisees. In a similar way, Samson had irritated Israel's enemies with his ambiguous riddles, so that I feel encouraged to also read Milton's first invocation of the muse in *Paradise Lost* as an example of a general tendency towards rendering language ambiguous.

Right at the beginning of Adam's existence in the Garden of Eden, God's interdiction to eat the fruit of the tree of knowledge had given this tree a significance that went far beyond its "tree-ness." Already here, language thus starts to lose the transparency that one might have expected in paradise. God himself uses ambiguous language in the course of the epic, and thus divine irony contributes to undermine mankind's faith in the clarity and unambiguousness of the linguistic sign. During the discussion about Adam's wish for a companion, Adam finds out that God does not always mean what he says, that he rather means Adam to disambiguate his ambiguous message. Although this is a pedagogically motivated deviation from an unambiguous use of language, it also marks a trend away from such a clear language towards rhetoric.

Such a deviation from an unambiguous language is also at the base of the message delivered by the archangel Raphael, who is sent by God to warn Adam of Satan's intrigues. Without having been told to do so, Raphael makes use of a strategy of accommodation and translation that shatters Adam's faith in the solid and clear coordination of things and names that he had encountered in his communication with God. Raphael himself, however, inadvertently hints at the possibility that the differences that he claims exist between heavenly and earthly spheres may not be so great and important after all.

Raphael's semiological strategies are motivated by his own understanding of his position in the heavenly hierarchies: as a divine messenger who has only limited insight into God's plans, he does not know and understand God's greater plan underlying the education of Adam. Thus he transfers the doctrine of absolute obedience to God's commands—on which his action in the War in heaven had depended—to God's relationship with Adam, and he does not realize that he himself is only a pedagogical tool in Adam's education that will turn the latter into an independent and self-reliable being in the course of a godgame. His message was only an ironical message meant to be deciphered by Adam.

If we analyze God's communication with Adam as ironical, we also see that the Father's way of treating the angels is often dominated by ironical strategies, even at a time when the earth has not yet been created. At first it seems to be Satan who makes use of ironical language when he uses the rhetoric of political speech in order rally his troops of fallen angels in Hell. But there had been a deviation from "prelapsarian language" even in heaven, and the earthly names of the fallen angels had lost their divine authorization. Even God had used ironical, non-monolithic language—if only to test his creatures.

If we read the Fall of language in *Paradise Lost* as the end of monolithic language in which there is a solid, clear, and divinely authorized coordination of word and thing, then this Fall must have taken place earlier than biblical exegesis had thought: way before the construction of the Tower of Babel, even before the apple was eaten in paradise. If one wants to reintroduce the unity of language, this is possible only through divine authorization and Frygian "words with power" in which faith brings word and thing (or, in a loosely semiotic sense, signifier and signified) together. Such a situation arises in *Paradise Regained*, when—on the pinnacle of the temple—Jesus refuses to be provoked by Satan and, in a paradoxical and literal fashion, proves obedient to God and his Word.

3.4. Educational Godgames: A Digression on Another Miltonic Paradigm

In the following pages, I would like show that my "linguistic" analysis of *Paradise Lost* opens up the possibility of a re-interpretation of the role of the Father's actions and of the archangel Raphael's somewhat inscrutable behaviour. In order to explain the "negative" role of the archangel Raphael in *Paradise Lost*—especially with regard to the "linguistic Fall" in *Paradise Lost* from a prelapsarian to a postlapsarian medium of communication—I suggest to have recourse to a traditional literary structure that has been known for centuries and is sometimes—rather fittingly—called *godgame*. This structure, I would claim, can be seen at work in several of Milton's texts: not only in *Paradise Lost*, but also as early as in works such as *Comus*. It thus puts the "linguistic" insights of my interpretation into perspective.

I would therefore like to suggest an innovative interpretation not only of Milton's epic but also of his "reformed masque."[316] It is, I hope, not just the result of an "ingenious facility for finding subtle new meanings in the masque"[317] that I am interested in the role played by the Attendant Spirit, because I intend to show that we can discern in his behaviour an educational strategy that might be seen as yet another type of "Miltonic paradigm" than the one identified by Stanley Fish. This paradigmatic educational strategy can then be seen at work not only in *Comus* but also—in a slightly different (but structurally comparable) way—in *Paradise Lost*. Furthermore, there are striking parallels between the teaching strategies in *Paradise Lost* and *Comus* and the game structure which has been around for several centuries, but which was only in our time—and intriguingly—baptized *godgame* by the novelist John Fowles, who makes use of it in various of his novels and especially in the meta-theatrical "masque" that plays a crucial role in *The Magus*.[318]

In *The Miltonic Moment*, J. Martin Evans claims that the following question lies at the heart of *Comus*: "Are fallen human beings capable of acting virtuously without supernatural assistance?"[319] On the one hand, Milton's masque shows that, in spite of the Lady's own strong convictions and her young brothers' active and forceful support, supernatural assistance is necessary for a happy ending of the trip through Comus's forest; on the other, the Attendant Spirit as the main representative of this more or less supernatural assistance—in his various incarnations as daemon, swain or shepherd—seems, according to Evans, to join "the angels guarding Eden in *Paradise Lost*" in being "curiously ineffectual, constantly hovering around the margins of the action but never intervening in it directly."[320] Critics highlight various aspects here: While Maryann Cale McGuire states that the children "undergo an educational experience that alters their basic assumptions about themselves and their world,"[321] Barbara Lewalski insists on the Spirit's limitations as a "teacher, dispensing heaven's aid through human means, not miracles."[322]

Still, with the exception of Evans's and McGuire's studies and perhaps Cedric Brown's chapter on "Spiritual Instructions,"[323] the Attendant Spirit has not received nearly enough scholarly attention so far, except for comments on the assumption that his role was presumably played by the musician Henry Lawes in the original production, Lawes being not only the composer of the accompanying music but also the teacher of the Bridgewater children who were the main performers in the masque.[324]

Among earlier commentaries on *Comus*, Brooks and Hardy's essay in their 1957 edition of the *Poems of Mr. John Milton* is quite helpful.[325] Preceding Evans for over forty years, Brooks and Hardy insist on the Spirit's tendency to refrain from involvement in the action, his function being "to help to *reveal* the meaning of the dramatic action" to the audience. They state that "he does not interfere; he is, in short, precisely what he is named, not the *moving* spirit of the play, but the *attendant*"[326]—paying service to the Miltonic insight, expressed in the last line of the sonnet on his blindness, that "They also serve who only stand and wait" (*CSP*328).

At first, the Attendant Spirit appears as a somewhat reluctant chorus character[327] presenting himself as a messenger sent down from heaven (although he is not an angel such as Raphael in *Paradise Lost*), his mansion being "Before the starry threshold of Jove's Court" (*Comus* 1).[328] His message is addressed to some select few who "by due steps aspire / To lay their just hands on that golden key / That opes the palace of eternity" (12-14), his task being to provide safe passage for the Lady and her Brothers on their way through the forest which is haunted by Comus, Circe's son, who threatens the travellers with "foul disfigurement" (74).

The Attendant Spirit later re-enters the scene as the shepherd Thyrsis, who tells the brothers about the Lady's encounter with Comus. Rather than saving her himself—as one at first assumes he might have done—he claims that "Longer I durst not stay" (577) and thus hurries on to alert the brothers and provide them with the powerful plant haemony. In spite of this herb, the Brothers' attack on Comus is not completely successful: Perhaps Thyrsis was not even truthful in ascribing various powers to the plant. In the end, Comus thus manages to escape with his wand, and the Lady must remain fastened to her seat by whatever "gums of glutinous heat" (916) may be.[329] The Spirit thus has to invoke the nymph Sabrina, who liberates the Lady, so that he can finally return the children safe and sound to their parents praising "Their faith, their patience, and their truth" (970) which led them "through hard assays" (971) to "triumph in victorious dance / O'er sensual folly, and intemperance" (973-74).[330] Now the Spirit withdraws in the spirit, as Roy Flannagan reminds us, of Shakespeare's Puck or Ariel.[331] His revels are now ended, and with a final insistence on the importance of virtue, he takes his adieu: "But now my task is smoothly done, / I can fly, or I can run" (1011-12).

The "curiously ineffectual" teacher in Milton's masque, who is often "conspicuously absent,"[332] may not be so ineffectual after all, however. The children's experience can be interpreted—in Elizabeth Frost's words—as "trial as a test of virtue,"[333] which has reminded many critics of Milton's attitude towards untried virtue in *Areopagitica*, and it may even show parallels to the strategies of the ideal humanist teacher whom Evans mentions and to the role that—in my view—the Father plays in his education of Adam and Eve in *Paradise Lost*, when he exposes them—as independent beings equipped with their own free will—to temptation. As Evans puts it,

> Thus, the reason the Attendant Spirit does not prevent Comus from tempting the Lady is the same as the reason the angels guarding paradise fail to prevent Satan from tempting Adam and Eve: if an individual is to function as a moral agent, he or she must be free to encounter temptation and to resist it.[334]

In order to make this point even more emphatically, however, it will first of all be useful to further introduce the concept of the godgame that I mentioned earlier on. John Fowles first uses this term in *The Aristos*, his collection of aphorisms. The central points of this concept involving, as Avrom Fleishman puts it, a "Greek or Pascalian God,"[335] are included in the following excerpt:

> Imagine yourself a god, and lay down the laws of a universe. You then find yourself in the Divine Predicament: good governors must govern all equally, and

all fairly. But no act of government can be fair to all, in all their different situations, except one.

The Divine Solution is to govern by not governing in any sense that the governed can call being governed; that is, to constitute a situation in which the governed must govern themselves.

If there had been a creator, his second act would have been to disappear.

Put dice on the table and leave the room; but make it seem possible to the players that you were never in the room.[336]

According to the person who—to my knowledge—introduced the term into contemporary literary studies, the Canadian scholar Robert Rawdon Wilson, in a godgame "one character (or several) is made a victim by another character's superior knowledge and power" so that "[c]aught in a cunningly constructed web of appearances, the victim, who finds the illusion impenetrable, is observed and his behavior is judged."[337] Both the situation of being "caught in a cunningly constructed web of appearances" and the phases of observation and judgment can easily be identified in *Comus*. Fowles's definition in *The Aristos* has an aspect to it which, I think, is lost in the short definition by Wilson, but not, of course, in his more elaborate statements. For example, he states at one point that "[t]he godgames of [Shakespeare's] *The Tempest*, [Cervantes's] *Don Quijote*, and [Calderón de la Barca's] *Life is a Dream* are, in pointing the reader toward a significant moral insight, sharply heuristic."[338] As the above quotation from *The Aristos* shows, for Fowles, the godgame is part of the process of good government, and the stress in this kind of godgame is not so much on the process of victimization but on that of positively influencing or teaching people, possibly even in such a way that they think they are not being influenced or taught.

Godgame is also the title Fowles originally intended for the novel that later came to be called *The Magus*, a novel in which the main character, Nicholas Urfe, has the impression that he may be nothing but a character in a game—or rather a "masque," as Urfe himself calls it—directed by the mysterious Mr. Conchis.[339] Even though godgames may be performed for any kind of motives such as sadism, psychological research or pure playfulness, one of the most important motivations is educational: The victim of a godgame will—or should have—learned something. And although the ending of Fowles's *The Magus* is open, one may assume that the godgame experience in Maurice Conchis's masque in the Greek island domaine of Bourani has taught Nicholas how to be a more responsible human being.[340]

One may take the parallels between Milton's masque and Fowles's masque in *The Magus* even further, as the unruly and threatening antimasque characters that Nicholas Urfe meets in the novel's central scene during his ordeal or trial in a cave—a "man with the head of a stag," a woman with a "malevolent mask," "a squat succubus with a Bosch-like snout" and so on[341]—resemble the "ougly-headed Monsters" (695) into which Comus's "orient liquor" (65) turns his victims so that

The express resemblance of the gods, is changed
Into some brutish form of wolf, or bear,
Or ounce, or tiger, hog, or bearded goat (69-71)

Although the term *godgame* may be new, the structure or paradigm to which it refers is—to quote Wilson again—"unmistakably transhistorical."[342] Wilson claims that "godgames recur persistently through baroque literature" and counts Shakespeare, Spenser, and Milton among its masters,[343] but unfortunately he does not go into much more detail about godgames in Milton's works. Nevertheless, one can clearly identify the outlines of an educational godgame structure in the behaviour of the Attendant Spirit. The three children within the masque learn about the importance—but also about the limits—of virtuous behaviour and/or temperance and/or virginity in their ordeal in the forest.

In *Paradise Lost*, the Father sends one of his most trustworthy archangels, Raphael, down to Earth in order to warn Adam and Eve of the danger that vengeful Satan means for mankind. Raphael is supposed to communicate and dine with Adam "as friend with friend" and warn him, although he of course knows right from the start that his mission is doomed to failure. Raphael's mission resembles that of those angels (amongst them Raphael himself) whom Empson describes at the gates of Hell: "They knew, and they knew that God knew that they knew, that this tiresome chore was completely useless."[344]

The ensuing description of Raphael's didactic mission, of his meeting with Adam and Eve in paradise, is a godgame directed by the Father. This insight has far-reaching consequences for the interpretation of the roles that the various characters involved play here. The Father himself is the teacher or magus in this case; Adam and Eve are the pupils, and the objective of the game is—as it was in Nicholas's case—the process of education bringing forth self-reliant and responsible human beings who will be able to find their own way in the world.

Adam is first approached by Raphael, who informs him about his responsibility and his duties towards God, only then to mention the danger that Satan may mean to him. Raphael tells him about the War in Heaven that forms the background of the new threat, i.e., the war between the armies of the obedient and the fallen angels that can only be won after the Father arms the Son, the Messiah, with his omnipotence. Still, this victory does not mean that Satan is no longer a threat, especially for Adam and Eve.

Both Adam in *Paradise Lost* and Nicholas in *The Magus* are warned not to try to understand the full complexity of the dramas in which they play only minor roles. For example, the archangel asks Adam not to occupy himself with "studious thoughts abstruse" (*PL* VIII.40) of astronomy. In the same way in which the other actors in *The Magus* are unwilling or unable to help Nicholas, Raphael is not ready to answer Adam's questions which should not concern him and the answers to which the Father has for some reason decided not to give him. That is why he advises

Adam to "Solicit not thy thoughts with matters hid," and to "be lowly wise" (*PL* VIII.167, 173).[345]

Adam first appreciates the chance to lead a simple and restricted life. He is not aware, of course, that the "wandering thoughts" and "notions vain" (*PL* VIII.187) he mentions already seem to be pointing towards the dangerous serpent and the "wandering mazes" in which one's thoughts can be lost. Adam's decision to restrict himself to his immediate and tangible environment is reminiscent of Milton's own reference to "solid things" in *Of Education* (but one has to admit that Milton in his pedagogical treatise saw the study of solid things as only a first step). Adam limits himself to "things at hand" (*PL* VIII.199) and wants to keep roving fancy under control.

The advice to be lowly wise seems to be addressed not only to Adam but also to the angels in *Paradise Lost*, who do not know that much more about the roles they play in the *godgame* than Adam does. Milton's angels have been shown the limitations of their power during the War in Heaven. And yet, self-restriction is not always the correct strategy in paradise. Every now and then, Adam is even encouraged to question the power structure imposed by the heavenly director and "ideal schoolmaster,"[346] for example in the "process of education by disputation with God."[347] Raphael's integration into the heavenly hierarchies keeps him from recognizing the Father's larger strategy. Although he claims to be able to explain the heavenly spheres to Adam, he is unable to see that his version of heavenly drama may not be the same as that of the divine director drawing the strings from Olympian heights. He is an angel who does not fully comprehend the structure of events in which he is embedded. For example, he accepts as God-given truth what I claim was only meant to be a challenge of Adam's mental capacity in the Father's script.

During his discussion with the Father in paradise, Adam himself has the impression that God responds positively towards human ability and willingness to argue and towards Adam's wish for a companion. Only at first sight does he deny this wish, but he changes his mind as soon as Adam has given him a convincing reason, and then he even admits that his denial of the wish had been nothing but a pedagogical trick meant to elicit Adam's demand. After Adam's brilliant performance, he admits that the test had been "for trial only brought, / To see how thou couldst judge of fit and meet" (*PL* VIII.447-448).

But Adam and Eve will in the end succumb to Satan's temptations, as the Father knows full well.[348] Owing to the Son's willingness to assume human shape and undergo punishment on their behalf, they are not annihilated, however, but only expelled from the Garden of Eden. Having undergone a sort of trial and education, they leave paradise, unhappy but able to trust in divine guidance and providence.

In the godgame in paradise, Adam and Eve obviously do not follow God's commandments and do not obey him. Having freely decided to disobey, they now have to pay for their behaviour. Their education in the sheltered environment of paradise has come to an end. This situation of Adam and Eve after the expulsion from paradise bears certain resemblances to the situation of Fowles's character

Nicholas Urfe after his "education" by Mr. Conchis on the Greek island, but of course there is an important difference between divine providence and the treatment by a psychologist, however good or innovative the latter's methods may be. In both cases, the temporary inhabitants of paradise have recognized the necessity to fall back on their own strengths.

In Fowles's *Magus,* Nicholas finds out that he does not need Conchis any longer. The god in his godgame has evaporated. What about the God in *Paradise Lost?* Can we extend the parallels between the texts so far as to claim that the Father in the end disappears after having fulfilled his educational function, so that the governor whom the young Milton sees abdicating in *Prolusion* VII[349] is a precursor of the governor in Fowles's *Aristos* and perhaps even of Milton's own God in *Paradise Lost?*

At first sight, one will probably respond negatively to such a question, especially since the Father sends the archangel Michael down to earth before he expels Adam and Eve. Michael is supposed to let Adam see the future of mankind, a future that is far from rosy but which is ensured of divine support and providence and in which "the earth / Shall all be Paradise, far happier place / Than this of Eden" (*PL* XII.463-465). On the other hand, human beings are now responsible for their own deeds, and these will lead to mistakes, even to deadly mistakes. After the archangels have guided Adam and Eve through the godgame in paradise, the Father withdraws in the same way as Mr. Conchis, the author and director of John Fowles's godgame, had absconded. He withdraws from this "other world" as he has promised in Book VII. He describes his unforced "resignation"—"necessity and chance / Approach not me" (*PL* VII.172-73)—as the process in which

> I uncircumscribed my self retire
> And put not forth my goodness, which is free
> To act or not. (*PL* VII.170-72)

Here my reading of Milton's epic corresponds to a certain degree not only to Denis Saurat's theory of "retraction"[350] and to William Empson's ideas as well as to some fascinating poststructuralist interpretations of *Paradise Lost,* but also to the position of at least some of Milton's contemporaries regarding the possibility of God's abdication.[351] Of course, the Father in *Paradise Lost* is more powerful than his secular twentieth-century successor, Mr. Conchis in *The Magus,* but he is as aware of the manipulative role he plays in his attempt to encourage self-reliant behaviour in his pupil.

So after all, the scenes in paradise and Comus's forest have something more in common than just being educational. The roles of the teachers show important parallels, which are also parallels to the role of "the conjuror-god" Conchis in *The Magus,* who "must silently abscond from the world that he has created if human freedom is ever to exist in that world."[352] In his ostensible inefficiency, or limited efficiency, the Attendant Spirit—according to Evans—not only resembles Milton's ideal humanist educator whose function it is "to instruct his students, not to protect them, to inform and advise them, not to guard them."[353] The Attendant Spirit, who intervenes in a situation in which the Fall is felt more than just briefly,[354] also foreshadows the educational structure of *Paradise Lost*. Of course, the motivation that I see behind this retraction could not be more different than those imputed by Empson for whom God's abdication is the only feature making "the whole picture of him just tolerable,"[355] but the structural parallels between the educational strategies in Milton's early masque and late epic remain.

That the situation in *Comus* resembles a play in which the main characters are unwittingly manipulated by a *magister ludi* has already been indicated by Brooks and Hardy in their interpretation of the Attendant Spirit's "ineffectuality" as "a variety of dramatic irony." They claim that "[t]his irony becomes double-edged, and much more complex, when we see how little the Spirit does to help them, or how little prepared they are to receive and make use of what he can give them in the form of advice."[356] Franklin Baruch furthermore points out, that "for reasons of pedagogy"—and from my critical perspective I would interpret this to mean 'because he has constructed a godgame situation for them'—"The Attendant Spirit does not speak the truth to the boys any more than Comus had to their sister."[357] He is playing a godgame.

In both *Comus* and *Paradise Lost*, a teacher figure, whether it be the Attendant Spirit or God, withdraws or remains inactive after his theoretical lesson to his pupils; he leaves them to fight for themselves for some time. In both cases, the educational experiment is only a qualified success. In both cases, the students still need help, and whereas the experiment is judged in a positive light at the end of *Comus*, the criticism and the consequences in *Paradise Lost* are a lot harsher, even if we see the Fall in *Paradise Lost* as an instance of *felix culpa* in the end.

Now it is especially interesting to see that in fact "the withdrawn, hidden (or disappearing) nature of the god"—the aspect that encourages me to draw the parallels between the Attendant Spirit and an Empsonian or Sauratian Father in *Paradise Lost*—is also mentioned by Robert Rawdon Wilson in his godgame theories, although he does not so much locate it in Milton's times but rather sees it as the "one striking difference between baroque and modern godgames."[358] Perhaps Milton is—at least in this respect—more modern than he had been thought to be.

While Adam and Eve—although they know that God is still with them—nevertheless have to leave paradise, in *Comus*, the Attendant Spirit comes back in order to save the Lady and her brothers with the help of Sabrina. In the end, he proudly presents them to their parents. Thus in *Comus*, a teacher character instructs his pupils, but rather than retracting completely after his theoretical lesson, he stays on in the background to help them, however ineffectual he may be in the end, having to call on yet another supporter, the nymph Sabrina.

Similar to the way in which Comus has been interpreted as an earlier incarnation of Satan, the Attendant Spirit's behaviour can be interpreted as pointing forward to the Father's actions in *Paradise Lost*, even though the Father's teaching strategies are much more complex than that of his precursor in the reformed court masque. For example, he delegates the task of teaching to an archangel whose reliability as a messenger is questioned by at least some critics. The Attendant Spirit's temporary withdrawal in *Comus* can thus be interpreted as an earlier instance—and a more benign one at that—of a recurring educational strategy, of a "Miltonic paradigm," that culminates in the Father's method in *Paradise Lost* of turning Adam and Eve into responsible and independent human beings who are "Sufficient to have stood, though free to fall" (*PL* III.99).[359]

Notes

1. In *The Western Canon: The Books and Schools of the Ages* (London: Macmillan, 1995), Harold Bloom counts him among the 26 authors forming the Western canon, and he remarks that his "place in the canon is permanent, even though he appears to be the major poet at present most deeply resented by feminist literary critics" (169). This statement does not do justice to recent feminist Milton criticism, however.

2. Kermode, Preface, *The Living Milton* ix.

3. See, for example, Stanley Fish, *Surprised by Sin.*

4. In *The Politics of Milton's Prose Style* (New Haven: Yale UP, 1975), Keith W. Stavely mentions Milton's "warm approval of Cicero," but also shows that "Ciceronian" has become a negative label referring to "pedantic imitators of Cicero satirized by Erasmus" (3).

5. Peter Auksi, "Milton's 'Sanctifi'd Bitternesse': Polemical Technique in the Early Prose," *Texas Studies in Literature and Language* 19 (1977): 376.

6. See Thomas N. Corns, *The Development of Milton's Prose Style* (Oxford: Clarendon, 1982) 65.

7. See Christopher Grose, *Milton's Epic Process: Paradise Lost and Its Miltonic Background* (New Haven: Yale UP, 1973) 37.

8. David Masson, *The Life of John Milton: Narrated in Connexion with the Political, Ecclesiastical, and Literary History of His Time*, 7 vols. (1877-96; Gloucester, MA: Peter Smith, 1965) I: 282.

9. See M. L. Donnelly, "Francis Bacon's Early Reputation in England and the Question of John Milton's Alleged 'Baconianism,'" *Prose Studies* 14.1 (1991): 1-20.

10. The term in the Latin version is *Americanus* (*WJM* XII: 276).

11. See also Masson I: 778.

12. See also William Riley Parker, *Milton: A Biography*, ed. Gordon Campbell, 2nd ed. (Oxford: Clarendon, 1996) I: 171.

13. Stevie Davies, *Milton* 49.

14. See Kathleen Swaim, *Before and After the Fall: Contrasting Modes in* Paradise Lost

(Amherst: U of Massachusetts P, 1986) 49.

15. David Loewenstein, "'An Ambiguous Monster': Representing Rebellion in Milton's Polemics and *Paradise Lost*," *Huntington Library Quarterly* 55 (1992): 297.

16. See John M. Major, "Milton's View of Rhetoric," *Studies in Philology* 64 (1967): 685.

17. Dayton Haskin, *Milton's Burden of Interpretation* (Philadelphia: U of Pennsylvania P, 1994) xiv, 67, xiv.

18. James Grantham Turner, "The Intelligible Flame," *John Milton*, ed. Annabel Patterson (London: Longman, 1993) 76.

19. William Riley Parker, "Education: Milton's Ideas and Ours," *College English* 24.1 (1962): 1.

20. Irby B. Cauthen, Jr., "'A Complete and Generous Education': Milton and Jefferson," *Virginia Quarterly Review* 55 (1979): 222.

21. See Hill, *Milton and the English Revolution*: 36, 158; on Bacon's influence on Milton's *Prolusions* and *Of Education*, see Snider, *Origin and Authority* 91, 201.

22. According to the *OED Online*, the verb *to repair* can have the meaning "[t]o renew, renovate (some thing or part); to restore to a fresh or sound condition by making up in some way for previous loss, waste, decay, or exhaustion," although it can of course also be interpreted as a synonym of *to mend*. Swaim seems to support the first interpretation: "Although it speaks of postlapsarian 'repair,' in fact *Of Education* addresses prelapsarian prospects" (*Before and After the Fall* 17). Twenty years later, Milton's more sober attitude is mirrored in the archangel Michael's words in Book XII of *Paradise Lost*. Ann Baynes Coiro highlights in "'To repair the ruins of our first parents': *Of Education* and Fallen Adam," *SEL* 28 (1988) "the profound difference between Milton's early sketch of an ideal education and his later dramatization" in *Paradise Lost* (143).

23. Joanna Picciotto, "Reforming the Garden: The Experimentalist Eden and *Paradise Lost*," *ELH* 72 (2005): 25. See also Bryson's statement in *The Tyranny of Heaven* that "To argue that education can 'repair' the ruins produced by the Fall of Adam and Eve is as radical a theological statement as I can find in Milton" (58).

24. Swaim takes the young Milton to be "a not inappropriate model for the later portrait of edenic Adam, though like the unfallen Adam this Milton too must learn to 'be lowly wise'" (*Before and After the Fall* 21). More than sixty years earlier, Murray W. Bundy had compared Milton's ideal students in *Of Education* (who were of course always already "by nature sinful") to Raphael's prelapsarian students in *Paradise Lost*. On the other hand, Bundy classifies Michael's teaching methods in *Paradise Lost* as postlapsarian ("Milton's View of Education in *Paradise Lost*," *Journal of English and Germanic Philology* 21 [1922]: 129-30). Coiro (133, 143) also draws fascinating parallels between the educational method described in *Of Education* and Adam's education by Michael in Books XI and XII.

25. Michael Lieb, "'The Sinews of Ulysses': Exercise and Education in Milton," *JGE: The Journal of General Education* 36.4 (1985): 247.

26. See the discussion of Milton's materialism and monism in my section on *Paradise Lost*.

27. Picciotto, "Reforming the Garden" 30.

28. While there are good reasons for locating the Fall of language in paradise, Milton in

Of Education still seems to follow the tradition of associating the Fall of language with the construction of the Tower of Babel: "And though a linguist should pride himselfe to have all the tongues that *Babel* cleft the world into, yet, if he have not studied the solid things in them as well as the words and lexicons, he were nothing so much to be esteem'd a learned man, as any yeoman or tradesman competently wise in his mother dialect only" (*CP* II: 369-70). In a footnote to *Of Education*, Donald C. Dorian points to an element distinguishing Milton from that school of linguists later ridiculed by Swift in *Gulliver's Travels*: "Milton does not make the mistake, however, of suggesting that education by way of ascending the Great Chain is alone sufficient for the salvation of fallen man: knowledge (. . .) may lead to virtue, 'which being united to the heavenly grace of faith makes up the highest perfection'" (*CP* II: 388, n. 84).

29. See William G. Riggs, "Poetry and Method in Milton's *Of Education*," *Studies in Philology* 89 (1992): 461.

30. See Balachandra Rajan, "Simple, Sensuous and Passionate (1945)," *Milton: Modern Essays in Criticism*, ed. Arthur E. Barker (London: OUP, 1965) 8.

31. Isabel Gamble MacCaffrey, Paradise Lost *as "Myth"* (Cambridge, MA: Harvard UP, 1959) 40.

32. See Harinder Singh Marjara, *Contemplation of Created Things* 4. Kester Svendsen writes for example in *Milton and Science* (Cambridge, MA: Harvard UP, 1956) that despite spectacular references to Galileo and others Milton was a representative of the "old science" (3). For the most recent treatment, see Angelica Duran, *The Age of Milton and the Scientific Revolution* (Pittsburgh: Duquesne UP, 2007).

33. Marjara 8.

34. See William Melczer, "Looking Back Without Anger: Milton's *Of Education*," *Milton and the Middle Ages*, ed. John Mulryan (Lewisburg, Pa.: Bucknell UP; London: Associated UPs, 1982) 92. As early as 1930, Ricardo Quintana claimed that Milton's educational ideas were quite wide-spread in seventeenth-century England ("Notes on English Educational Opinion During the Seventeenth Century," *Studies in Philology* 27 [1930]: 281).

35. Donald C. Dorian in *CP* II: 373, n. 29.

36. Hill, *Milton and the English Revolution* 148, and Oliver M. Ainsworth, *Milton on Education: The Tractate* Of Education *with Supplementary Extracts from Other Writings of Milton* (1928; New York: AMS Press, 1970) 20. Webster also finds "clear traces of the influence of Comenius and Bacon" in *Of Education*, but this does not surprise him as "their views were completely assimilated into a humanistic framework" (*The Great Instauration* 190). In his introduction to the Yale edition, Ernest Sirluck also sceptically points out that Milton is generally seen as a member of the Comenian reform movement, and he remarks that if one wants to construct a relationship of dependence, then this should exist between Bacon and Milton: "But the debt is a limited one, and Milton's tractate is scarcely more Baconian than Comenian; indeed, as Jones makes clear, Comenianism is for the most part Baconianism in the field of education" (*CP* II: 186, n. 9).

37. Comenius in *Comenius in England*, ed. Robert Fitzgibbon Young (Oxford: OUP; London: Humphrey Milford, 1932) 31.

38. See Linda C. Mitchell, *Grammar Wars: Language as Cultural Battlefield in 17th and 18th Century England* (Aldershot: Ashgate, 2001) 67.

39. Tony Davies, "The Ark in Flames: Science, Language, and Education in Seventeenth-Century England," *The Figural and the Literal: Problems of Language in the History of Science and Philosophy 1630-1800*, eds. Andrew E. Benjamin, Geoffrey N. Cantor and John R.R. Christie (Manchester: Manchester UP, 1987) 96-97. See also Barbara Kiefer Lewalski, "Milton and the Hartlib Circle: Educational Projects and Epic *Paideia*," *Literary Milton: Text, Pretext, Context*, eds. Diana Treviño and Michael Lieb (Pittsburgh: Duquesne UP, 1994) 202-03; William G. Riggs, "The Temptation of Milton's Eve: 'Words, Impregn'd / With Reason,'" *JEPG* 94.3 (1995): 366; Karen L. Edwards, "Comenius, Milton, and the Temptation to Ease," *Milton Studies* 32 (1996); Gauri Viswanathan, "Milton and Education," *Milton and the Imperial Vision*, eds. Balachandra Rajan and Elizabeth Sauer (Pittsburgh: Duquesne UP, 1999) 273-293. For an early study of these connections, see George H. Turnbull, *Hartlib, Dury and Comenius: Gleanings from Hartlib's Papers* (Liverpool: UP of Liverpool; London: Hodder and Stoughton, 1947). Coiro insists that "the philosophy and direction of Milton's argument are pointedly different from Hartlib's" ("'To Repair the ruins of our first parents'" 145).

40. See Riggs, "Poetry and Method" 448. We do not know to what extent Milton relied on the older version of Ramus prepared by Downham.

41. In order to become comprehensible for fallen human beings, the divine message undergoes a process of accommodation. See Swaim, *Before and After the Fall* 52.

42. *CP* II: 650. On prudence, see Monika Gomille, *Prudentia in Miltons Paradise Lost* (Heidelberg: Winter, 1990) and Victoria Kahn, *Rhetoric, Prudence and Skepticism in the Renaissance* (Ithaca: Cornell UP, 1985). For another *méthode de prudence* certainly known to Milton, see my discussion of Milton's Ramist logic.

43. David Loewenstein, *Milton and the Drama of History: Historical Vision, Iconoclasm, and the Literary Imagination* (Cambridge: CUP, 1990) 57.

44. *CP* IV.1: 339. This personal attack of course invites a rebuttal on the same personal level, for example in the conservative satirist Samuel Butler's "Fragments of an Intended Second Part of the Foregoing Satire (1670)," *Milton: The Critical Heritage*, ed. John T. Shawcross (London: Routledge, 1970) 76.

45. The clear identification of Milton as the author of *De Doctrina* would of course support his classification as a heretic and unorthodox Christian. Arguments in this respect are to be found in Gordon Campbell *et al.*, "The Provenance of *De Doctrina Christiana*," *Milton Quarterly* 31.3 (1997): 67-121. For the most comprehensive recent discussion of *De Doctrina*, see Lieb, *Theological Milton.*

46. *CP* VI: 44. See Shullenberger's "Linguistic and Poetic Theory in Milton's *De Doctrina Christiana*," probably the first reference in Milton criticism to Ferdinand de Saussure. Shullenberger relies, however, on a different Saussurean dichotomy—that of *langue* and *parole*—than I do in my own interpretation of *Paradise Lost*. Starting out from the reference to the Son as *the Word* (Latin *sermo*), he interprets God as the personification of the theoretical gift of language—"the generative rules and limits of formation of all possible articulate existence" included in the concept of *langue*—and the Son as the actual and human form of these abilities on the level of *parole* (268). Shullenberger almost goes so far as to co-opt Milton's semiotics as a precursor of Saussurean structuralism.

47. Heretically, one might wonder if Milton's description of the (no longer completely)

tri-une God is not already a deviation from unambiguous language. For a defence of Milton against the accusation of being heretical, see the contributions to *Bright Essence: Studies in Milton's Theology*, eds. William B. Hunter, C.A. Patrides and J.H. Adamson (Salt Lake City: U of Utah P, 1973).

48. William Kerrigan, *The Sacred Complex: On the Psychogenesis of* Paradise Lost (Cambridge, MA: Harvard UP, 1983) 237, 238.

49. John Guillory, *Poetic Authority: Spenser, Milton, and Literary History* (New York: Columbia UP, 1983) 152.

50. The process of Adam's giving names to the animals is also mentioned in *De Doctrina*: "Since man was formed in the image of God, he must have been endowed with natural wisdom, holiness and righteousness. . . . Moreover he could not have given names to the animals in that extempore way, without very great intelligence" (*CP* VI: 324).

51. Austin Woolrich comments that Barker "observes in *The Readie & Easie Way* a partial return to the humanistic confidence of that tract of 1644" (*CP* VII: 184).

52. Grose, *Milton's Epic Process* 125 suggests the period from 1629 to 1632.

53. Esterhammer follows Shullenberger's study of *De Doctrina* in pointing out parallels between Ramist logic (e.g., the distinction between the general and the special) and the binary system of modern structuralist grammar (Esterhammer, *Creating States* 67), even though such a point of view is rejected by many historical linguists (e.g., Padley, *Grammatical Theory in Western Europe* 24). Nevertheless, there is a suggestive similarity between the Ramist binary system as it is illustrated by a diagram in Perry Miller's *The New England Mind* and the tree diagrams of structuralist grammar.

54. Ong in *CP* VIII: 204.

55. See Gordon Campbell, "Milton's *Accedence Commenc't Grammar*," *Milton Quarterly* 10 (1976): 40.

56. See Walter J. Ong, Introduction (*CP* VIII: 155). Ong traces the separation of logic and rhetoric, "the posttypographic desocialization of logic" (155), back to the spreading of the printing press which liberates the art of argumentation from oral performance (156-157).

57. Ong writes: "All speech, poetry included, was assumed to be probatory or disprobatory unless there were positive indications to the contrary—as there almost never were. Indeed, following Ramus (and many others), Milton can discern 'proof' and 'refutation' in passages that to the twentieth-century mind appear patently nonpolemic utterances of fact or fancy" (*CP* VIII: 160-61).

58. The passages in italics indicate formulations that Milton has taken directly from Ramus.

59. Ong describes this subdivision in the following way: "Artificial arguments 'argue' of themselves, 'by an innate and proper force.' Since they are situated within the 'art' of logic, their power derives from within this art. . . . Artificial arguments are those found under cause, effect, disparates, and indeed all arguments except those derived from testimony, under which fall all the inartificial arguments; for to argue from what someone says about a matter is to step outside the art of logic into actual history" (*CP* VIII: 175).

60. Grose, *Milton's Epic Process* 124. Cf. Grose's earlier essay, "Milton on Ramist Similitude," *Seventeenth-Century Imagery: Essays on Uses of Figurative Language from Donne to Farquhar*, ed. Earl Miner (Berkeley: U of California P, 1971)103-116.

61. Further down, Milton states: "An argument is derived more often and more firmly from name than from notation: for example, he is a man (*homo*), therefore he is from earth (*humus*); it is a hearth (*focus*), therefore it warms (*fovet*). But not with the same force is an argument derived from notation: for example, he is from earth, therefore he is a man; it warms everything, therefore it is a hearth" (*CP* VIII: 296).

62. See Entzminger, *Divine Word* 89 and Swaim, *Before and After the Fall* 52.

63. Cf. Grose, "Milton on Ramist Similitude": "Although Milton does not specify the source of all this confusion—the Fall of Man—it is assumed throughout, and the art of logic exists precisely to remedy the terrible defect. Like *Of Education*, then, the *Art of Logic* helps us 'repair the ruins of our first parents,' and it is to that end that it points" (112).

64. Ong in *CP* VIII: 204.

65. In the English translation of 1574, this method is also called "the craftie and secrete methode" (Petrus Ramus, *The Logike*, ed. and trans. Rolland M'Kilwein [1574; rpt. Menston: Scolar Press, 1970] 100).

66. See the discussion of the *Prolusions* in my prose section.

67. For an excellent philological comment on aspects of multilingualism and intertextuality in Milton's poetry, see especially John K. Hale, *Milton's Languages: The Impact of Multilingualism on Style* (Cambridge: CUP, 1997).

68. Qtd. in A.S.P. Woodhouse and Douglas Bush, *The Minor English Poems: A Variorum Commentary on the Poems of John Milton II* (New York: Columbia UP, 1972) 137.

69. See Gale H. Carrithers and James D. Hardy, *Milton and the Hermeneutic Journey* (Baton Rouge: Louisiana UP, 1994) 197, and Cedric C. Brown, *John Milton* 7.

70. See Woodhouse and Bush, *The Minor English Poems* 138.

71. Parker, *Milton: A Biography* I: 46.

72. In her study *Before and After the Fall*, Swaim also points out that Milton here still hopes for a return to the "prelapsarian condition" which is symbolized by music and language.

73. Carey in *CSP* 148 suggests 1632 as the year of its composition.

74. See Woodhouse and Bush, *The Minor English Poems* 401 and Carey in *CSP* 290.

75. Maryann Cale McGuire, *Milton's Puritan Masque* (Athens: U of Georgia P, 1983) 118.

76. Unfortunately, this aspect is given almost no room in Woodhouse and Bush's *Variorum* volume. David Gay, however, points to "the specific concern for language in the masque tradition" ("'Rapt Spirits': 2 Corinthians 12.2-5 and the Language of Milton's *Comus*," *Milton Quarterly* 29 [1995]: 78), and John Steadman in *The Hill and the Labyrinth: Discourse and Certitude in Milton and His Near-Contemporaries* (Berkeley: U of California P, 1984) sees the "sensual rhetorician" Comus as the prototype of Belial in *Paradise Lost*, "the most dissolute but also the most polished orator in Milton's Hell" (55).

77. According to Gay ("'Rapt Spirits'" 77), "Milton bases his treatment of language in *Comus* rather broadly on Paul's struggle against false apostles who led the Corinthians astray on matters of doctrine and morality (2 Cor. 11.5-15)."

78. Stephen Orgel, *The Jonsonian Masque* (Cambridge, MA: Harvard UP, 1965) 152.

79. Grose, *Milton's Epic Process* 87.

80. See Frye, *Words With Power*.

81. McGuire 117.

82. Angus Fletcher, *The Transcendental Masque: An Essay on Milton's* Comus (Ithaca: Cornell UP, 1971) 21.

83. See Stanley Fish, *How Milton Works* (Cambridge: Harvard UP, 2001) *passim.* Fish's argument contradicts McGuire's interpretation according to which Milton "posited that stasis is impossible in the fallen world, that individual and collective organisms must either grow spiritually or die" (McGuire 76).

84. Joseph Wittreich, *Interpreting* Samson Agonistes (Princeton: Princeton UP, 1986) 297.

85. Heather Asals, "Rhetoric Agonistic in *Samson Agonistes*," *Milton Quarterly* 11 (1977): 1, 2.

86. Entzminger, *Divine Word* 145.

87. Entzminger, *Divine Word* 146.

88. Entzminger, *Divine Word* 156. One may here construct certain parallels between the fates of Samson and Milton himself that would in fact speak in favour of seeing *Samson Agonistes* as a late work of Milton's and explain parallels to the relatively sober style of the last parts of *Paradise Lost* and especially *Paradise Regained.* Such an interpretation of the style of *Samson Agonistes* would contradict Carey's view of it as a product of the revolutionary years 1647-53 (*CSP* 328) and speak in favour of the "venerable tradition" (Hughes, *CPMP* 531) of seeing it as a late work in which we can identify Milton with the blind suffering hero.

89. Marcia Landy, "Language and the Seal of Silence in *Samson Agonistes*," *Milton Studies* 2 (1970): 176.

90. Landy 176.

91. Entzminger, *Divine Word* 145. Cf. Henry McDonald, "A Long Day's Dying: Tragic Ambiguity in *Samson Agonistes*," *Milton Studies* 27 (1991): "For Samson, . . . language, or what he calls 'the popular noise,' is something to make oneself deaf to, just as visual images have disappeared as a result of his blindness" (278).

92. Entzminger, *Divine Word* 146.

93. Fish does not share the "regenerative" interpretation of *Samson Agonistes* in his "Spectacle and Evidence in *Samson Agonistes*," *Critical Inquiry* 15.3 (1989): 585.

94. Robert Entzminger, "*Samson Agonistes* and the Recovery of Metaphor," *SEL* 22 (1982): 141, 156.

95. See for example Thomas Ellwood's praise of "Lofty Fancy, deep Conceit, / Style concise and Language great" in his "Epitaph on Milton (1675)," *Milton: The Critical Heritage*, ed. John T. Shawcross (London: Routledge, 1970) 87.

96. Charles Gildon, "Vindication of *Paradise Lost* (1694)," *Milton: The Critical Heritage*, ed. John T. Shawcross 107.

97. Joseph Addison, *Notes Upon the Twelve Books of* Paradise Lost (1712), *Milton: The Critical Heritage*, ed. John T. Shawcross 161.

98. Jonathan Richardson, "Explanatory Notes and Remarks on Milton's *Paradise Lost* (1734)," *Milton:* Paradise Lost, eds. A.E. Dyson and Julian Lovelock (Houndmills, Basingstoke: Macmillan, 1973) 40.

99. Quoted in Lalia Phipps Boone, "The Language of Book VI, *Paradise Lost*," *SAMLA*

Studies in Milton: Essays on John Milton and His Works, ed. J. Max Patrick (Gainesville: U of Florida P, 1953) 114-15.

100. Samuel Johnson, "Milton (1779)," *Samuel Johnson*, ed. Donald Greene (Oxford: OUP, 1984) 711, 714-15.

101. Lalia Phipps Boone, "The Language of Book VI" 127. See Fowler in *PL* 15. But cf. Hale, *Milton's Languages* 105-07.

102. Frank Kermode, *The Living Milton* ix.

103. See James Whaler, "The Miltonic Simile," *PMLA* 46 (1931): 1034.

104. Kingsley Widmer, "The Iconography of Renunciation: The Miltonic Simile," *ELH* 25 (1958): 259.

105. T.S. Eliot, "The Metaphysical Poets (1921)," *Selected Essays* (London: Faber, 1951) 281-291.

106. Terry Eagleton, "The God that Failed," *Re-membering Milton: Essays on the Texts and Traditions*, eds. Mary Nyquist and Margaret W. Ferguson (New York: Methuen, 1987) 347. Geoffrey Hartman, however, rather thinks that Milton's brilliant similes are the effect of a Miltonic counterplot expressing "God's omnipotent knowledge that the creation will out-live death and sin" ("Milton's Counterplot," *Milton: Modern Essays in Criticism*, ed. Arthur Barker [New York: OUP, 1965] 388).

107. See for example Sherry, "Speech in *Paradise Lost*" 247-249.

108. J.B. Broadbent, "Milton's 'Mortal Voice' and his 'Omnific Word,'" *Approaches to Paradise Lost: The York Tercentenary Lectures*, ed. C.A. Patrides (London: Edward Arnold, 1968) 104.

109. Herman Rapaport, *Milton and the Postmodern* (Lincoln: U of Nebraska P, 1983) 12. Other important works on this topic from the 1980s and 90s are Entzminger, *Divine Word*; Leonard Mustazza, *"Such Prompt Eloquence": Language as Agency and Character in Milton's Epics* (Lewisburg: Bucknell; London: Associated UPs, 1988); and Leonard, *Naming in Paradise*.

110. Stevie Davies, *Milton* 25. Ronald W. Cooley in "Reformed Eloquence: Inability, Questioning, and Correction in *Paradise Lost*," *University of Toronto Quarterly* 62.2 (1993) identifies "reformed eloquence" as Milton's linguistic ideal: "a rhetoric clearly dependent on classical and humanist conventions, but stripped of the duplicity characteristic of Satan's dis-course" (232), whereas Regina M. Schwartz, in *Remembering and Repeating: On Milton's Theology and Poetics* (1988; Chicago: U of Chicago P, 1993), sees Milton as "the poet and philosopher who labored over the power and meaning of language, regarding it as both a snare and our means of redemption" (xi). Alvin Snider writes that *Paradise Lost* "represents truth as the reanimation of a suppressed but nevertheless retrievable origin, even while it casts the quest for certain origins and transparent language into doubt" (*Origin and Authority* 14).

111. Esterhammer, *Creating States* 66.

112. Christopher Ricks, *Milton's Grand Style* (Oxford: Clarendon, 1963) 70.

113. Entzminger, *Divine Word* 145. Cf. Fish, *How Milton Works*.

114. Fish, *Surprised by Sin* 128.

115. Snider, *Origin and Authority* 136.

116. Haskin, *Milton's Burden of Interpretation* 224.

117. Haskin 224.

118. Carrithers and Hardy, *Milton and the Hermeneutic Journey* 2.

119. See Harold Toliver, "Symbol-Making and the Labors of Milton's Eden," *Texas Studies in Literature and Language* 18 (1976): 449. See also André Verbart, *Fellowship in Paradise Lost: Vergil, Milton, Wordsworth* (Amsterdam: Rodopi, 1995). Even though his analyses of Milton's ambiguous use of language are convincing, Verbart goes a bit far in denying that Milton has a coherent theology.

120. Dennis Danielson, *Milton's Good God: A Study in Literary Theodicy* (Cambridge: CUP, 1982) 164.

121. John Owen, *A Display of Arminianisme* [London, 1643], qtd. in Danielson, *Milton's Good God* 165.

122. See George Musacchio, *Milton's Adam and Eve: Fallible Perfection* (New York: Lang, 1991). Entzminger denies, too, that Milton's Adam and Eva ever lived "in the Paradise of denotative language seventeenth-century linguists hoped to regain" (*Divine Word* 72).

123. See Herbert Marks, "The Blotted Book," *Re-membering Milton*, eds. Nyquist and Ferguson 214: "Milton never shared . . . the philological optimism of the adamic speculators."

124. See G.K. Hunter, *Paradise Lost* (London: Allen & Unwin, 1980) 143: "he allows that there is a connection, however broken-up and circuitous." Victoria Silver would, however, probably see this as a case of accommodation establishing "the most facile correspondence between creator and creature in the poem," which can "dangerously expect real continuities where there can at best be only artificial contiguity of ideas" and "ostensible equality" (*Imperfect Sense* 49, 49-50, 221).

125. See Grose, *Milton's Epic Process* 12 and Schwartz, *Remembering and Repeating* 1. On the unreliability of Milton's narrative voices, especially Raphael, but even the Father, see Peter C. Herman, *Destabilizing Milton* 51-57, 125.

126. Although these further developments would not necessarily have been authorized by Saussure, his name is meant to stand for all contemporary models based on his basic ideas regarding a dyadic structure of the linguistic sign.

127. For the distinction of *plot* and *story,* see E.M. Forster, *Aspects of the Novel* (1927; Harmondsworth: Penguin, 1976) 87.

128. See Berry, "Melodramatic Faking in the Narrator's Voice, *Paradise Lost,*" *Milton Quarterly* 10 (1976): 1.

129. Anne Ferry, *Milton's Epic Voice: The Narrator in* Paradise Lost, 2nd ed. (Chicago: U of Chicago P, 1983) 16.

130. For the term "restricted voice," see Rodney Delasanta, *The Epic Voice* (The Hague: Mouton, 1967) 82.

131. At least some critics assume that Adam had been endowed with the knowledge necessary for his existence on earth without having to undergo a process of education. See Peter A. Fiore, *Milton and Augustine: Patterns of Augustinian Thought in* Paradise Lost (University Park: Pennsylvania State UP, 1981) 26 and C.S. Lewis, *A Preface to* Paradise Lost (1942; London: OUP, 1960). But cf. Danielson, *Milton's Good God* 178.

132. Steven Blakemore, "Language and Logos in *Paradise Lost,*" *Southern Humanities Review* 20 (1986): 336.

133. Valerie Carnes, "Time and Language in Milton's *Paradise Lost*," *ELH* 37 (1970): 520.

134. See John Lyons, *Linguistic Semantics* (Cambridge: CUP, 1995) 26: "Not only do most English words have more than one form. They may also have more than one meaning; and in this respect English is typical of all natural languages."

135. See Lyons, *Linguistic Semantics* 79.

136. Carrithers and Hardy, *Milton and the Hermeneutic Journey* 26.

137. Carnes, "Time and Language in Milton's *Paradise Lost*" 521.

138. Carrithers and Hardy 134, 136.

139. Snider's position is even more radical, as he claims that "we have little reason to think that the Edenic language corresponds perfectly and uniquely to truth, signifying things in their essences" and that it is "a fabrication, a 'man-made' entity, although brought into being with divine assistance" (*Origin and Authority*, 131).

140. Robert L. Entzminger, "Epistemology and the Tutelary Word in *Paradise Lost*," *Milton Studies* 10 (1977): 104.

141. Michael Lieb, "'Holy Name': A Reading of *Paradise Lost*," *Harvard Theological Review* 67 (1974): 322.

142. Lieb, "'Holy Name'" 322.

143. Entzminger, *Divine Word* 31.

144. See Winfried Nöth, *Handbook of Semiotics* (Bloomington: Indiana UP, 1990) 56-63.

145. See Nöth, "Arbitrariness and Motivation: The Language Sign," *Handbook of Semiotics* 240-46.

146. For earlier uses of Saussurean theories in Milton studies see Shullenberger, "Linguistic and Poetic Theory in Milton's *De Doctrina Christiana*" and Esterhammer, *Creating States*.

147. Mustazza, *"Such Prompt Eloquence"* 71.

148. Haskin claims that "although Adam is given the prerogative of naming, the names that he confers are not merely arbitrary but correspond to some pre-existing language" (*Milton's Burden of Interpretation* 192).

149. Christopher, *Milton and the Science of the Saints* 101.

150. Esterhammer, *Creating States* 111.

151. See Trabant, *Elemente der Semiotik* 41.

152. The metalinguistic communication about the act of naming occupies yet another level (*PL* VIII.343-344).

153. Harada, "Self and Language in the Fall" 222.

154. See Edward Le Comte, *A Dictionary of Puns in Milton's English Poetry* (New York: Columbia UP, 1981) 186, who quotes these lines as an example of Milton's ambiguous use of the preposition *to*. In his edition of *Paradise Lost, John Milton: Paradise Lost—Samson Agonistes—Lycidas* (New York: New American Library, 1981), Le Comte remarks: "The normal prose order would be: 'And justify to men the ways of God.'" (37). See also the parallel to Raphael's formulation "the ways of God with man" (*PL* VIII.226).

155. R.A. Shoaf, Milton, *Poet of Duality: A Study of Semiosis in the Poetry and Prose* (New Haven: Yale UP, 1985) 12. Bryson even states in *The Tyranny of Heaven* that "Milton

is appropriating and reversing the process through which Man is reconciled to God. Rather than reconciling Man to God, Milton is reconciling God to Man" (120).

156. Davies, *Milton* 102.

157. Referring to Milton's use of allegory in the description of Satan, Sin and Death, Victoria Kahn suggests in *Machiavellian Rhetoric: From the Counter-Reformation to Milton* (Princeton: Princeton UP, 1994) "that the structures of linguistic difference and indifference that we observed in the Sin and Death episode—the emphasis on the mediation of signs and the varied uses of rhetorical figures—are constitutive of prelapsarian experience as well" (225).

158. Mustazza, *"Such Prompt Eloquence"* 15.

159. Denis Saurat, *Milton: Man and Thinker* (1925; New York: AMS Press, 1975) 231.

160. E.M.W. Tillyard, *Milton* (Harmondsworth: Penguin, 1968) 253.

161. For another interpretation of God's language as ambiguous, see Carnes, "Time and Language in Milton's *Paradise Lost*" 525.

162. David Aers and Bob Hodge, "'Rational Burning': Milton on Sex and Marriage," *Literature, Language and Society in England 1580-1680*, eds. David Aers, Bob Hodge and Gunther Kress (Dublin: Gill and Macmillan; Totowa: Barnes & Noble, 1981) 145.

163. One may well wonder if Adam's use of double negatives is here influenced by the many cases of litotes in the style of his heavenly visitor Raphael.

164. Entzminger also interprets the dialogue between God and Adam as part of God's pedagogical strategy ("Epistemology and the Tutelary Word in *Paradise Lost*" 96). Christopher, too, reads this scene as "a hermeneutic test for Adam" (*Milton and the Science of the Saints* 113).

165. Bryson, *The Tyranny of Heaven* 70, 117.

166. John E. Parish, "Milton and an Anthropomorphic God," *Studies in Philology* 56 (1959): 624. For Hugh MacCallum, in *Milton and the Sons of God: The Divine Image in Milton's Epic Poetry* (Toronto: UTP, 1986), this scene is an example of "education by disputation with God" (100).

167. Bryson, *The Tyranny of Heaven* 125.

168. Entzminger, *Divine Word* 43.

169. Mary Nyquist, "Reading the Fall: Discourse in Drama in *Paradise Lost*," *English Literary Renaissance* 14 (1984): 202.

170. Fowler mentions A.J.A. Waldock and Dennis H. Burden. See Burden, *The Logical Epic: A Study of the Argument of* Paradise Lost (London: Routledge, 1967) 79 and William B. Hunter, Jr., "Eve's Demonic Dream," *ELH* 13 (1946): 255.

171. See Fowler in his edition and Thomas H. Blackburn, "'Uncloistered Virtue': Adam and Eve in Milton's Paradise," *Milton Studies* 3 (1971): 119, 124.

172. David Loewenstein, *Milton:* Paradise Lost (Cambridge: CUP, 1993) xv.

173. Wayne A. Rebhorn, "The Humanist Tradition and Milton's Satan: The Conservative as Revolutionary," *SEL* 13 (1973): 93.

174. In *Origin and Originality in Renaissance Literature: Versions of the Source* (New Haven: Yale UP, 1983), David Quint reads the exaltation as "God's self-authorizing fiction, a piece of political propaganda which, like the encomiastic Renaissance court spectacle, attempts to give a mask of legitimacy to the present regime" so that "Satan concludes that sig-

nification is an autonomous system controlled arbitrarily by the powers that be, and ... aspires to that power himself: it is his word against the Word of God" (208).

175. See Fish, *Self-Consuming Artifacts*, and Patterson's remark quoted in my introduction.

176. Cf. the title of Danielson's study, *Milton's Good God*.

177. Margaret Olofson Thickstun, *Milton's* Paradise Lost: *Moral Education* (New York: Palgrave Macmillan, 2007) 105.

178. Eckhard Lobsien calls this situation the „Raphael-Problem" in *Wörtlichkeit und Wiederholung: Phänomenologie poetischer Sprache* (Munich: Fink, 1995) 114. Cf., however, Ira Clark, "A Problem of Knowing Paradise in *Paradise Lost*," *Milton Studies* 27 (1991): 183.

179. Lee A. Jacobus, *Sudden Apprehension: Aspects of Knowledge in* Paradise Lost (The Hague: Mouton, 1976) 48.

180. See John S. Lawry, *The Shadow of Heaven: Matter and Stance in Milton's Poetry* (Ithaca: Cornell UP, 1968) 194.

181. See John R. Knott, Jr., "The Visit of Raphael: *Paradise Lost*, Book V," *Philological Quarterly* 47 (1968): 38.

182. Michael Allen, "Divine Instruction: *Of Education* and the Pedagogy of Raphael, Michael, and the Father," *Milton Quarterly* 26 (1992): 115.

183. See Kerrigan, *The Sacred Complex* 236. Recent critics such as Silver would of course disagree.

184. William G. Madsen, "Earth the Shadow of Heaven: Typological Symbolism in *Paradise Lost*," *Milton: Modern Essays in Criticism*, ed. Arthur Barker 246. See also Walter Clyde Curry, *Milton's Ontology, Cosmogony and Physics* (Lexington: U of Kentucky P, 1957) 160 and Arthur E. Barker, "'Paradise Lost': The Relevance of Regeneration," Paradise Lost: *A Tercentenary Tribute*, ed. Balachandra Rajan (Toronto: UTP, 1967) 62.

185. Stephen Fallon, *Milton among the Philosophers: Poetry and Materialism in Seventeenth-Century England* (Ithaca: Cornell UP, 199) 11. See also Kermode, "Adam UnParadised," *The Living Milton* 104-05, William B. Hunter, "Milton's Materialistic Life Principle," *Journal of English and Germanic Philology* 45 (1946): 68-76, Harold Toliver, "Complicity of Voice in *Paradise Lost*," *Modern Language Quarterly* 25 (1964): 153-70, and John Reichert, *Milton's Wisdom: Nature and Scripture in* Paradise Lost (Ann Arbor: U of Michigan P, 1992) 125.—The counterpart of this chain of being in the field of language would be a linguistic development within *Paradise Lost* from a monist prelapsarian language towards a dualist postlapsarian language: a *great chain of language*. See Blakemore, "Language and Logos in *Paradise Lost*" 335.

186. The same is true for Roland Hagenbüchle's idea presented in *Sündenfall und Wahlfreiheit in Miltons* Paradise Lost of a golden chain of reason through which the "qualitative abyss" between man and God is bridged and turned into a gradual one (135).

187. Thickstun 54.

188. See George Williamson, "The Education of Adam," *Modern Philology* 61 (1963): 99.

189. Cf. Mary Ann Radzinowicz, "'Man as a Probationer of Immortality': *Paradise Lost* XI-XII," *Approaches to* Paradise Lost: *The York Tercentenary Lectures*, ed. C.A. Patrides

(London: Edward Arnold, 1968) 34.

190. Don Cameron Allen, *The Harmonious Vision: Studies in Milton's Poetry*, enlarged ed. (Baltimore: Johns Hopkins UP, 1970) xii. Raphael might have justified his decision to use accommodation by referring to Milton's discussion of *similitude* in chapter 21 of the *Art of Logic*, where the latter writes that "a high fictitious similarity" may have the same power of conviction as a factual one (*CP* VIII: 287).

191. Thomas F. Merrill, "Miltonic God-Talk: The Creation in *Paradise Lost*," *Language and Style* 16 (1983): 303. See also Merrill, *Epic God-Talk* 68.

192. John S. Diekhoff, *Milton's* Paradise Lost: *A Commentary on the Argument* (1946; New York: Humanities Press, 1963) 10; see also Lawrence Babb, *The Moral Cosmos of* Paradise Lost (East Lansing: Michigan State UP, 1970) 6.

193. See Leopold Damrosch, *God's Plot and Man's Stories: Studies in the Fictional Imagination from Milton to Fielding* (Chicago: U of Chicago P, 1985) 75, 76.

194. See Lobsien, *Wörtlichkeit und Wiederholung* 115.

195. See C.A. Patrides, "*Paradise Lost* and the Theory of Accommodation," *Texas Studies in Literature and Language* 5 (1963): 60. Cf. Ira Clark, "A Problem of Knowing" 189.

196. The positive view is Brown's in *John Milton* 158. The more sceptical view is held by Michael Allen, "Divine Instruction" 114.

197. Another arbitrary sign that is almost indecipherable is that of the scales at the end of Book IV. Its meaning is even impenetrable for the angels so that Satan, who had just been caught by Ithuriel, can profit from this moment of confusion and flee.

198. See Robert Kellogg: "Except for the forbidden tree itself, everything in Eden was what it appeared to be. Sign and signified were the same. Except for the tree, the things that looked good and tasted good and felt good *were* good" ("The Harmony of Time in *Paradise Lost*," *Oral Tradition* 2.1 [1987]: 261). One has to take into account, however, that Kellogg's use of the word *sign* is different from Milton's in lines 428-29.

199. Following a Saussurean line of interpretation, there are now two linguistic signs relating to one and the same referent. One might be tempted to interpret the deviation from a clear one-to-one relationship in the case of "tree of knowledge" / apple tree as one of the first cases of an ambiguous sign which is still authorized (and even created) by God. According to Milton's classification in his *Logic*, this would probably be an "inartificial argument" relying on divine authority, such as the sacraments. The *Doctrina*, however, seems to speak against such an interpretation: Whereas sacraments are created to be used (*ad usum*), "The tree of the knowledge of good and evil was not a sacrament, as is commonly thought, for sacraments are meant to be used, not abstained from; but it was a kind of pledge or memorial of obedience" (*CP* VI: 352). See also Blackburn, "'Uncloister'd Virtue'" 125. Another interesting point is made by Clark, who argues that "naming the tree *of knowledge of good and evil* appears in warnings to and discussions by Adam and Eve as an accommodation for our fallen understanding; before the fall the tree went nameless" (Clark, "A Problem of Knowing" 201). As Irene Samuel points out in "Milton on Learning and Wisdom," *PMLA* 64 (1949), the term *tree of the knowledge of good and evil* is the "most fatal *double entendre* in literature" as it refers to "the experience of evil, as Adam too late recognizes (IX, 1071-73), and not the understanding of good and evil that Adam and Eve enjoyed before the fall" (714).

200. As in Milton's predecessor Du Bartas (at least in Joshua Sylvester's English translation), the apple changes from a mere fruit into a "sign of obedience." In the first part of Du Bartas' *Seconde Semaine*, the tree's identity as a "sacred signe" becomes obvious (qtd. in Watson Kirkconnell, *The Celestial Cycle: The Theme of Paradise Lost in World Literature with Translations of the Major Analogues* [1952; New York: Gordian Press, 1967] 64). Shoaf suggests an interpretation relying on the Saussurean principle of *différence* by creating a parallel between the Fall and the creation of a sign system. The dichotomy *sin/sign* of course invites deconstructionist word-play: "The non-differentiation from which signs emerge is a pretext invented by Sin (and Satan), and hence Milton's coupling of *Sin* and *sign* in the same breath" (*Milton, Poet of Duality* 27). This fascinating explanation is, however, not fully convincing as I think Shoaf is wrong in claiming that all signs are "post-sin" (28): "Milton plots the fall into language on the same graph as the fall into sin and finds the curve for much of the way identical" (xii). I would argue that the signs in *Paradise Lost* already exist before the Fall, even signs the meaning of which is not clear. See for example Adam and Eve's discussion of the meaning of the word *death* after God has threatened them with death if they eat the fruit of the tree of knowledge (*PL* IV.425-427).

201. Umberto Eco, "On the Possibility of Generating Aesthetic Messages in an Edenic Language," *The Role of the Reader: Explorations in the Semiotics of Texts* (Bloomington: Indiana UP, 1979) 94.

202. Eco, "On the Possibility" 95.

203. Eco, "On the Possibility" 95, 103. As I will show, it is also possible to interpret the Father's action as a pedagogical strategy rather than a mistake.

204. Raphael's theory of accommodation can also be interpreted differently. For example, Michael Murrin argues in "The Language of Milton's Heaven," *The Allegorical Epic: Essays in Its Rise and Decline* (Chicago: U of Chicago P, 1980) that Milton used a special language derived from the Bible in order to dissuade the reader from "literalist readings," in other words from equating heavenly signs and earthly referents (154).

205. Mustazza, *"Such Prompt Eloquence"* 81.

206. According to Don Cameron Allen: "A little tradition and some bad Hebrew stood behind the remark" ("Milton and the Name of Eve," *Modern Language Notes* 74 [1959]: 682-83). Riggs points out the contrast between "this harsh repudiation of Eve" and Adam's "prelapsarian naming of the animals" ("The Temptation of Milton's Eve" 365).

207. Marc D. Cyr, "The Archangel Raphael: Narrative Authority in Milton's War in Heaven," *The Journal of Narrative Technique* 17.3 (1987): 309.

208. See Murrin, "The Language of Milton's Heaven" 161, and Delasanta, *The Epic Voice* 83.

209. See Grossman, *"Authors to Themselves"* 95.

210. Barbara Lewalski, Paradise Lost *and the Rhetoric of Literary Forms* (Princeton: Princeton UP, 1985) 39.

211. Ricks claims, however, that "Milton's process of speech is so compact that it can even reflect divine immediacy" (*Milton's Grand Style* 65). Grose argues that one has to distinguish between Raphael's and Milton's own "process of speech" "through which alone we can 'repair the ruins of our first parents'" (*Milton's Epic Process* 18).

212. According to William Myers, there is "abundant evidence that Milton himself was

aware of *différance* (without, of course, knowing the word) and that he understood presence and so the classical subject in its light" ("The Spirit of *Différance*," *John Milton*, ed. Annabel Patterson 106; see also Myers, *Milton and Free Will: An Essay in Criticism and Philosophy* [London: Croom Helm, 1987]).

213. Walter R. Davis, "The Languages of Accommodation and the Styles of *Paradise Lost*," *Milton Studies* 18 (1983): 105. See also Entzminger, *Divine Word* 18-19.

214. See William J. Kennedy, *Rhetorical Norms in Renaissance Literature* (New Haven: Yale UP, 1978) 175.

215. See John Lyons, *Semantics* (Cambridge: CUP, 1977), vol. 1: 235.

216. Swaim, *Before and After the Fall* 54.

217. Even though she interprets rhetoric and dialectics as a consequence of the greater flexibility of postlapsarian language, Isabel Gamble MacCaffrey insists that "Stylistically, Milton's vision of a single interconnected universe meant that, even when he used metaphor and simile, the vehicle could almost without warning shift and become the tenor" (Paradise Lost *as "Myth"* 108). This may answer Riggs who wonders whether "Milton's powerful sense of fallen deficiency extend[ed] to his own linguistic means" ("The Temptation of Milton's Eve: 'Words, Impregn'd / With Reason'" 365). While Riggs criticizes Milton's "aggressive imposition of 'fallen' difficulties (. . .) onto the conditions of pre-lapsarian purity" (367), I would rather blame this on the archangel. Such a view would also unexpectedly back up Christopher's statement that "Milton comes no nearer to explaining the Fall than his predecessors did, but he gives it a literary rather than a metaphysical cast: in *Paradise Lost* God's word *is* vocal" and that "Milton . . . treats the primal sin as a literary lapse, a misconstruction of a divine text" (*Milton and the Science of the Saints* 90).

218. See Delasanta in *The Epic Voice*: "Milton's theory of restricted angelic knowledge . . . should logically and artistically preclude the possibility of his merely giving over to Raphael the omniscience of his own voice" (84). Cf. Fowler's argument that only God and the Messiah are always aware of all the implications of their actions: "Only they participate in the dramatic ironies" (*PL* 36). That angels, even archangels, have only limited knowledge is also stated in *De Doctrina Christiana* (*CP* VI: 347-48). See also Mildred Gutkin, "'Sufficient to Have Stood': The Mimesis of Free Will in *Paradise Lost*," *English Studies in Canada* 10.1 (1984): 11-21.

219. See Stevie Davies, *Milton* 100. Sauer, however, sees Raphael's voice as authoritative (*Barbarous Dissonance* 63).

220. Schwartz, *Remembering and Repeating* 42.

221. Guillory, *Poetic Authority: Spenser, Milton, and Literary History* 158.

222. Arnold Stein, "Milton's War in Heaven: An Extended Metaphor," *ELH* 18 (1951): 201.

223. For G.K. Hunter, too, Raphael is "unwilling to allow any large gap to appear between the corporeal forms it presents and the actual truth it conveys" (*Paradise Lost* 29). For MacCallum, Milton's unorthodox version of the begetting of the Son in Book V establishes "the significance of angelic experience as analogue to that of man" (*Milton and the Sons of God* 80). See Davis, "The Languages of Accommodation" 112, and Norbrook, *Writing the English Republic* 477-78.

224. See also Mustazza, *"Such Prompt Eloquence"* 14.

225. Grossman, *"Authors to Themselves"* 187.

226. For parallels to the views of Origen, see Harry F. Robins, *If This Be Heresy: A Study of Milton and Origen* (Urbana: U of Illinois P, 1963) 39.

227. Robert H. West, *Milton and the Angels* (Athens: U of Georgia P, 1955) 114. See also Thomas N. Corns, *Regaining* Paradise Lost (London: Longman, 1994) 31, Tillyard, *Milton* 232, and Curry, *Milton's Ontology, Cosmogony and Physics* 15.

228. R.D. Bedford, "Milton and Philosophy," *Milton Quarterly* 26 (1992): 53. But cf. William B. Hunter, Jr., "Eve's Demonic Dream" 257 and Silver, *Imperfect Sense,* who very much insists on the ontological difference between creator and creature.

229. For examples of seventeenth-century scholars seeing angels as material and not only spiritual beings, see West, *Milton and the Angels* 21. Blakemore, in "Language and Logos in *Paradise Lost*," sees "the Word's naming of the universe" as an "onomastic model for Adam's Edenic naming and, by extension, all appropriate future naming, albeit fallen": "Beginning with the 'word' and the premise that names are a primary source of power and being, Milton suggests that as the angels were created by the Word, their essence is profoundly linguistic" (325). Consequently, Blakemore interprets the fallen angels' loss of their original names as "simultaneously a fall from language and being" and concludes: "Because Satan and his followers rebel against God's Word, their fall is significantly linguistic" (325). Blakemore refers to Satan's "first linguistic fall" as "a semantic revolution that inverts the prelapsarian meaning of words" (331).

230. See, for example, Rumrich, *Milton Unbound* 17. In the late 1940s, C.S. Lewis had criticized in his *Preface to* Paradise Lost (70) that Milton had "made the unfallen already so voluptuous and kept the fallen still so poetical that the contrast is not so sharp as it ought to have been." Coming from a somewhat different perspective, Frye writes that "the sense of alienation traditionally attached to the fall may be latent in the original creation too" (*The Great Code: The Bible and Literature* [1981; Toronto: Academic Press, 1983] 111). Approaching the epic from a "heretical" point of view, Hill claims that "the differences between angels and men, soul and body, spirit and matter, are of degree, not of kind. This enables Milton to suggest in *Paradise Lost* that heaven may be more like earth than we assume, and so opens up a world of allegory" (*Milton and the English Revolution* 331). See also Diane Kelsey McColley, *Milton's Eve* (Urbana: U of Illinois P, 1983) 103 and MacCallum, *Milton and the Sons of God* 125. Schwartz concludes from the fact that Raphael compares "great things with small" that "they are obviously comparable" (*Remembering and Repeating* 27). For a different point of view, see Carrithers and Hardy who insist on an "essential difference in being and consciousness between levels of being" so that "applied to God, perfectly useful words lose their sharp bite of definition, become slippery, vague, their meaning blunted" (*Milton and the Hermeneutic Journey* 52).

231. Russell E. Smith, Jr., "Adam's Fall," *ELH* 35 (1968): 533.

232. For Arthur Lovejoy, Raphael's "lesson in usefulness" (Schwartz) represents "an obscurantist utilitarianism hostile to all disinterested intellectual curiosity and to all inquiry into unsolved problems about the physical world" (Lovejoy, "Milton's Dialogue on Astronomy," *Reason and the Imagination,* ed. J.A. Mazzeo [New York: Columbia UP, 1962] 142, qtd. in Schwartz, *Remembering and Repeating* 44). If we see Raphael as a reliable representative of the Father, criticism of Raphael's position will also affect our view of Milton.

Svendsen claims that Milton was not interested in the contradictions of recent cosmological theories and that "here Raphael would seem his spokesman, particularly since Milton did not attempt a system of natural philosophy like his system of divinity" (*Milton and Science* 5). Entzminger, however, sees Raphael's appeal to be "lowly wise" as Milton's support of an "empirical, Baconian method of inquiry," while Adam stands for a "speculative, Cartesian one" (*Divine Word* 37). See also Michael Bryson's statement that "Such advice does not represent any recognizable Miltonic epistemology" (*The Tyranny of Heaven* 59-60).

233. Fowler remarks that critics interpret lines such as "But what created mind can comprehend / Their number, or the wisdom infinite / That brought them forth" (*PL* III.705-07) as evidence "that God keeps some knowledge secret even from the angels" (*PL* 187). For the Son, of course, even the position of a fighting angel means a sort of humiliation. See Albert C. Labriola, "'Thy Humiliation Shall Exalt': The Christology of *Paradise Lost*," *Milton Studies* 15 (1981) 36.

234. See Entzminger, *Divine Word* 47, Mary Nyquist, "The Father's Word/Satan's Wrath," *PMLA* 100 (1985): 190, and Christopher, *Milton and the Science of the Saints* 95.

235. Perhaps Raphael rather than his creator Milton should be blamed for God' words in VI.684-703 which Ricks finds so disappointing in *Milton's Grand Style* 19.

236. Barbara Kiefer Lewalski points out that "We ought to recall here that at the outset of Adam's career in the Garden God was similarly delighted when Adam urged him down on the question of a mate" ("Innocence and Experience in Milton's Eden," *New Essays on Paradise Lost*, ed. Thomas Kranidas [Berkeley: U of California P, 1971] 116).

237. Michael Allen, "Divine Instruction" 115.

238. Rumrich, *Milton Unbound* 17.

239. Although E.M.W. Tillyard claims that this "process of replenishment" is prohibited by the Fall—"that process is not through a fall and a redemption but through a ripening of unfallen powers" (*Studies in Milton* [1951; London: Chatto & Windus, 1960] 67)—this does not necessarily have to be so, especially since God had foreknowledge of the Fall.

240. This interpretation only holds, of course, if we do not grant the narrative voice in *Paradise Lost* access to a special type of *metadialogue* that would be comparable to Thomas F. Merrill's *God-talk* (see Carrithers and Hardy 129, cf. Merrill, *Epic God-Talk*).

241. MacCallum, *Milton and the Sons of God* 106. See Bryson, *The Tyranny of Heaven* 34.

242. Berry, "Melodramatic Faking in the Narrator's Voice, *Paradise Lost*," calls this situation "one of the most baffling passages in the entire poem" (2). See Rumrich, *Milton Unbound* 130.

243. Irene Samuel, "The Dialogue in Heaven: A Reconsideration of *Paradise Lost*, III.1-417," *Milton: Modern Essays in Criticism*, ed. Arthur E. Barker 235.

244. See Verbart, *Fellowship in Paradise Lost: Vergil, Milton, Wordsworth* 98.

245. On irony and hypocrisy, see Grossman, *"Authors to Themselves"* 169; on deconstruction, see Thomas L. Martin, "On the Margin of God: Deconstruction and the Language of Satan in *Paradise Lost*," *Milton Quarterly* 29 (1995): 41-47. Mustazza calls Satan the "father of persuasive political rhetoric" (*"Such Prompt Eloquence"* 16).

246. As Swaim (*Before and After the Fall* 53) points out, among the fallen angels the originally motivated connection between names and character traits has long become com-

pletely arbitrary.

247. Mustazza, *"Such Prompt Eloquence"* 21. On the use of the words *ambiguous* and *debate*, see S.G. Hornsby, Jr., "'Ambiguous Words': Debate in *Paradise Lost*," *Milton Quarterly* 14 (1980): 60-62.

248. Entzminger, *Divine Word* 46. For Nyquist, Satan here plays "the role Protestant logocentrism has assigned him, the role of the adversary devoted both to detaching the Word from its transcendental origin and to death" ("The Father's Word/Satan's Wrath" 195).

249. Guillory (*Poetic Authority* 149) compares "Satan's shape-changing" to a trope and argues that "Milton sees no need to distinguish between the two so long as Ithuriel's spear happens to be around." In his phenomenological reading, Lobsien (*Wörtlichkeit und Wiederholung* 125) claims Satan's manipulative use of the words *heaven* and *hell* in Book IV.73-78 empties them of any meaning so that they become mere variables on a scale of personal evaluations.

250. Christopher, *Milton and the Science of the Saints* 59.

251. This is at least how one would argue from a position that sees the Father in a positive light, but of course there have been more critical attitudes towards him, before and after William Empson's *Milton's God*. See for example Corns's statement that "The godly—even the Godhead—may use guile" and that "the politic control of information is central to the orchestration of the tests faced by Satan and by Adam and Eve" (*Regaining* Paradise Lost 137). Corns's formulation is reminiscent of Curry's statement that God is an "arbitrary King" (*Milton's Ontology, Cosmogony and Physics* 47) who does not hesitate to hold information back from his enemies. See also Aers and Hodge, "'Rational Burning'" 144.

252. Fowler points out that as early as 1953, Millicent Bell claimed "that prelapsarian man was pretty much like the passionate, sinful, post-lapsarian man we are familiar with" (*PL* 32). Bell stated that "Milton's Adam and Eve, like the universe at large, are never purely Good, but fallen and capable of redemption from the start" ("The Fallacy of the Fall in *Paradise Lost*," *PMLA* 68 [1953]: 883; for a counter-position see H.V.S. Ogden, "The Crisis of *Paradise Lost* Reconsidered," *Milton: Modern Essays in Criticism*, ed. Arthur E. Barker 308-27). For another position that does not rely on an Augustinian interpretation of the Fall, see Harold Fisch, "Hebraic Style and Motifs in *Paradise Lost*," *Language and Style in Milton*, eds. Ronald D. Emma and John T. Shawcross (New York: Ungar, 1967) 50.

253. Wendy Furman, Christopher Grose and William Shullenberger, Preface, *Milton Studies* 28 [1992]: vii.

254. See Haskin, *Milton's Burden of Interpretation* 184.

255. Snider interprets the search for a paradisal clarity of language as an attempt "to loose philosophy from the grip of endless interpretation," but "Adam's original perfection in no way prevents his experiencing doubt and uncertainty, or undergoing a process of intellectual growth" (*Origin and Authority* 3, 124).

256. See Haskin, *Milton's Burden of Interpretation* 186. Merrill (*Epic God-Talk* 107) also thinks that it is plausible "to assume that Milton calculated a *linguistic* fall for Eve prior to her actual lapse." One of the earliest representatives of this theory is Tillyard in *Studies in Milton*. He "accuses" Milton of narrative "faking": "He anticipates the Fall by attributing to Eve and Adam feelings which though nominally felt in the state of innocence are actually not compatible with it" (10-11). Haskin is however opposed to "[t]he widely popular doctrine

according to which the whole Western tradition is pervaded by linguistic ambiguities and structured by binary oppositions" (Haskin 186).

257. Tillyard even sees Eve's wish to work on her own as an ironical challenge of Adam's authority, a "mild trap" rather than a "sincere" argument (*Studies in Milton* 17). For more recent interpretations, see Schwartz, *Remembering and Repeating* (65) and Dayton Haskin, *Milton's Burden of Interpretation* (187); Louis Martz states that "the problem of making the right choice, the problem of the right exercise of freedom, is shown to be as difficult before the Fall as it is afterwards" (*Poet of Exile: A Study of Milton's Poetry* [New Haven: Yale UP] 140). For Nyquist, "With varying degrees of explicitness, much of the recent literature on *Paradise Lost* suggests that Eve and Adam begin developing, rather than falling, before the Fall" ("Reading the Fall" 199). Dennis Danielson integrates this view into his discussion of theodicy in *Milton's Good God* (109): "In accordance with the goodness and justice of God, fallen man is given a chance of avoiding damnation. However, something analogous is required for prelapsarian man. The unavoidability of the Fall for Adam and Eve would have the same negative implications for theodicy as would the unavoidability of damnation for their offspring."

258. Haskin, *Milton's Burden of Interpretation* 188. See Kahn, "Allegory and the Sublime in *Paradise Lost*," *John Milton*, ed. Annabel Patterson 185-201, and my own "The End of Monolithic Language: Raphael's Sematology in *Paradise Lost*," *English Studies in Canada* 15.3 (1989): 263-276.

259. Entzminger, *Divine Word* 1, 28. McColley also interprets the act of seduction as a linguistic act, as "an attempt to confuse Eve's mind by divorcing language from actuality, or sign from what it pretends to signify" (*Milton's Eve* 196). Satan's medium is "that by which in the Renaissance mind God most clearly presents himself to men and men to one another: the word."

260. MacCallum (*Milton and the Sons of God* 139) sees this dream inspired by Satan as "[t]he catalyst of further development," and Leonard Mustazza (*"Such Prompt Eloquence"* 58) states that the dream has influenced "her receptivity to the idea of exaltation and liberation."

261. Myers, "The Spirit of *Différance*" 104.

262. Entzminger, *Divine Word* 63. I have my reservations about Entzminger's use of the preposition *despite*, though, as I would argue that the archangel's teaching is part of God's great plan.

263. Mustazza, *"Such Prompt Eloquence"* 69.

264. Grossman, *"Authors to Themselves"* 194.

265. MacCallum (*Milton and the Sons of God* 106) shows how this debate leads towards incarnation, which depends upon the Son's voluntary acceptance of the role of the mediator and saviour: "The richness of tone humanizes the deity, making us aware that his ways are accessible to our minds and hearts. The climax of the process achieves the integration of man with God through the Son."

266. Mustazza, *"Such Prompt Eloquence"* 22. See also Samson's "literalization" of metaphors in *Samson Agonistes*.

267. Christopher, *Milton and the Science of the Saints* 21. Leonard Mustazza (*"Such Prompt Eloquence"* 120) points out that "In effect, the Father is saying that some people will

be saved through the use of heartfelt words, words that reflect precisely their true obedience and repentance, unlike Satanic words, which are meant to dissemble."

268. Esterhammer (*Creating States* 65) quotes from *The Censure of the Rota Upon Mr Miltons Book, Entituled, The Ready and Easie Way to Establish A Free Common-wealth* (1660): "you are very solicitous about [words] as if they were charmes, or had more in them then what they signifie: For no Conjurer's Devill is more concerned in a spell, then you are in a meer word, but never regard the things which it serves to expresse."

269. See Frye, *Words With Power*.

270. Ferry, *Milton's Epic Voice* 88.

271. See Frye, *The Great Code* 5-6.

272. As Reichert points out in *Milton's Wisdom*, "In short, nature, or the book of the creatures, will continue to signify, for those who can read it, just what it signified before the Fall: namely, the omnipresence, goodness, and love of the Creator" (40). From a structuralist or poststructuralist perspective, it is tempting pursue the Augustinian *vestigia* or traces mentioned by Martz (*Poet of Exile* 174). See also Rapaport, *Milton and the Postmodern* (16) and Myers, *Milton and Free Will* (199) as well as Myers, "The Spirit of *Différance*" (115); another application of Derridean concepts is Michael McCanles, "From Derrida to Bacon and Beyond," *Francis Bacon's Legacy of Texts: "The Art of Discovery Grows with Discovery,"* ed. William A. Sessions (New York: AMS Press, 1990) 25-46. Loewenstein claims that Michael turns his pupil into a "semiologist," "training him in the art of reading and interpreting God's signs in fallen history" (*Milton and the Drama of History* 108).

273. John R. Knott, *Milton's Pastoral Vision: An Approach to* Paradise Lost (Chicago: U of Chicago P, 1971) 14.

274. Christopher, *Milton and the Science of the Saints* 151.

275. Frye, *The Great Code* 55.

276. Grossman, *"Authors to Themselves"* 180.

277. Harold Bloom, *Ruin the Sacred Truths: Poetry and Belief from the Bible to the Present* (1987; Cambridge: Harvard UP, 1989) 91. See also Barker, *Milton and the Puritan Dilemma 1641-1660* 318-319, Jacobus, *Sudden Apprehension,* and most recently, Fish, *How Milton Works*, but cf. Silver, *Imperfect Sense* 359-63.

278. Bloom names W.B.C. Watkins as the original representative of the idea that Milton was a monist accepting "the whole range from the physical, specifically the senses, to the ultimate Divine as *absolutely unbroken*" (qtd. in Bloom, *Ruin the Sacred Truths* 94). Bloom also points out another interesting fact that becomes important for the interpretation of the Bible and *Paradise Lost*: "The Hebrew word behind Saint John's *logos* is *davhar*, as Milton knew, and *davhar* is both a deed and a thought, a word for 'word' that does not allow any dualism" (94). The dualistic meaning of *davhar* or *dabar* is also mirrored in the Latin translation of the Greek *logos*. As Christopher shows in *Milton and the Science of the Saint*, Erasmus's translation of the biblical *logos* as *sermo* (speech) instead of *verbum* (reason, "the static philosophical idea") led to Martin Luther's "realistic" interpretation of the Bible shifting "the locus of religious experience from visual symbol and ritual action to verbal action" (4). Entzminger shows that Milton (?) in his *Christian Doctrine* also translates *logos* as *sermo* (*Divine Word* 12, 16).

279. Harold Skulsky interprets *sermo* as "the word as the principle of talk itself: the di-

vine communicativeness" in *Language Recreated: Seventeenth-Century Metaphorists and the Act of Metaphor* (Athens: U of Georgia P, 1992) 33.

280. Christopher, *Milton and the Science of the Saints* 21; see also Ong, *The Presence of the Word* 12-13, and Kerrigan, *The Prophetic Milton* 36.

281. Christopher, *Milton and the Science of the Saints* 21.

282. Grossman, *"Authors to Themselves"* 4.

283. Referring to the written version of God's message in the second part of his *Great Code*, Frye discusses polysemous meaning in the context of Dante's four senses of interpretation in order to reject Milton's criticism of "polysemous meaning" in *De Doctrina Christiana*. While Milton fears the arbitrariness possibly arising from polysemy and insists that "[e]ach passage of scripture has only a single sense, though in the Old Testament this sense is often a combination of the historical and the typological" (*CP* VI: 581), Frye states that "[f]or Dante 'polysemous' does not really imply different meanings, suggesting that the chosen meaning of a given passage is purely relative" but rather "a single process growing in subtlety and comprehensiveness" (221).

284. Hughes in *CPMP* 198.

285. The tears of the fallen angel once more indicate that angels and human beings have more in common than Raphael would have Adam believe. See Fowler's notes in *PL* 80.

286. See Lee Jacobus's comparison of Raphael's and Michael's strategies in *Sudden Apprehension* (90): "The first accommodates slightly; the second mightily." Or, as Hartman puts it in "Adam on the Grass With Balsamum," *ELH* 36 (1969): "Accommodation becomes typology" (180).

287. See also Tillyard's opinion that Eve's behaviour is nothing but a test for Adam (*Studies in Milton* 17).

288. Hale, *Milton's Languages* 145.

289. Delasanta (*The Epic Voice* 100) interprets Adam's understandable yearning for a higher status instead of remaining "lowly wise" as "Adam's tragic flaw," a flaw exacerbated by his uxoriousness.

290. Georgia B. Christopher, "The Verbal Gate to Paradise: Adam's 'Literary Experience' in Book X of *Paradise Lost*," *PMLA* 90 (1975): 74.

291. Rapaport (*Milton and the Postmodern* 39) expresses this in a quasi-Saussurean fashion by stating that "things are no longer signifieds, but signifiers; things are not archetypes, but only copies of archetypes. It is as if nature suddenly turns into a book and man into a reader or interpreter of the signs written in that book. Things have faded, and all that remains is their residual semiotic significance."

292. See Mary Ann Radzinowicz, *Toward Samson Agonistes: The Growth of Milton's Mind* (Princeton: Princeton UP, 1978) 304: "Nimrod's crew have removed from their one language its necessary link to one reality, its dependency upon reason." There are good arguments, however, in favour of locating the "linguistic Fall," the first moment of manifest linguistic arbitrariness, much earlier, i.e., in paradise. Radzinowicz, too, points in this direction when she writes that "Promptly upon deciding to eat the apple, Adam became a linguistic relativist. He rationalized a defense of joining Eve in disobedience; by his rationalization he made words mean what he willed them to mean" (305).

293. Mary Ann Radzinowicz, "The Politics of *Paradise Lost*," *Politics of Discourse:*

The Literature and History of Seventeenth-Century England, eds. Kevin Sharpe and Steven N. Zwicker (Berkeley: U of California P, 1987) 229.

294. Barbara Kiefer Lewalski, *Milton's Brief Epic: The Genre, Meaning, and Art of Paradise Regained* (Providence: Brown UP; London: Methuen, 1966) 332.

295. Northrop Frye, "The Typology of *Paradise Regained*," *Milton: Modern Essays in Criticism*, ed. Arthur E. Barker 440.

296. William E. McCarron, "The 'persuasive Rhetoric' of *Paradise Regained*," *Milton Quarterly* 10 (1976): 15).

297. Carey, *CSP* 424. See also Haskin's interpretation of *Paradise Regained* as "a veritable 'hermeneutic combat'" (*Milton's Burden of Interpretation* 148).

298. Leonard Mustazza, "Language as Weapon in Milton's *Paradise Regained*," *Milton Studies* 18 (1983): 195.

299. Stevie Davies, *Milton* 154, 169. See Gomille, *Prudentia in Miltons* Paradise Lost (88) for Milton's anti-Hobbesian position here. For a more radical and poststructuralist linguistic interpretation, see Myers: "To fix a meaning, as Satan wishes to, is to consume the sign: instead Jesus accepts his self-reading as 'play, activity, production, practice.' Thus the difference between Satan and Jesus is in their responses to *différance*, upon which Satan seeks to impose totalitarian closure, but in which Jesus discerns by faith his Father's will" ("The Spirit of *Différance*" 117).

300. For the role of obedience, see the obedient behaviour of angels such as Raphael and Abdiel through which a "literal" interpretation of God's commands becomes possible.

301. Mustazza, "Language as Weapon in Milton's *Paradise Regained*" 197.

302. See John Spencer Hill, *John Milton: Poet, Priest and Prophet* (London: Macmillan, 1979) 175: "what did the Father mean in proclaiming him 'my beloved Son'?—for the phrase (as Satan later observes) is ambiguous."

303. Stevie Davies, *Milton* 177.

304. Mustazza, "Language as Weapon in Milton's *Paradise Regained*" 201.

305. See Lewalski, *Milton's Brief Epic* 343.

306. See McCarron, "The 'persuasive Rhetoric' of *Paradise Regained*" 15.

307. Milton's attitude towards the function of knowledge and education seems to have undergone quite a change in comparison to his earlier position in *Of Education*, a development that is also apparent in his later prose regarding the education of theologians. Irene Samuel satirizes the explanations of this change devised by critics: "[T]hat Milton changed from his early enthusiasm for learning to a dour Puritanical anti-intellectualism," which—put so brutally—is certainly wrong; "that he could not have meant what he said, or meant it only as a repudiation of pride of intellect," which recent interpretations seem to believe; "that he was tired and disillusioned," which would be biographically understandable; and finally, "that he was romantic, mystic, stoical" ("Milton on Learning and Wisdom" 708). She finishes by pointing out "that Jesus is rejecting things possibly good enough in themselves, but somehow tainted by the mode of their offer" (715). See also Carey's discussion in *CSP* 503-04.

308. Walter MacKellar, *A Variorum Commentary on the Poems of John Milton*, vol. IV: *Paradise Regained*, gen. ed. Merritt Y. Hughes (London: Routledge, 1975) 33.

309. MacKellar sees both Satan's "injunction to stand" and Christ's reaction as ironical:

"For the first and only time Christ complies with Satan's suggestion; but he does so *not* in surrender to Satan, not as finding his motive in the suggestion, but in obedience to God" (30).

310. Entzminger, *Divine Word* 116. See also Stanley Fish, "Inaction and Silence: The Reader in *Paradise Regained*," *Calm of Mind: Tercentenary Essays on* Paradise Regained *and* Samson Agonistes *in Honor of John S. Diekhoff*, ed. Joseph Anthony Wittreich, Jr. (Cleveland: Case Western Reserve UP, 1971) 42.

311. Donald Swanson and John Mulryan, "The Son's Presumed Contempt for Learning in *Paradise Regained*: A Biblical and Patristic Solution," *Milton Studies* 27 (1991): 248.

312. While Fish claims that the final identity of God's and Christ's will is expressed in the Son's silence—"when the Son rejects the arts of language he does what he has been doing all along: he refuses to play God" ("Inaction and Silence" 41)—Shoaf argues that "*Paradise Regained* completes the argument begun in *Paradise Lost* regarding the sign and its repair" (*Milton, Poet of Duality* 154). Entzminger also shows that "[o]bediently withstanding temptation, Christ will recover what Adam lost through disobedience," and that "his defeat of Satan becomes complete when he fully realizes the significance of himself as the Incarnate Word, a paradox whose mystery overcomes Satan even as it restores to language the possibility of expressing divinity" (*Divine Word* 103). Cf. Stevie Davies (*Milton* 159): "Language is presented as the riddling problem of *Paradise Regained*. But the right words, presented in the form of a riddle, are the key to that problem."

313. Silver, *Imperfect Sense* 10.

314. Carey in *CSP* 425.

315. William Blake, *The Marriage of Heaven and Hell* (1790), *Milton*: Paradise Lost, eds. A.E. Dyson and Julian Lovelock (Houndmills, Basingstoke: Macmillan, 1973) 44.

316. Barbara K. Lewalski, "Genre," *A Companion to Milton*, ed. Thomas N. Corns (Oxford: Blackwell, 2001) 8.

317. John G. Demaray, *Milton and the Masque Tradition: The Early Poems, "Arcades," and* Comus, Cambridge, MA: Harvard UP, 1968. 2.

318. John Fowles, *The Magus: A Revised Version* (1965/1978; New York: Dell-Laurel, 1985).

319. J. Martin Evans, *The Miltonic Moment* (Lexington: UP of Kentucky, 1998) 64.

320. Evans 66.

321. McGuire 61.

322. Barbara K. Lewalski, "Milton's *Comus* and the Politics of Masquing," *The Politics of the Stuart Court Masque*, eds. David Bevington and Peter Holbrook (Cambridge: CUP, 1998) 314.

323. Cedric C. Brown, *John Milton's Aristocratic Entertainments* (Cambridge: CUP, 1985) 104-131. Brown also draws attention to the function of "protective spirits" in both *Arcades* and *Comus* (38). McGuire refers to the Spirit as "a truth-teller, as one who educates by verbally setting forth necessary information" (119).

324. As for Lawes's function, see for example Elizabeth A. Frost, "The Didactic *Comus*: Henry Lawes and the Trial of Virtue," *Comitatus: A Journal of Medieval and Renaissance Studies* 22 (1991): 87-103.

325. Cleanth Brooks and John Edward Hardy, "*Comus*," *Poems of Mr. John Milton:*

The 1645 Edition with Essays in Analysis, eds. Brooks and Hardy (London: Dobson, 1957) 187-237.

326. Brooks and Hardy 190.

327. See Fish, *How Milton Works* 261 for a comment on his "posture of reluctance."

328. For Neoplatonic and, above all, Christian overtones in this description, see McGuire 78. See also Fletcher's statement that "One standard Elizabethan theatrical term for the space above the stage was 'the heavens,' and therefore whenever an ascent or descent from the heavens occurred in the masque, there might be a double sense to the stage direction, symbolic as well as theatrical" (79).

329. See Debora Shuger, "'Gums of Glutinous Heat' and the Stream of Consciousness: The Theology of Milton's *Maske*," *Representations* 60 (1997): 1-21.

330. See Leah S. Marcus, "John Milton's *Comus*," *A Companion to Milton*, ed. Thomas N. Corns (Oxford: Blackwell, 2001) 237.

331. Note to l. 613 in Roy Flannagan's *Riverside Milton*.

332. Frost 91.

333. Frost 88.

334. Evans 66.

335. Avrom Fleishman, "*The Magus* of the Wizard of the West," *Critical Essays on John Fowles*, ed. Ellen Pifer (Boston: G.K. Hall, 1986) 79.

336. John Fowles, *The Aristos*, rev. ed. (n.p.: Triad/Granada, 1981) 18-19.

337. R. Rawdon Wilson, *In Palamedes' Shadow: Explorations in Play, Game, and Narrative Theory* (Boston: Northeastern UP, 1990) 123.

338. Wilson, *In Palamedes' Shadow* 130.

339. Conchis even refers to his masque as the dramatic form of *meta-theatre* (see Fowles, *The Magus* 411, 415) in which—and this is of course a parallel to the seventeenth-century court masque, real life persons—such as the Egerton children in *Comus*—are drawn into the masque so that the distinction between the world of the masque and the real world disappears.

340. See, for example, Paul H. Lorenz, "Heraclitus Against the Barbarians: John Fowles's *The Magus*," *Twentieth-Century Literature* 42.1 (1996), who claims that the "events of the godgame are meant to be instructive" (72).

341. Fowles, *The Magus* 507, 508, 509.

342. Wilson, *In Palamedes' Shadow* 125.

343. Wilson, *In Palamedes' Shadow* 126.

344. William Empson, *Milton's God* (1961; Cambridge: CUP, 1981) 110.

345. Herman also sees the possibility that Adam may at times be "politely complimenting Raphael while correcting the angel's mistaken version" (*Destabilizing Milton* 53).

346. Michael Allen, "Divine Instruction" 115.

347. Hugh MacCallum, *Milton and the Sons of God* 100.

348. Norbrook, on the other hand, sees the Father as experimenting rather than directing a play: "Like the English republicans, the poem's God undertakes a series of experiments in freedom and finds them confounded to the point of arousing his enemies' derisive laughter" (*Writing the English Republic* 490).

349. See Hill, *Milton and the English Revolution* 304.

350. Saurat, *Milton: Man and Thinker passim.*

351. Cf. Empson, *Milton's God* 130: "I thus suddenly realized, what M. Saurat was not intending to prove, that Milton did expect God to abdicate." For a reference by the very young Milton to the principle of abdication, see his Prolusio VII. See also Hill, *Milton and the English Revolution* 286, 304; Tillyard, *Milton* 233 and Rumrich, *Milton Unbound* 142-143. For an innovative approach, see Brian Johnson, "Sacred Silence: The Death of the 'Author' and *Paradise Lost*," *Milton Quarterly* 29 (1995): 65-76. In *If This Be Heresy: A Study of Milton and Origen*, Harry F. Robins shows that the idea of God's retraction was not uncommon among the Church Fathers (48-49). See also Leon Howard, "'The Invention' of Milton's 'Great Argument'" 169-170, and David Norbrook, *Writing the English Republic* 112.

352. William J. Palmer, *The Fiction of John Fowles: Tradition, Art, and the Loneliness of Selfhood* (Columbia: U of Missouri P, 1974) 12.

353. Evans 66-67. McGuire, too, shows that the Attendant Spirit, although a "divine agent," restricts himself to "earthly antidotes" (152).

354. Brown, *John Milton's Aristocratic Entertainments* 57: "If [in *Arcades*] the Fall is felt briefly [. . .] in Genius' nightly care over mundane evils on the estate, it will be felt more directly, often in the Ludlow masque."

355. Empson, *Milton's God* 137.

356. Brooks and Hardy 214.

357. Franklin R. Baruch, "Milton's *Comus*: Skill, Virtue, and Henry Lawes," *Milton Studies* 5 (1973): 298.

358. Wilson 131.

359. Another question regarding divine instruction through godgames would be whether we can also read *Paradise Regained* as a godgame in which Jesus learns about his divine identity. I would like to thank Neil Forsyth and Helen Lynch for an enlightening discussion about this point.

4 Conclusion

The "literal" interpretation of the role of the Word underlying this study of Milton's poetics was a consequence of the Reformation. As Regina Schwartz puts it in *Remembering and Repeating*: "In thus empowering words, Milton heeds the Bible even as he anticipates contemporary debates about the illocutionary force of language."[1] By relying on faith in God's word, we can communicate with God: "Milton argued that in believers 'the intellect is to a very large extent restored to its former [i.e., prelapsarian] state of enlightenment.'"[2]

As the Father promises in Book VII of *Paradise Lost*, heaven and earth will finally come together und be united through the deeds of the Son, "thou my Word" (*PL* VII.163). God's Word is the origin of creation, and if there is anything arbitrary about this word and its relationship to what it signifies, then this arbitrariness is God's own arbitrariness: At this level of monolithic language as it is spoken by Adam and Eve in paradise, connotations do not yet exist.

Prelapsarian language is God-given or at least authorized by God, as could be seen in the scene in which a divinely inspired Adam gives names to the animals. Still, the term *monolithic* used in connection with this language is in a way misleading: according to many seventeenth-century philosophers and theologians, word and thing are always already separate entities and no longer identical, even though they are clearly and unambiguously coordinated. Even Bishop Wilkins no longer feels able to postulate a "necessary and natural correspondence between things and words"[3] and offers instead a systematic model reducing "all things and notions unto such a frame, as may express their natural order, dependence, and relations."[4]

The archangel Raphael and modern linguists show that language in paradise already bears the features of a dual system: What seventeenth-century philosophers of language imagined to be a universal language was a language in which the relationship between names and things was a generally accepted or divinely inspired convention, but its reliance on these two co-ordinated kinds of elements—names and things, signifiers and signifieds—existed right from the start. If it did not exist (or come into being later), Milton's system of theodicy relying on the coordination of these elements by human will or faith would be in danger.

The introduction of connotations and ambiguity into human communication in paradise is made by Raphael, an angel with a semi-divine but still—I would claim —limited intelligence who cannot understand divine irony because he has been taught to obey the Father's commands without questioning them. He thus cannot see that he himself is only playing a role in a greater godgame.

In God's "game," the archangel Raphael plays a role that Adam may have been meant to see through, and he brings a message down to earth that Adam may have been meant to disambiguate. As Raphael accepts as God-given truth what had only been meant to be a challenge for Adam's intellect, the archangel does not realize that he is only a paedagogical instrument in Adam's socialization. Instead, his explanation of the difference between divine and earthly spheres, which Adam might have rejected or at least questioned, turns into the basis of "fallen" linguistics leading to the necessity of translation—and to the possibilities of a rhetorical use of language.

My interpretation of the role of the archangel Raphael is radically different from traditional interpretations in that it does not necessarily accept him as an infallible, omniscient and trustworthy messenger. It partially suggests to revise Kathleen Swaim's interpretation of the teaching methods of Raphael and Michael which states that "Michael makes disjunctive the realms of earthly and heavenly that for Raphael were continuous and unified;" whereas "for Michael nature and grace are dichotomous alternatives, from which informed reasoners will opt for the absolute not the mundane, the eternal not the temporal, wisdom not knowledge, faith not reason."[5] Whereas it is above all Michael's task to re-establish the unity of the Word through methods of interpretation such as typology, Raphael obviously believed that such a process of disambiguating the divine message through accommodation was already necessary in prelapsarian times.[6] It is not only Michael who uses "ambiguity, sometimes appearing to mislead Adam deliberately in order to crystallize the false interpretation which must be rejected,"[7] but already Raphael, who mistakenly thinks that this is part of the task.

Milton, I argue in this study, has largely lost the linguistic optimism of seventeenth-century philosophers of language such as Wilkins and shows a "somewhat ambiguous relation to his own century's theories of language."[8] On the one hand, he mistrusts figurative language, but on the other he does not have his contemporaries' "faith in the imminent removal of this error, the apocalyptic union of word and thing" through the sciences.[9]

For the Milton of *Paradise Lost*, a truly monolithic language in which word and things are identical was an illusion. The "recreation" of an Edenic language would mean a clear and unambiguous correspondence between thing and word, but for Milton this ideal was already almost impossible in the Garden of Eden and was even undermined—for paedagogical reasons, of course—by God himself. Furthermore, Milton resembled many of his contemporaries in having "mixed feelings" about the "art of effective expression known as rhetoric."[10]

As Stanley Fish already indicated in *Surprised by Sin*, it is impossible to rebuild Paradise through linguistic reform. The archangel Michael's reference to a "paradise within" shows us the only remaining possibility of establishing a one-to-one relationship between words and concepts. The "sudden apprehension" that Lee Jacobus alludes to in the title of his interpretation of *Paradise Lost*, can only be brought forth through an act of faith, and linguistics might well be counted among those methods that Jacobus rejects as useless in solving the "problem of knowledge for the Christian in *Paradise Lost*."[11]

Such an experience of faith and such a "literary" interpretation of the Word would turn *Paradise Lost* into a "sacramental vessel through which the *viva vox Christi* could issue and overwhelm all the mighty rhetoric of Satan."[12] This insight is the final point of a development leading from early optimism (such as in *Of Education*) to later pessimism regarding the effect of linguistic reforms and activities. Whereas at the beginning the linguistic "repair of the ruins of our first parents" was the pragmatic centre of Milton's program, this repair later was restricted to the realm of individual faith.

As I have shown in this "linguistic" interpretation of his works, Milton's experience in the fields of political and diplomatic discourse led him not only to reject the ideal of the reconstruction of a paradisal linguistic situation in postlapsarian times; he even goes so far as to wonder whether such an ideal linguistic state may ever have existed in heaven or paradise. The search for an original "unfallen" language leads us back to the beginning of linguistic communication . . . and perhaps even further back than that.

Notes

1. Schwartz, *Remembering and Repeating* 63. See also Bloom, *Ruin the Sacred Truths*.
2. Hill, *Milton and the English Revolution* 148.
3. Cohen, *Sensible Words* 31.
4. Wilkins, *An Essay Towards a Real Character* 1.
5. Swaim, *Before and After the Fall* ix, 33.
6. Swaim herself hints at this: "Raphael's teaching is aimed precisely at inducing Adam to read between the lines and to penetrate behind the veils of, for example, vegetation or solar phenomena to apprehend their full divine meaning" (*Before and After the Fall* 164).
7. Hugh MacCallum in "Milton and Sacred History," qtd. in Swaim, *Before and After the Fall* 64.

8. Patricia Parker, *Inescapable Romance: Studies in the Poetics of a Mode* (Princeton: Princeton UP, 1979) 135-136. For Parker, Milton "shares both the Puritan and the Baconian distrust of metaphor, the impulse which led John Wilkins to propose a language free of 'Synonymous words,' 'Equivocals' or words of 'several significations, and of metaphors, those 'infected ornaments' which 'prejudice the native simplicity of speech.'"

9. Parker, *Inescapable Romance* 136.

10. John M. Major, "Milton's View of Rhetoric" 685.

11. Jacobus, *Sudden Apprehension* 211.

12. Christopher, "The Verbal Gate to Paradise" 76.

Works Cited and Consulted

Editions of Milton's Works

The Works of John Milton. Gen. ed. Frank Allen Patterson. New York: Columbia UP, 1931-38. Quoted as *WJM.*

Complete Prose Works. Gen. ed. Don M. Wolfe. New Haven: Yale UP, 1953-82. Quoted as *CP.*

Complete Poems and Major Prose. Ed. Merritt Y. Hughes. Indianapolis: Odyssey, 1957. Quoted as *CPMP.*

Complete Shorter Poems. Ed. John Carey. London: Longman, 1971. Quoted as *CSP.* If not indicated otherwise, quotations are to book and line numbers from this edition. *A Masque Presented at Ludlow Castle, Paradise Regained* and *Samson Agonistes* are quoted as *Comus, PR* or *SA.*

Paradise Lost. Ed. Alastair Fowler. London: Longman, 1971. Quoted as *PL.* References are to book and line numbers of this edition.

John Milton: Paradise Lost – Samson Agonistes – Lycidas. Ed. Edward Le Comte. New York: New American Library, 1981.

The Riverside Milton. Ed. Roy Flannagan. Boston: Houghton Mifflin, 1998.

Secondary Sources

Aarsleff, Hans. *From Locke to Saussure: Essays on the Study of Language and Intellectual History.* London: Athlone, 1982.

Achinstein, Sharon. *Milton and the Revolutionary Reader.* Princeton: Princeton UP, 1994.

Addison, Joseph. *Notes Upon the Twelve Books of* Paradise Lost (1712). Shawcross, *Milton: The Critical Heritage* 147-220.

Aers, David, and Bob Hodge. "'Rational Burning': Milton on Sex and Marriage." *Literature, Language and Society in England 1580-1680.* Eds. David Aers, Bob Hodge and Gunther Kress. Dublin: Gill and Macmillan; Totowa: Barnes & Noble, 1981. 122-51.

Ainsworth, Oliver M. *Milton on Education: The Tractate* Of Education *with Supplementary Extracts from Other Writings of Milton.* 1928. New York: AMS P, 1970.

Allen, Don Cameron. *The Harmonious Vision: Studies in Milton's Poetry.* Enlarged ed. Baltimore: Johns Hopkins UP, 1970.

——. "Milton and the Name of Eve." *Modern Language Notes* 74 (1959): 681-83.

——. "Some Theories of the Growth and Origin of Language in Milton's Age." *Philological Quarterly* 28.1 (1949): 5-16.

Allen, Michael. "Divine Instruction: *Of Education* and the Pedagogy of Raphael, Michael, and the Father." *Milton Quarterly* 26 (1992): 113-21.

Andrade, E(dward) N. da C. *A Brief History of the Royal Society.* London: Royal Society, 1960.

Arakelian, Paul G. "The Myth of a Restoration Style Shift." *The Eighteenth Century* 20/21 (1979): 227-45.

Asals, Heather. "Rhetoric Agonistic in *Samson Agonistes*." *Milton Quarterly* 11 (1977): 1-4.

Augustine. *The Confessions of St. Augustine.* Trans. John K. Ryan. Garden City, NY: Doubleday-Image, 1961.

——. *De Doctrina Christiana.* Ed. and trans. R.P.H. Green. Oxford: Clarendon, 1995.

Auksi, Peter. "Milton's 'Sanctifi'd Bitternesse': Polemical Technique in the Early Prose." *Texas Studies in Literature and Language* 19 (1977): 363-81.

Babb, Lawrence. *The Moral Cosmos of* Paradise Lost. East Lansing: Michigan State UP, 1970.

Bacon, Francis. *Works.* 1858-74. Eds. James Spedding, Robert L. Ellis and Douglas D. Heath. 14 vols. Stuttgart-Bad Canstatt: Frommann, 1963.

Barker, Arthur E. *Milton and the Puritan Dilemma 1641-1660.* Toronto: UTP, 1942.

——. "'Paradise Lost': The Relevance of Regeneration." Paradise Lost: *A Tercentenary Tribute.* Ed. Balachandra Rajan. Toronto: UTP, 1967. 48-78.

——, ed. *Milton: Modern Essays in Criticism.* London: OUP, 1965.

Barthes, Roland. *Mythologies. Oeuvres complètes.* Ed. Éric Marty. Paris: Seuil, 1993. I: 561-719.

Baruch, Franklin R. "Milton's *Comus*: Skill, Virtue, and Henry Lawes." *Milton Studies* 5 (1973): 298-308.

Bedford, R.D. "Milton and Philosophy." *Milton Quarterly* 26 (1992): 52-54.

Bell, Millicent. "The Fallacy of the Fall in *Paradise Lost*." *PMLA* 68 (1953): 863-83.

Belsey, Catherine. *John Milton: Language, Gender, Power.* Oxford: Blackwell, 1988.

Benveniste, Emile. *Probleme der allgemeinen Sprachwissenschaft.* Trans. Wilhelm Bolle. Frankfurt: Syndikat, 1977.

Berry, Boyd M. "Melodramatic Faking in the Narrator's Voice, *Paradise Lost*." *Milton Quarterly* 10 (1976): 1-5.

Blackburn, Thomas H. "'Uncloister'd Virtue': Adam and Eve in Milton's Paradise." *Milton Studies* 3 (1971): 119-37.

Blake, William. *The Marriage of Heaven and Hell* (1790). Dyson and Lovelock 44.

Blakemore, Steven. "Language and Logos in *Paradise Lost*." *Southern Humanities Review* 20 (1986): 325-40.

Bloom, Harold. *The Anxiety of Influence: A Theory of Poetry.* New York: OUP, 1973.

——. *Ruin the Sacred Truths: Poetry and Belief from the Bible to the Present.* 1987. Cambridge, Mass.: Harvard UP, 1989.

——. *The Western Canon: The Books and Schools of the Ages.* 1994. London: Macmillan, 1995.

Boone, Lalia Phipps. "The Language of Book VI, *Paradise Lost*." *SAMLA Studies in Milton: Essays on John Milton and His Works.* Ed. J. Max Patrick. Gainesville: U of Florida P, 1953. 114-27.

Borst, Arno. *Der Turmbau zu Babel: Geschichte der Meinungen über Ursprung und Vielfalt der Sprachen und Völker*. 4 vols. Stuttgart: Hiersemann, 1957-63.

Broadbent, J.B. "Milton's 'Mortal Voice' and his 'Omnific Word.'" Patrides, *Approaches* 99-117.

Brooks, Cleanth, and John Edward Hardy. *"Comus." Poems of Mr. John Milton: The 1645 Edition with Essays in Analysis*. Eds. Brooks and Hardy. London: Dobson, 1957. 187-237.

Brown, Cedric C. *John Milton: A Literary Life*. New York: St. Martin's P, 1995.

———. *John Milton's Aristocratic Entertainments*. Cambridge: CUP, 1985.

Bryson, Michael. *The Tyranny of Heaven: Milton's Rejection of God as King*. Newark: U of Delaware P; London: Associated UPs, 2004.

Bundy, Murray W. "Milton's View of Education in *Paradise Lost*." *Journal of English and Germanic Philology* 21 (1922): 127-52.

Burden, Dennis H. *The Logical Epic: A Study of the Argument of* Paradise Lost. London: Routledge, 1967.

Butler, Samuel. "Fragments of an Intended Second Part of the Foregoing Satire (1670)." Shawcross, *Milton: The Critical Heritage* 76.

Campbell, Gordon. "Milton's *Accedence Commenc't Grammar*." *Milton Quarterly* 10 (1976): 39-48.

———, et al. "The Provenance of *De Doctrina Christiana*." *Milton Quarterly* 31.3 (1997): 67-121.

Carnes, Valerie. "Time and Language in Milton's *Paradise Lost*." *ELH* 37 (1970): 517-39.

Carrithers, Gale H., Jr., and James D. Hardy, Jr. *Milton and the Hermeneutic Journey*. Baton Rouge: Louisiana UP, 1994.

Cauthen, Irby B., Jr. "'A Complete and Generous Education': Milton and Jefferson." *Virginia Quarterly Review* 55 (1979): 222-33.

Christensen, Francis. "John Wilkins and the Royal Society's Reform of Prose Style." *Modern Language Quarterly* 7 (1946): 179-87, 279-90.

Christopher, Georgia B. "The Verbal Gate to Paradise: Adam's 'Literary Experience' in Book X of *Paradise Lost*." *PMLA* 90 (1975): 69-77.

———. *Milton and the Science of the Saints*. Princeton: Princeton UP, 1982.

Clark, Ira. "A Problem of Knowing Paradise in *Paradise Lost*." *Milton Studies* 27 (1991): 183-207.

Cohen, Murray. *Sensible Words: Linguistic Practice in England, 1640-1785*. Baltimore: Johns Hopkins UP, 1977.

Coiro, Ann Baynes. "'To Repair the ruins of our first parents': *Of Education* and Fallen Adam." *SEL* 28 (1988): 133-47.

Colish, Marcia L. *The Mirror of Language: A Study in the Medieval Theory of Knowledge*. Rev. ed. Lincoln: U of Nebraska P, 1983.

Cooley, Dennis. *Dedications*. Saskatoon: Thistledown P, 1988.

Cooley, Ronald W. "Reformed Eloquence: Inability, Questioning, and Correction in *Paradise Lost*." *University of Toronto Quarterly* 62.2 (1993): 232-55.

Cope, Jackson I. *The Metaphoric Structure of* Paradise Lost. 1962. New York: Octagon, 1979.

Corns, Thomas N. *The Development of Milton's Prose Style*. Oxford: Clarendon, 1982.

———. *Regaining* Paradise Lost. London: Longman, 1994.

———, ed. *A Companion to Milton*. Oxford: Blackwell, 2001.

Croll, Morris W. "Attic Prose: Lipsius, Montaigne, Bacon (1923)." Fish, *Seventeenth-Century Prose* 3-25.

Crowley, Tony. "John Locke." *Proper English? Readings in Language, History and Cultural Identity.* London: Routledge, 1991. 13-15.

Curry, Walter Clyde. *Milton's Ontology, Cosmogony and Physics.* Lexington: U of Kentucky P, 1957.

Cyr, Marc D. "The Archangel Raphael: Narrative Authority in Milton's War in Heaven." *Journal of Narrative Technique* 17.3 (1987): 309-16.

Dabydeen, David. "On Not Being Milton: Nigger Talk in England Today." *Proceedings of the XIIth Congress of the International Comparative Literature Association / Actes du XIIIe congrès de l'Association internationale de littérature comparée.* Eds. Roger Bauer and Douwe Fokkema. Munich: Iudicium, 1990. I: 80-90.

Damrosch, Leopold, Jr. *God's Plot and Man's Stories: Studies in the Fictional Imagination from Milton to Fielding.* Chicago: U of Chicago P, 1985.

Danielson, Dennis Richard. *Milton's Good God: A Study in Literary Theodicy.* Cambridge: CUP, 1982.

Davies, Stevie. *Milton.* New York: Harvester Wheatsheaf, 1991.

Davies, Tony. "The Ark in Flames: Science, Language, and Education in Seventeenth-Century England." *The Figural and the Literal: Problems of Language in the History of Science and Philosophy 1630-1800.* Eds. Andrew E. Benjamin, Geoffrey N. Cantor and John R.R. Christie. Manchester: Manchester UP, 1987. 83-102.

Davis, Walter R. "The Languages of Accommodation and the Styles of *Paradise Lost*." *Milton Studies* 18 (1983): 103-27.

De Grazia, Margreta. "The Secularization of Language in the Seventeenth Century." *Journal of the History of Ideas* 41.2 (1980): 319-29.

Delasanta, Rodney. *The Epic Voice.* The Hague: Mouton, 1967.

Demaray, John G. *Milton and the Masque Tradition: The Early Poems, "Arcades," and Comus.* Cambridge, MA: Harvard UP, 1968.

Diekhoff, John S. *Milton's* Paradise Lost*: A Commentary on the Argument.* 1946. New York: Humanities P, 1963.

Donnelly, M.L. "Francis Bacon's Early Reputation in England and the Question of John Milton's Alleged 'Baconianism'." *Prose Studies* 14.1 (1991): 1-20.

Duran, Angelica. *The Age of Milton and the Scientific Revolution.* Pittsburgh: Duquesne UP, 2007.

Dyson, A.E. and Julian Lovelock, ed. *Milton:* Paradise Lost. Houndmills, Basingstoke: Macmillan, 1973.

Eagleton, Terry. "The God that Failed." Nyquist and Ferguson 342-49.

Eco, Umberto. "On the Possibility of Generating Aesthetic Messages in an Edenic Language." *The Role of the Reader: Explorations in the Semiotics of Texts.* Bloomington: Indiana UP, 1979. 90-104.

Edwards, Karen L. "Comenius, Milton, and the Temptation to Ease." *Milton Studies* 32 (1996): 23-43.

Eliot, T.S. "The Metaphysical Poets." *Selected Essays.* 1921. London: Faber, 1951. 281-91.

——. *Milton: Two Studies* (1936/1947). London: Faber, 1968.

Ellwood, Thomas. "Epitaph on Milton (1675)." Shawcross, *Milton: The Critical Heritage* 85-87.

Emma, Ronald D. and John T. Shawcross, eds. *Language and Style in Milton*. New York: Ungar, 1967.

Empson, William. *Milton's God*. 1961. Cambridge: CUP, 1981.

Entzminger, Robert L. *Divine Word: Milton and the Redemption of Language*. Pittsburgh: Duquesne UP, 1985.

——. "Epistemology and the Tutelary Word in *Paradise Lost*." *Milton Studies* 10 (1977): 93-109.

——. "*Samson Agonistes* and the Recovery of Metaphor." *SEL* 22 (1982): 137-56.

Esterhammer, Angela. *Creating States: Studies in the Performative Language of John Milton and William Blake*. Toronto: UTP, 1994.

Evans, J. Martin. *The Miltonic Moment*. Lexington: UP of Kentucky, 1998.

Fallon, Stephen M. *Milton among the Philosophers: Poetry and Materialism in Seventeenth-Century England*. Ithaca: Cornell UP, 1991.

Ferry, Anne. *Milton's Epic Voice: The Narrator in* Paradise Lost. 2nd ed. Chicago: U of Chicago P, 1983.

Fiore, Peter A. *Milton and Augustine: Patterns of Augustinian Thought in* Paradise Lost. University Park: Pennsylvania State UP, 1981.

Fisch, Harold. "Hebraic Style and Motifs in *Paradise Lost*." Emma and Shawcross 30-64.

Fish, Stanley. *How Milton Works*. Cambridge, MA: Harvard UP, 2001.

——. "Inaction and Silence: The Reader in *Paradise Regained*." *Calm of Mind: Tercentenary Essays on* Paradise Regained *and* Samson Agonistes *in Honor of John S. Diekhoff*. Ed. Joseph Anthony Wittreich, Jr. Cleveland: Case Western Reserve UP, 1971. 25-47.

——. *Self-Consuming Artifacts: The Experience of Seventeenth-Century Literature*. Berkeley: U of California P, 1972.

——. "Spectacle and Evidence in *Samson Agonistes*." *Critical Inquiry* 15.3 (1989): 556-86.

——. *Surprised by Sin: The Reader in* Paradise Lost. London: Macmillan; New York: St. Martin's P, 1967.

——, ed. *Seventeenth-Century Prose: Modern Essays in Criticism*. New York: OUP, 1971.

Flasch, Kurt. *Augustin: Einführung in sein Denken*. 1980. Stuttgart: Reclam, 2003.

Flasdieck, Hermann J. *Der Gedanke einer englischen Sprachakademie in Vergangenheit und Gegenwart*. Jena: Frommann, 1928.

Fleishman, Avrom. "The Magus of the Wizard of the West." *Critical Essays on John Fowles*. Ed. Ellen Pifer. Boston: G.K. Hall, 1986. 77-93.

Fletcher, Angus. *The Transcendental Masque: An Essay on Milton's* Comus. Ithaca: Cornell UP, 1971.

Formigari, Lia. *Language and Experience in 17th-Century British Philosophy*. Amsterdam: Benjamins, 1988.

Forster, E.M. *Aspects of the Novel*. 1927. Harmondsworth: Penguin, 1976.

Fowles, John. *The Aristos: A Self-Portrait in Ideas*. London: Cape, 1965.

——. *The Magus: A Revised Version*. 1978. New York: Dell-Laurel, 1985.

Frost, Elizabeth A. "The Didactic *Comus*: Henry Lawes and the Trial of Virtue." *Comitatus: A Journal of Medieval and Renaissance Studies* 22 (1991): 87-103.

Frye, Northrop. *The Great Code: The Bible and Literature*. 1981. Toronto: Academic P, 1983.

——. *The Double Vision: Language and Meaning in Religion*. Toronto: UTP, 1991.

——. "The Typology of Paradise Regained." Barker, *Milton: Modern Essays* 429-46. Rpt. from *Modern Philology* 53 (1956): 227-38.

———. *Words With Power: Being a Second Study of "The Bible and Literature."* 1990. Harmondsworth: Penguin, 1992.

Furman, Wendy, Christopher Grose and William Shullenberger. Preface. *Milton Studies* 28 (1992): vii-x.

Gay, David. "'Rapt Spirits': 2 Corinthians 12.2-5 and the Language of Milton's *Comus.*" *Milton Quarterly* 29 (1995): 76-86.

Geissler, Heinrich. *Comenius und die Sprache.* Heidelberg: Quelle und Meyer, 1959.

Genette, Gérard. "L'envers des signes." *Figures I.* Paris: Seuil, 1966. 185-204.

Gilbert, Sandra M., and Susan Gubar. "Milton's Bogey: Patriarchal Poetry and Women Readers." *The Madwoman in the Attic: The Woman Writer and the Nineteenth-Century Imagination.* New Haven: Yale UP, 1979. 187-212.

Gildon, Charles. "Vindication of *Paradise Lost* (1694)." Shawcross, *Milton: The Critical Heritage* 107-08.

Gomille, Monika. *Prudentia in Miltons Paradise Lost.* Heidelberg: Winter, 1990.

Grant, Patrick. *Images and Ideas in Literature of the English Renaissance.* London: Macmillan, 1979.

Grose, Christopher. "Milton on Ramist Similitude." Miner 103-16.

———. *Milton's Epic Process: Paradise Lost and Its Miltonic Background.* New Haven: Yale UP, 1973.

Grossman, Marshall. *"Authors to Themselves": Milton and the Revelation of History.* Cambridge: CUP, 1987.

Guillory, John. *Poetic Authority: Spenser, Milton, and Literary History.* New York: Columbia UP, 1983.

Gutkin, Mildred. "'Sufficient to Have Stood': The Mimesis of Free Will in *Paradise Lost.*" *English Studies in Canada* 10.1 (1984): 11-21.

Hagenbüchle, Roland. *Sündenfall und Wahlfreiheit in Miltons* Paradise Lost*: Versuch einer Interpretation.* Bern: Francke, 1967.

Hale, John K. *Milton's Languages: The Impact of Multilingualism on Style.* Cambridge: Cambridge UP, 1997.

Harada, Jun. "Self and Language in the Fall." *Milton Studies* 5 (1973): 213-28.

Harris, Roy. *Reading Saussure: A Critical Commentary on the* Cours de linguistique générale. London: Duckworth, 1987.

Hartman, Geoffrey. "Adam on the Grass With Balsamum." *ELH* 36 (1969): 168-92.

———. "Milton's Counterplot." Barker, *Milton: Modern Essays* 386-97. Rpt. from *ELH* 25 (1958): 1-12.

Haskin, Dayton. *Milton's Burden of Interpretation.* Philadelphia: U of Pennsylvania P, 1994.

Herman, Peter C. *Destablizing Milton: Paradise Lost and the Poetics of Incertitude.* New York: Palgrave Macmillan, 2005.

Hewes, Gordon Winant. *Language Origins: A Bibliography.* 2nd ed. The Hague: Mouton, 1975.

Hill, Christopher. *Milton and the English Revolution.* London: Faber, 1977.

———. *A Nation of Change and Novelty: Radical Politics, Religion and Literature in Seventeenth-Century England.* London: Routledge, 1990.

———. *The World Turned Upside Down: Radical Ideas during the English Revolution.* London: Temple Smith, 1972.

Hill, John Spencer. *John Milton: Poet, Priest and Prophet.* London: Macmillan, 1979.

Hobbes, Thomas. *Leviathan. The English Works of Thomas Hobbes*. Ed. William Molesworth. Vol. III. 1839. London: Bohn; Aalen: Scientia, 1966.

Hornsby, S.G., Jr. "'Ambiguous Words': Debate in *Paradise Lost.*" *Milton Quarterly* 14 (1980): 60-62.

Howard, Leon. "'The Invention' of Milton's 'Great Argument': A Study of the Logic of 'God's Ways to Men'." *Huntington Library Quarterly* 9.2 (1946): 149-73.

Howatt, A.P.R. *A History of English Language Teaching*. Oxford: OUP, 1984.

Howell, A.C. "*Res et Verba*: Words and Things." *ELH* 13 (1946): 131-42.

Howell, Wilbur Samuel. *Logic and Rhetoric in England, 1500-1700*. 1956. New York: Russell and Russell, 1961.

Hüllen, Werner. *"Their Manner of Discourse": Nachdenken über Sprache im Umkreis der Royal Society*. Tübingen: Narr, 1989.

Hunter, G.K. *Paradise Lost*. London: Allen & Unwin, 1980.

Hunter, William B., Jr. "Eve's Demonic Dream." *ELH* 13 (1946): 255-65.

——. "Milton's Materialistic Life Principle." *Journal of English and Germanic Philology* 45 (1946): 68-76.

——, C.A. Patrides, and J.H. Adamson. *Bright Essence: Studies in Milton's Theology*. Salt Lake City: U of Utah P, 1973.

Isermann, Michael. *Die Sprachtheorie im Werk von Thomas Hobbes*. Münster: Nodus, 1991.

Jacobus, Lee A. *Sudden Apprehension: Aspects of Knowledge in Paradise Lost*. The Hague: Mouton, 1976.

Johnson, Brian. "Sacred Silence: The Death of the 'Author' and *Paradise Lost.*" *Milton Quarterly* 29 (1995): 65-76.

Johnson, Samuel. "Milton (1779)." *Samuel Johnson*. Ed. Donald Greene. Oxford: OUP, 1984. 698-716.

Jones, Richard Foster. "Science and English Prose Style, 1650-75 (1930)." Fish, *Seventeenth-Century Prose* 53-89.

——. "Science and Language in England of the Mid-Seventeenth Century (1932)." Fish, *Seventeenth-Century Prose* 94-111.

Kahn, Victoria. "Allegory and the Sublime in *Paradise Lost.*" Patterson 185-201

——. *Machiavellian Rhetoric: From the Counter-Reformation to Milton*. Princeton: Princeton UP, 1994.

——. *Rhetoric, Prudence and Skepticism in the Renaissance*. Ithaca: Cornell UP, 1985.

Kamm, Jürgen. *Der Diskurs des heroischen Dramas: Eine Untersuchung zur Ästhetik dialogischer Kommunikation in der englischen Restaurationszeit*. Trier: WVT, 1996.

Katz, David S. "The Language of Adam in Seventeenth-Century England." *History and Imagination. Essays in Honor of H.R. Trevor-Roper*. Eds. Hugh Lloyd-Jones, Valerie Pearl and Blair Worden. 1981. New York: Holmes and Meier, 1982. 132-45.

Keeble, N.H. *The Literary Culture of Nonconformity in Later Seventeenth-Century England*. Leicester: Leicester UP, 1987.

Kellogg, Robert. "The Harmony of Time in *Paradise Lost.*" *Oral Tradition* 2.1 (1987): 260-72.

Kennedy, William J. *Rhetorical Norms in Renaissance Literature*. New Haven: Yale UP, 1978.

Kermode, Frank. "Adam Unparadised." *The Living Milton: Essays by Various Hands*. Ed. Frank Kermode. London: Routledge, 1960. 85-123.

Kerrigan, William. *The Prophetic Milton*. Charlottesville: UP of Virginia, 1974.

——. *The Sacred Complex: On the Psychogenesis of Paradise Lost.* Cambridge, Mass.: Harvard UP, 1983.

Kirkconnell, Watson. *The Celestial Cycle: The Theme of Paradise Lost in World Literature with Translations of the Major Analogues.* 1952. New York: Gordian P, 1967.

Klein, Wolf Peter. *Am Anfang war das Wort: Theorie- und wissenschaftsgeschichtliche Elemente frühneuzeitlichen Sprachbewußtseins.* Berlin: Akademie Verlag, 1992.

Knott, John R., Jr. *Milton's Pastoral Vision: An Approach to* Paradise Lost. Chicago: U of Chicago P, 1971.

——. "The Visit of Raphael: *Paradise Lost*, Book V." *Philological Quarterly* 47 (1968): 36-42.

Knowlson, James. *Universal Language Schemes in England and France, 1600-1800.* Toronto: UTP, 1975.

Kroll, Richard W.F. *The Material Word: Literate Culture in the Restoration and Early Eighteenth Century.* Baltimore: Johns Hopkins UP, 1991.

Labriola, Albert C. "'Thy Humiliation Shall Exalt': The Christology of *Paradise Lost*." *Milton Studies* 15 (1981): 29-42.

Landy, Marcia. "Language and the Seal of Silence in *Samson Agonistes*." *Milton Studies* 2 (1970): 175-94.

Lawry, John S. *The Shadow of Heaven: Matter and Stance in Milton's Poetry.* Ithaca: Cornell UP, 1968.

Le Comte, Edward. *A Dictionary of Puns in Milton's English Poetry.* New York: Columbia UP, 1981.

Leonard, John. *Naming in Paradise: Milton and the Language of Adam and Eve.* Oxford: Clarendon, 1990.

Lewalski, Barbara Kiefer. "Genre." Corns, *A Companion* 3-21.

——. "Innocence and Experience in Milton's Eden." *New Essays on* Paradise Lost. Ed. Thomas Kranidas. Berkeley: U of California P, 1971. 86-117.

——. "Milton and the Hartlib Circle: Educational Projects and Epic *Paideia*." *Literary Milton: Text, Pretext, Context.* Eds. Diana Treviño Benet and Michael Lieb. Pittsburgh: Duquesne UP, 1994. 202-19.

——. *Milton's Brief Epic: The Genre, Meaning, and Art of* Paradise Regained. Providence: Brown UP; London: Methuen, 1966.

——. "Milton's *Comus* and the Politics of Masquing." *The Politics of the Stuart Court Masque.* Eds. David Bevington and Peter Holbrook. Cambridge: CUP, 1998. 296-320.

——. Paradise Lost *and the Rhetoric of Literary Forms.* Princeton: Princeton UP, 1985.

——. *Protestant Poetics and the Seventeenth-Century Religious Lyric.* Princeton: Princeton UP, 1979.

Lewis, C.S. *A Preface to* Paradise Lost. 1942. London: OUP, 1960.

Lieb, Michael. "'Holy Name': A Reading of *Paradise Lost*." *Harvard Theological Review* 67 (1974): 321-39.

——. "'The Sinews of Ulysses': Exercise and Education in Milton." *JGE: The Journal of General Education* 36.4 (1985): 245-56.

——. *Theological Milton: Deity, Discourse and Heresy in the Miltonic Canon.* Pittsburgh: Duquesne UP, 2006.

Lobsien, Eckhard. *Wörtlichkeit und Wiederholung: Phänomenologie poetischer Sprache.* Munich: Fink, 1995.

Locke, John. *An Essay Concerning Human Understanding.* Ed. Peter H. Nidditch. Oxford: Clarendon, 1975.

Loewenstein, David. "'An Ambiguous Monster': Representing Rebellion in Milton's Polemics and *Paradise Lost,*" *Huntington Library Quarterly* 55 (1992): 295-315.

——. *Milton and the Drama of History: Historical Vision, Iconoclasm, and the Literary Imagination.* Cambridge: CUP, 1990.

——. *Milton: Paradise Lost.* Cambridge: CUP, 1993.

Lorenz, Paul H. "Heraclitus Against the Barbarians: John Fowles's *The Magus.*" *Twentieth-Century Literature* 42.1 (1996): 69-87.

Lyons, John. *Linguistic Semantics: An Introduction.* Cambridge: CUP, 1995.

——. *Semantics.* Cambridge: CUP, 1977.

MacCabe, Colin. "Language, Linguistics, and the Study of Literature." *Modern Criticism and Theory: A Reader.* Ed. David Lodge. London: Longman, 1988. 432-44.

——. "'So truth be in the field': Milton's Use of Language." *Teaching the Text.* Eds. Susanne Kappeler and Norman Bryson. London: Routledge, 1983. 18-34.

MacCaffrey, Isabel Gamble. Paradise Lost *as "Myth."* Cambridge, MA: Harvard UP, 1959.

MacCallum, Hugh. *Milton and the Sons of God: The Divine Image in Milton's Epic Poetry.* Toronto: UTP, 1986.

McCanles, Michael. "From Derrida to Bacon and Beyond." *Francis Bacon's Legacy of Texts: "The Art of Discovery Grows with Discovery."* Ed. William A. Sessions. New York: AMS P, 1990. 25-46.

McCarron, William E. "The 'persuasive Rhetoric' of *Paradise Regained.*" *Milton Quarterly* 10 (1976): 15-21.

McColley, Diane Kelsey. *Milton's Eve.* Urbana: U of Illinois P, 1983.

McDonald, Henry. "A Long Day's Dying: Tragic Ambiguity in *Samson Agonistes.*" *Milton Studies* 27 (1991): 263-83.

McGuire, Maryann Cale. *Milton's Puritan Masque.* Athens: U of Georgia P, 1983.

MacKellar, Walter. *A Variorum Commentary on the Poems of John Milton.* Vol IV: *Paradise Regained.* Gen. ed. Merritt Y. Hughes. London: Routledge, 1975.

Madsen, William G. "Earth the Shadow of Heaven: Typological Symbolism in *Paradise Lost.*" Barker, *Milton: Modern Essays* 246-63. Rpt. from *PMLA* 75 (1960): 519-26.

Major, John M. "Milton's View of Rhetoric." *Studies in Philology* 64 (1967): 685-711.

Marcus, Leah S. "John Milton's *Comus.*" Corns, *A Companion* 234-45.

Marjara, Harinder Singh. *Contemplation of Created Things: Science in* Paradise Lost. Toronto: UTP, 1992.

Markley, Robert. *Fallen Languages: Crises of Representation in Newtonian England, 1660-1740.* Ithaca: Cornell UP, 1993.

——. *Two-Edg'd Weapons: Style and Ideology in the Comedies of Etherege, Wycherley, and Congreve.* Oxford: Clarendon, 1988.

Marks, Herbert. "The Blotted Book." Nyquist and Ferguson 211-233.

Martin, Thomas L. "On the Margin of God: Deconstruction and the Language of Satan in *Paradise Lost.*" *Milton Quarterly* 29 (1995): 41-47.

Martz, Louis L. *Poet of Exile: A Study of Milton's Poetry.* New Haven: Yale UP, 1980.

Masson, David. *The Life of John Milton: Narrated in Connexion with the Political, Ecclesiastical, and Literary History of His Time.* 7 vols. 1877-96. Gloucester, Mass.: Peter Smith, 1965.

Mazzeo, Joseph Anthony. "St. Augustine's Rhetoric of Silence: Truth vs. Eloquence and Things vs. Signs." *Journal of the History of Ideas* 23.2 (1962): 175-96.

Melczer, William. "Looking Back Without Anger: Milton's *Of Education.*" Mulryan 91-102.

Menne, Albert. *Einführung in die Logik.* 5. Auflage. Tübingen: Francke, 1993.

Merrill, Thomas F. *Epic God-Talk: Paradise Lost and the Grammar of Religious Language.* Jefferson, NC: McFarland and Company, 1986.

——. "Miltonic God-Talk: The Creation in *Paradise Lost.*" *Language and Style* 16 (1983): 296-312.

Miller, Perry. *The New England Mind: The Seventeenth Century.* 1939. Cambridge, Mass.: Harvard UP, 1971.

Miner, Earl, ed. *Seventeenth-Century Imagery: Essays on Uses of Figurative Language from Donne to Farquhar.* Berkeley: U of California P, 1971.

Mintz, Samuel I. "The motion of thought: intellectual and philosophical backgrounds." Patrides and Waddington 138-69.

Mitchell, Linda. C. *Grammar Wars: Language as cultural battlefield in 17th and 18th century England.* Aldershot: Ashgate, 2001.

Mulryan, John, ed. *Milton and the Middle Ages.* Lewisburg, Pa.: Bucknell UP; London: Associated UPs, 1982.

Murrin, Michael. "The Language of Milton's Heaven." *The Allegorical Epic: Essays in Its Rise and Decline.* Chicago: U of Chicago P, 1980. 153-71.

Musacchio, George. *Milton's Adam and Eve: Fallible Perfection.* New York: Lang, 1991.

Mustazza, Leonard. "Language as Weapon in Milton's *Paradise Regained.*" *Milton Studies* 18 (1983): 195-216.

——. *"Such Prompt Eloquence": Language as Agency and Character in Milton's Epics.* Lewisburg: Bucknell; London: Associated UPs, 1988.

Myers, William. *Milton and Free Will: An Essay in Criticism and Philosophy.* London: Croom Helm, 1987.

——. "The Spirit of *Différance.*" Patterson 102-19.

Neve, Philip. "Milton (1789)." *Milton 1732-1801: The Critical Heritage.* Ed. John T. Shawcross. London: Routledge, 1972. 350-62.

Nöth, Winfried. *Handbook of Semiotics.* Bloomington: Indiana UP, 1990.

Norbrook, David. *Writing the English Republic: Poetry, Rhetoric and Politics, 1627-1660.* Cambridge: CUP, 1999.

Nyquist, Mary. "The Father's Word/Satan's Wrath." *PMLA* 100 (1985): 187-202.

——. "Reading the Fall: Discourse in Drama in *Paradise Lost.*" *English Literary Renaissance* 14 (1984): 199-229.

——, and Margaret W. Ferguson, eds. *Re-membering Milton: Essays on the Texts and Traditions.* New York: Methuen, 1987.

Ogden, H.V.S. "The Crisis of *Paradise Lost* Reconsidered." Barker, *Milton: Modern Essays* 308-27. Rpt. from *Philological Quarterly* 36 (1957): 1-19.

Ong, Walter J. *The Presence of the Word: Some Prolegomena for Cultural and Religious History.* New Haven: Yale UP, 1967.

Orgel, Stephen. *The Jonsonian Masque.* Cambridge, MA: Harvard UP, 1965.

Padley, G.A. *Grammatical Theory in Western Europe 1500-1700: Trends in Vernacular Grammar I.* Cambridge: CUP, 1985.

Palmer, William J. *The Fiction of John Fowles: Tradition, Art, and the Loneliness of Selfhood.* Columbia: U of Missouri P, 1974.

Parish, John E. "Milton and an Anthropomorphic God." *Studies in Philology* 56 (1959): 619-25.

Parker, Patricia. *Inescapable Romance: Studies in the Poetics of a Mode.* Princeton: Princeton UP, 1979.

Parker, William Riley. "Education: Milton's Ideas and Ours." *College English* 24.1 (1962): 1-14.

——. *Milton: A Biography.* 2nd ed. 2 vols. Ed. Gordon Campbell. Oxford: Clarendon, 1996.

Patrides, C.A. "*Paradise Lost* and the Theory of Accommodation." *Texas Studies in Literature and Language* 5 (1963): 58-63.

——, ed. *Approaches to* Paradise Lost: *The York Tercentenary Lectures.* London: Edward Arnold, 1968.

——, and Raymond B. Waddington, ed. *The Age of Milton: Backgrounds to Seventeenth-Century Literature.* Manchester: Manchester UP; Totowa, NJ: Barnes & Noble, 1980.

Patterson, Annabel, ed. *John Milton.* London: Longman, 1993.

Picciotto, Joanna. "Reforming the Garden: The Experimentalist Eden and *Paradise Lost.*" *ELH* 72 (2005): 23-78.

Pratt, Mary Louise. *Toward a Speech Act Theory of Literary Discourse.* Bloomington: Indiana UP, 1977.

Quint, David. *Origin and Originality in Renaissance Literature: Versions of the Source.* New Haven: Yale UP, 1983.

Quintana, Ricardo. "Notes on English Educational Opinion During the Seventeenth Century." *Studies in Philology* 27 (1930): 265-92.

Radzinowicz, Mary Ann. "'Man as a Probationer of Immortality': *Paradise Lost* XI-XII." Patrides, *Approaches* 31-51.

——. *Toward Samson Agonistes: The Growth of Milton's Mind.* Princeton: Princeton UP, 1978.

——. "The Politics of *Paradise Lost.*" Sharpe and Zwicker 204-229.

Rajan, Balachandra. "Simple, Sensuous and Passionate (1945)." Barker, *Milton: Modern Essays* 3-19. Rpt. from *Review of English Studies* 21: 289-301.

Ramus, Petrus. *The Logike.* 1574. Ed. and trans. Rolland M'Kilwein. Menston: Scolar P, 1970.

Rapaport, Herman. *Milton and the Postmodern.* Lincoln: U of Nebraska P, 1983.

Rebhorn, Wayne A. "The Humanist Tradition and Milton's Satan: The Conservative as Revolutionary." *SEL* 13 (1973): 81-93.

Reichert, John. *Milton's Wisdom: Nature and Scripture in* Paradise Lost. Ann Arbor: U of Michigan P, 1992.

Richardson, Jonathan. "Explanatory Notes and Remarks on Milton's *Paradise Lost* (1734)." Dyson and Lovelock 40.

Ricks, Christopher. *Milton's Grand Style.* Oxford: Clarendon, 1963.

Ricœur, Paul. *The Rule of Metaphor: Multi-disciplinary Studies of the Creation of Meaning in Language.* Trans. Robert Czerny with Kathleen McLaughlin and John Costello, SJ. Toronto: UTP, 1981.

Riggs, William G. "Poetry and Method in Milton's *Of Education.*" *Studies in Philology* 89 (1992): 445-69.

——. "The Temptation of Milton's Eve: 'Words, Impregn'd / With Reason.'" *JEPG* 94.3 (1995): 365-92.

Risse, Wilhelm. *Die Logik der Neuzeit*. Vol. 1.: *1500-1640*. Stuttgart-Bad Canstatt: Friedrich Frommann, 1964.

Robins, Harry F. *If This Be Heresy: A Study of Milton and Origen*. Urbana: U of Illinois P, 1963.

Roston, Murray. *Milton and the Baroque*. Pittsburgh: U of Pittsburgh P, 1980.

Rumrich, John Peter. *Milton Unbound: Controversy and Reinterpretation*. Cambridge: CUP, 1996.

——. "Uninventing Milton." *Modern Philology* 87 (1990): 249-65.

Samuel, Irene. "The Dialogue in Heaven: A Reconsideration of *Paradise Lost*, III.1-417." Barker, *Milton: Modern Essays* 233-45. Rpt. from *PMLA* 72 (1957): 601-11.

——. "Milton on Learning and Wisdom." *PMLA* 64 (1949): 708-23.

Sauer, Elizabeth. *Barbarous Dissonance and Images of Voice in Milon's Epics*. Montreal: McGill-Queen's UP, 1996.

Saurat, Denis. *Milton: Man and Thinker*. 1925. New York: AMS P, 1975.

Saussure, Ferdinand de. *Cours de linguistique générale*. 1916. Ed. Tullio de Mauro. Paris: Payot, 1991.

——. *Cours de linguistique générale: Edition critique*. Ed. Rudolf Engler. Vol. 1. Wiesbaden: Harassowitz, 1968.

——. *Course in General Linguistics*. Trans. Wade Baskin. London: Peter Owen, 1974.

Scholes, Robert. *Semiotics and Interpretation*. New Haven: Yale UP, 1982.

Schreyer, Rüdiger. "Die Tradition der Philosophischen Grammatik in England." *Sprachtheorien der Neuzeit II: Von der "Grammaire de Port-Royal" (1660) zur Konstitution moderner linguistischer Disziplinen*. Ed. Peter Schmitter. Tübingen: Narr, 1996. 44-93.

Schwartz, Regina. *Remembering and Repeating: On Milton's Theology and Poetics*. 1988. Chicago: U of Chicago P, 1993.

Sharpe, Kevin, and Steven N. Zwicker, ed. *Politics of Discourse: The Literature and History of Seventeenth-Century England*. Berkeley: U of California P, 1987.

Shawcross, John T. , ed. *Milton: The Critical Heritage*. London: Routledge, 1970.

Sherry, Beverley. "Speech in *Paradise Lost*." *Milton Studies* 8 (1975): 247-66.

Shoaf, R.A. *Milton, Poet of Duality: A Study of Semiosis in the Poetry and Prose*. New Haven: Yale UP, 1985.

Shuger, Debora. "'Gums of Glutinous Heat' and the Stream of Consciousness: The Theology of Milton's *Maske*." *Representations* 60 (1997): 1-21.

Shullenberger, William. "Linguistic and Poetic Theory in Milton's *De Doctrina Christiana*." *ELN* 19 (1982): 262-78.

Skulsky, Harold. *Language Recreated: Seventeenth-Century Metaphorists and the Act of Metaphor*. Athens: U of Georgia P, 1992.

Silver, Victoria. *Imperfect Sense: The Predicament of Milton's Irony*. Princeton: Princeton UP, 2001.

Smith, Russell E., Jr. "Adam's Fall." *ELH* 35 (1968): 527-39.

Snider, Alvin. *Origin and Authority in Seventeenth-Century England: Bacon, Milton, Butler*. Toronto: UTP, 1994.

Sprat, Thomas. *History of the Royal Society*. Eds. Jackson I. Cope and Harold Whitmore Jones. St. Louis: Washington University Studies; London: Routledge, 1959.

Stavely, Keith W. *The Politics of Milton's Prose Style*. New Haven: Yale UP, 1975.

Steadman, John M. *The Hill and the Labyrinth: Discourse and Certitude in Milton and His Near-Contemporaries*. Berkeley: U of California P, 1984.

Stein, Arnold. "Milton's War in Heaven: An Extended Metaphor." *ELH* 18 (1951): 201-20. Rpt. in Barker, *Milton: Modern Essays* 264-83.

Svendsen, Kester. *Milton and Science*. Cambridge, Mass.: Harvard UP, 1956.

Swaim, Kathleen M. *Before and After the Fall: Contrasting Modes in* Paradise Lost. Amherst: U of Massachusetts P, 1986.

Swanson, Donald, and John Mulryan. "The Son's Presumed Contempt for Learning in *Paradise Regained*: A Biblical and Patristic Solution." *Milton Studies* 27 (1991): 243-61.

Thickstun, Margaret Olofson. *Milton's* Paradise Lost*: Moral Education*. New York: Palgrave Macmillan, 2007.

Tillyard, E.M.W. *Milton*. Harmondsworth: Penguin, 1968.

——. *Studies in Milton*. 1951. London: Chatto & Windus, 1960.

Todorov, Tzvetan. "The Birth of Occidental Semiotics." *The Sign: Semiotics Around the World*. Eds. R.W. Bailey, L. Matejka and P. Steiner. Ann Arbor: U of Michigan, 1978.

Toliver, Harold. "Complicity of Voice in *Paradise Lost*." *Modern Language Quarterly* 25 (1964): 153-70.

——. "Symbol-Making and the Labors of Milton's Eden." *Texas Studies in Literature and Language* 18 (1976): 433-50.

Trabant, Jürgen. *Elemente der Semiotik*. Tübingen: Francke, 1996.

Turnbull, George H. *Hartlib, Dury and Comenius: Gleanings from Hartlib's Papers*. Liverpool: UP of Liverpool; London: Hodder and Stoughton, 1947.

Turner, James Grantham. „The Intelligible Flame." Patterson 74-86.

Van Dijk, Teun A., ed. *Discourse and Literature*. Amsterdam: Benjamins, 1985.

Verbart, André. *Fellowship in Paradise Lost: Vergil, Milton, Wordsworth*. Amsterdam: Rodopi, 1995.

Viswanathan, Gauri. "Milton and Education." *Milton and the Imperial Vision*. Eds. Balachandra Rajan and Elizabeth Sauer. Pittsburgh: Duquesne UP, 1999. 273-93.

Von Maltzahn, Nicholas. "Laureate, Republican, Calvinist: An Early Response to Milton and *Paradise Lost* (1667)." *Milton Studies* 29 (1992): 181-98.

Waldock, A.J.A. Paradise Lost *and Its Critics*. 1947. Cambridge: CUP, 1966.

Watson, Thomas Ramey. *Perversions, Originals, and Redemptions in* Paradise Lost*: The Typological Scheme and Sign Theory that Unify Milton's Epic*. Lanham, MD: University Press of America, 2007.

Webster, Charles. *The Great Instauration: Science, Medicine and Reform 1626-1660*. London: Duckworth, 1975.

West, Robert H. *Milton and the Angels*. Athens: U of Georgia P, 1955.

Whaler, James. "The Miltonic Simile." *PMLA* 46 (1931): 1034-74.

Widmer, Kingsley. "The Iconography of Renunciation: The Miltonic Simile." *ELH* 25 (1958): 258-69.

Wilkins, John. *An Essay Towards a Real Character, And a Philosophical Language*. 1668. Menston, England: Scolar P, 1968.

Williamson, George. "The Education of Adam." *Modern Philology* 61 (1963): 96-109. Rpt. in Barker, *Milton: Modern Essays* 284-307.

Wilson, Robert Rawdon. *In Palamedes' Shadow: Explorations in Play, Game, and Narrative Theory*. Boston: Northeastern UP, 1990.

Wittreich, Joseph. *Interpreting* Samson Agonistes. Princeton: Princeton UP, 1986.

Woodhouse, A.S.P., and Douglas Bush. *The Minor English Poems. A Variorum Commentary on the Poems of John Milton II.* Gen. ed. Merritt Y. Hughes. New York: Columbia UP, 1972.

Young, Robert Fitzgibbon, ed. *Comenius in England.* Oxford: OUP; London: Humphrey Milford, 1932.

Zwierlein, Anne-Julia. *Majestick Milton: British Imperial Expansion and Transformations of Paradise Lost, 1667-1837.* Münster: Lit Verlag, 2001.

Index

About the Author

Martin Kuester is professor of English literature at the University of Marburg in Germany and director of the Marburg Centre for Canadian Studies. He teaches English literature from Shakespeare to the present and has a special interest in the New Literatures in English as well as in Milton. He completed his M.A. at the University of Trier (Germany), his PhD at the University of Manitoba (Winnipeg, Canada), and a Dr. phil. habil. at the University of Augsburg (Germany). He has written and/or edited numerous articles and several books on Canadian and British literatures and cultures, among them *Framing Truths: Parodic Structures in Contemporary English-Canadian Historical Novels* (University of Toronto Press, 1992). He is also the co-author of a handbook of literary terminology for university students, *Basislexikon anglistische Literaturwissenschaft* (Munich: Fink, 2007).